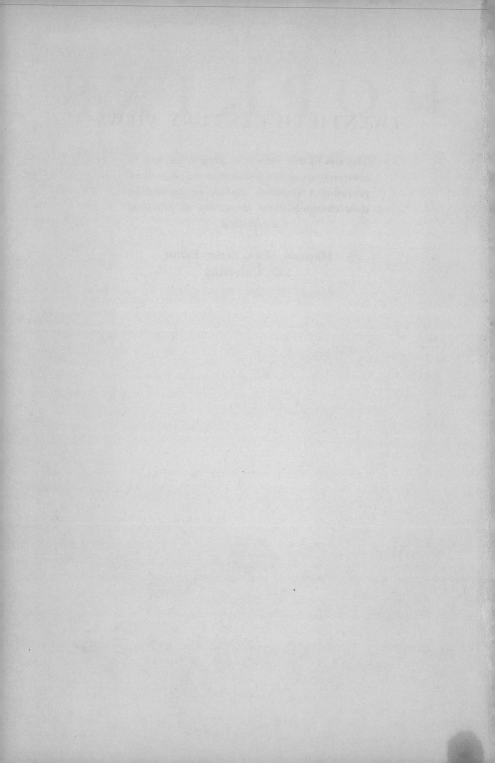

TWENTIETH CENTURY VIEWS

The aim of this series is to present the best in contemporary critical opinion on major authors, providing a twentieth century perspective on their changing status in an era of profound revaluation.

Maynard Mack, *Series Editor*
Yale University

HOPKINS

A COLLECTION OF CRITICAL ESSAYS

Edited by

Geoffrey H. Hartman

Prentice-Hall, Inc. *Englewood Cliffs, N.J.*

A SPECTRUM BOOK

The editor wishes to thank the following publishers
for permission to use their material in this volume:
Oxford University Press for the selections from
Hopkins' poetry throughout the essays; The Clarendon
Press for "Low Barometer" and "London Snow" by
Robert Bridges; and Alfred A. Knopf, Inc. for "The
Course of a Particular" from *Opus Posthumous* by
Wallace Stevens.

For Austin Warren

Contents

vii

HOPKINS

Introduction:
Poetry and Justification

by Geoffrey H. Hartman

When Yeats said that Hopkins' style was merely "the last development of poetic diction," [1] he spoke like a contrary old man, but he spoke
shrewdly. The manneristic element in Hopkins, whether nurtured by
traditional rhetoric or by the force of the vernacular, is the dragon that
lies in the gates of his verse. Hopkins' small and idiosyncratic produc-
tion, much of it fragments, must have seemed to Yeats a threat to what
had already been achieved without it. Yeats' desire was not for singularity
but for a new and modern species of universal poetry, and Hopkins was
judged to contribute an interesting but dead mutation to this evolving
species. It was ironical, therefore, that he should have become a test case
in the struggle for the recognition of modern poetry which achieved a
certain intensity at Cambridge around 1930. I. A. Richards, William
Empson, and F. R. Leavis championed Hopkins as the classic example
of the modern poet. They agreed that his strength was bound up with
the immediacy of his relation to words: he seemed to fulfill the dream
that poetry was language speaking about itself, language uttering complex words that were meanings *as* words. Yeats challenged their estimate:
he suggested that Hopkins was to be counted among the decadents rather
than the innovators, that in a curious way his strong new style was the
sweet old style brought to a terminal contortion. This is not unlike the
feeling of Bridges, who first published the poems of Hopkins in 1918
with strictures on their "luxurious experiments."

Yeats' minority opinion has been refined by Giorgio Melchiori, but it
has not been cast out. After almost fifty years of close reading and superb
editing, Hopkins' verse remains something of a scandal. For we continue
to be uncertain as to whether Hopkins, like Spenser, "writ no language,"
or whether he coins a radically new idiom. The basic questions about his
greatness, direction and even plain-sense are not yet answered. Almost

---

[1] *The Oxford Book of Modern Verse* (1936), pp. xxxix-xl.

1

every one of his poems has cruxes (like "Buckle" in "The Windhover") that defeat exegetical activity. There is a strange absence, among so many books and articles, of any that can be called definitive—definitive on some aspects of interpretation.

The one thing that has been clarified is that we must rethink the whole matter of Hopkins' "diction." There is hardly an essay in this anthology which does not touch upon it. Austin Warren's scrupulous account of its lineage and John Wain's essay on its relation (or absence of relation) to Victorian literature are complemented by Sigurd Burkhardt's reflections on the changing status of words in the consciousness of poets from Herrick to Wallace Stevens. Hillis Miller has shown what Hopkins learned about language from Parmenides; and we know modern philosophy and poetry are both implicated in a verbal thinking about words. Still missing is a consideration of how Hopkins relates to the Romantic poets on the matter of diction; the remarks of Yvor Winters on his "Romantic" eccentricities do not speak to this point but to the loss of logical or analogical poetic structure. Yet F. O. Mathiessen noted in passing Hopkins' relation to Whitman and the Romantic revolt against "poetic diction."

The Romantic revolt was, on one level, a reaction in the name of life, passion or imagination against everything dead: dead language as well as dead emotions and the deadening intellect. But the maturer intent of that revolt was to make our powers, hopes, and even sufferings more ours. Whatever stood between man and life was thought to be spurious; and language too was suspected of being a false mediation. Poetry, moreover, instead of purifying language, seemed to have fallen into the hands of a literary caste that claimed to deal in universals externalized as "poetic diction." Poetry had to be cleansed of these, often inauthentic, universals by becoming more concrete in form and thought. The end of Romantic poetry, then, is not concreteness or particularity for its own sake; rather it is the discovery from within nature or felt experience of truly universal universals, concepts and words that could spread, like joy, "in widest commonality." Wordsworth in his greatness encouraged a new Vulgate for the imagination: poetry written in the strongest and simplest language, "words that speak of nothing more than what we are."

Yeats' remark on Hopkins and poetic diction reflects this Wordsworthian ideal of a difficult simplicity which Yeats himself rarely attained before his last decade. Hopkins also could not ignore the ancient truth revived by Wordsworth that the poet writes in a tongue that is like the things it describes, issuing from their very heart; yet he remembered another truth, equally ancient, that the poet is peculiarly learned and respectful of tradition. His religious beliefs, moreover, strengthened this latter, esoteric conception of poetry. Catholicism, compared to Protestantism, is a mystery religion, and the ambiance in which Hopkins reached intellectual maturity, the Oxford of the 1860s, found the Church of England divided by a reform movement that had insisted on mystery, ritual, and the authority of tradition. Thus Hopkins relived at its source the double nature of the poet who is always both popular and learned, natural and artificial, holy and profane. The Protestantism into which he was born had come to regard poetry as the most viable and open aspect of religion, its vernacular as it were; while the Catholic faith to which he converted recalled him to the mystery, discipline, and tradition indispensable for a real presence of the spirit.

No wonder, then, that Hopkins' poetry is an uneasy blend of natural and learned elements, and that its vivid surface leads on occasion not to clarity but to darkness. There is in many poems a residue of obscurity difficult to remove; Yvor Winters has blamed it on the convenient scapegoat of "Romantic" individualism. But it may equally well be blamed on something very different from Romanticism: Hopkins' desire for an impersonal and esoteric discipline. We know that his urge towards a sacrifice of intellect and a true religious anonymity was very strong; his letters to Dixon reveal an unremitting conflict between the priest and the poet as well as between the priest and the scholar. The Jesuit order seemed to demand a sacrifice of everything that might have led to fame and away from a daily *imitatio Christi;* and though we will never know how thoroughly Hopkins mortified himself before the "incredible condescension" of the incarnation—an ideal of service, unself-consciousness, and sacrifice to the calling—he significantly refers to the burning of his early poems as a "slaughter of the innocents." One wonders how many slaughters there were, since we do not possess any of the works on Greek scansion which flushed him with an enthusiasm bordering on megalomania. Yet despite his own aspirations to anonymity, his service to the poetry of others was unstinting: his letters to Bridges, Patmore, and Dixon are full of exact and scrupulous remarks on art. He does not actively raise the question of a radical conflict between poetry and religion, and indeed seems to hope that poetry can be justified. But what is a justified poem?

All poets lay restrictions on themselves, if only for the sake of poetry. In this spirit Valéry defined form as *difficulté vaincue.* A finished poem, impressive as a thing in itself, is more impressive for the threshold pressures apparently overcome. In Hopkins precariousness is a religious quality that becomes a poetic quality. Sometimes, of course, we feel merely the pressures and the poet's failing spirit. But here too, in the

kind of religious scruple he shows, Hopkins is modern. As a post-Roman-
tic he identified poetry with "Selfyeast of spirit," and the question was
whether poetry could authentically be anything more. Could one pass
beyond the self to its "other side"? In an eloquently obscure passage of
Trinitarian speculation, he tries to reconcile self, self-sacrifice, and creation. "It is," he writes, "as if the blissful agony or stress of selving in God
had forced out drops of sweat or blood, which drops were the
world. . . ." One is tempted to adapt the parable and say, "which drops
were the poem." It was a matter of coming to terms, in poetry, with his
own strength, of going out, by means of poetry, to the strength in nature,
and of going through that to Christ. Each mortal thing "Selves—goes itself, *myself* it speaks and spells."

   This procession is highly problematic, but the most hermetic poetry
speaks and spells—opens on something. "Go forth," writes Bridges, in
his envoi to the first edition of his friend's poetry, "amidst our chaffinch
flock display/Thy plumage of far wonder and heavenly flight." If Hopkins has not quite "gone forth" even today, if he is still an exotic bird—a
rara avis—it is because we think of his inner conflict as only a curious
product of his orthodoxy. A similar conflict, however, between the religious (esoteric) and naturalistic (exoteric) conception of poetry is found
in the Symbolist movement on the Continent, and continues to disturb
the more candid speech of Yeats and Stevens. Despite obvious differences, Hopkins' seven-years' abnegation of poetry is comparable to
Valéry's silence, and his hesitations may have an affinity with Mallarmé's
"glacier" of stillborn flights. A religious or quasi-religious pressure of
justification weighed on them all. To understand, in Hopkins' case, the
form of that pressure clears even our secular judgment.

   We begin with the well-known fact that Hopkins was familiar with
Ignatian methods of meditation. The extent to which he was obliged
to practice them, and the degree to which he exercised his obligation,
are documented in his devotional writings. Yet the relevance of this kind
of meditation, to all and not only Christian poetry, has not been fully
understood. The meditational technique of Ignatius of Loyola, perhaps
the most powerful spiritual technique invented by the West, adapts
the mimetic principle to the life of Christ. Meditation is not primarily
speculative, not thought or intellectual exploration moving from a
relatively arbitrary point of departure to an adventurous conclusion.
It is nearer to imitation in the older, religious meaning of the word.
We say that art is imitation; and even in Aristotle, who modifies the
sense of the word, the root-notion of *imitatio,* or serious miming, persists.

The aim of Ignatian meditation is to prepare a fuller *imitatio Christi* by bringing the mind as close as possible to the primal scene.

The first peculiarity, and justifying characteristic, of Hopkins' poetry is that it mimes what it represents. Not all miming is overtly religious: in "Hurrahing in Harvest," or "The Windhover," the first sighting of the subject is an exceptionally pure act of sense-prehension—deictic, vocative, evocative. Yet to enter so strongly into things, to speak, as it were, for or from nature, argues an exceptionally trained power of identification. If being divinely "possessed" means anything, it means speaking for or from the desired mode of being. This initial encounter, on its own terms, with nature or beauty, is doubtless a lesser *imitatio,* a propaedeutic for the larger acting out to come. Thus the *downing* motion in the second part of "Hurrahing in Harvest" (a similar downing occurs in "The Windhover"),

> I walk, I lift up, I lift up heart, eyes,
> Down all that glory in the heavens to glean our Saviour,

is a mimic and optative gesture that recalls, together with the distance between heaven and earth, the spanning mystery of Incarnation. Having met nature "barbarous in beauty," and having transcended, or rather downed it in the name of a greater beauty, the poet at the end of his mime begins to "ascend wingèd." His transcendence we may feel to be a trick; but it acts out a Christian doctrine without intellectual sleight or theological complication. The justifying end of such poetry is for the poet to become Christ, to act Christ, who "plays in ten thousand places" of nature and man; and the justifying doctrine is that of the Incarnation harmonized with Romans 1:20 and 8:17 ff.

The impulse to imitation-as-miming is already central in "The Wreck of the Deutschland" which launched Hopkins' sacred poetry. It is felt in the style, in the ritual crying of thoughts, and in passages of unusual rhythmic mimicry. *Imitatio,* religious participation, is in fact the burden of the poem. Hopkins enters the scene he evokes, the nun enters by anticipation into glory, all things are said to "go" to Christ. The objective and subjective, narrative and lyrical, parts of the theme are interwoven, so that turns of the action become (after stanza 11) turns in the poet's mind, and narrator is transformed to celebrant. Thus the illumination which redeems the catastrophe is Hopkins' own illumination: it is he who delivers the meaning of the nun's call to Christ, and it is he who labors for it. The cry, and its meaning, are brought forth by an empathic spiritual maieutics: "heart-throe, birth of brain, Word."

Though the meaning of that Word (specifically, the nun's cry) re-

mains less clear than the impulse of the whole poem, it suggests the
theme of participation once more. The nun calls for her bridegroom
and the consummation of her mystical marriage. She does not do this,
Hopkins is careful to say, for her own glory or from spiritual impatience.
Her cry, rather, recalls that of Job: as in "Carrion Comfort," there is a
wrestling with, if not a constraining of, God. "Her will was bent at God,"
Hopkins says of Margaret Clitheroe; and what he admires in the nun is
the claim she rises to. She seizes the occasion with a daring and energy
already divine.[2] But this is the dangerous fruit of *imitatio,* its hardest,
most ambiguous venture: to call up one's calling, to chose what one is
chosen for. "It is as if a man said: That is Christ playing at me and me
playing at Christ, only that it is no play but truth; That is Christ *being
me* and me being Christ." Hopkins is always on this shadowy ground
where personality, free will, and grace intertwine. It was merely a "hint"
from his Superior which made him break a seven year silence and com-
pose "The Wreck of the Deutschland." There must be a call, and the
hint must have become that call: the paradox in Hopkins' early poem,
"Elected silence sing to me / And beat upon my whorléd ear," is genuine.

   Here appears a further characteristic closely allied to *imitatio* and
justification. Hopkins' style is as vocative as possible. This holds for
sound, grammar, figures of speech, and actual performance. Tell and toll
become cognates. God, in that first vocative of "The Wreck of the
Deutschland," is giver of *breath* and *bread*—two staples only a smallest
voicing apart. We find cries within cries as in: "Not, / I'll not, / carrion
comfort, / Despair, / not feast on thee." The poet's situation is essentially that of the "heart in hiding" which is called: by the call of the
nun, by the sighting of a falcon, by the rudeness of God. What is man,
says Job, that Thou shouldst contend with him? Yet, as in Job, we feel
the calling more than the being called—a voice constraining the void.
The true contender is man, who cries for justice. So with Hopkins who
strains ears and eyes to transform the *not yet* into the *now:*

---

[2] The formalized hesitations in stanza 28 of "The Wreck of the Deutschland"
suggest the enormity of the thought the poet is about to express: that the nun, in
extremity, turns from that aspect of the Imitation of Christ which Hopkins calls the
root of all moral good, namely "the holding of himself back, and not snatching at
the highest and truest good . . . his own being and self," to the claim (the snatching)
she frankly makes. The poet's holding-back issues in the exceptional not-holding-back
and vision of Christ as glorious master rather than as servant: "Let him ride, her
pride, in his triumph, despatch and have done with his doom there." In "The
Windhover" the same notion of mastery stirs the heart in hiding (cf. the "I was at
rest" of stanza 24 of the "Deutschland") but the imitation of Christ-servant prevails.
See also Philippians 2:5-11, and Fr. Devlin's introduction to *The Sermons and Devotional Writings* (London: Oxford University Press, 1959), pp. 107 ff.

> like a lighted empty hall
> Where stands no host at door or hearth
> Vacant creation's lamps appall.
>
>   ("Nondum")

The more he packs his verse the more we sense his Pascalian horror at that vacancy. "Verily thou art a God that hidest thyself."

In a stray comment Hopkins once urged what he names *"contentio, or strain of address."* No phrase can better describe his own strain of style. *Contentio* is a term from rhetoric designating an antithetical or pointed repetition of words. But in Hopkins' mind the term has somehow fused with the Jobean *contentio,* with a raising of the voice to God, with a like insistence of address. "You must not slovenly read it with the eyes but with your ears," he writes to Bridges about a poem, "as if the paper were itself declaiming it at you. . . . Stress is the life of it." And by such stress and strain of address, maintained until all parts of speech, all figures seem to partake in the vocative, Hopkins revolutionized poetic style. He made forever questionable the neutral or high-objective mode of which Tennyson was the eminent nineteenth century practitioner. This style, called Parnassian by Hopkins, was a last try at the grand manner. It wished to combine the noble simplicity of Greek or Roman epic with the intensity of lyric and the modern interest in the picturesque. The result: a charming frigidity. "A horrible thing has happened to me," Hopkins writes in 1864, "I have begun to *doubt* Tennyson." And to illustrate the Parnassian mode he quotes from the latter's *Enoch Arden.* It is a passage worth reproducing:

> The mountain wooded to the peak, the lawns
> And winding glades high up like ways to Heaven,
> The slender coco's drooping crown of plumes,
> The lightning flash of insect and of bird,
> The lustre of the long convolvuluses
> That coil'd around the stately stems, and ran
> Ev'n to the limit of the land, the glows
> And glories of the broad belt of the world,
> All these he saw.

The destruction of the Parnassian style is accomplished by an extroversion of language that pushes verbal matter into the foreground. As color for the radical nineteenth century painters is no longer a ground (like the good earth) which does its carrying function quietly, but is obtruded as part of the subject, so words come forward in Hopkins' poetry to reclaim what he calls their "inscape," their immediate power of address.

They do not, for all that, exist in themselves or by some automatic virtue of revelation. On the contrary, they mimic, paint ("that is a lie, so to speak, of Lessing's, that pictures ought not to be painted in verse, a damned lie—so to speak"), and participate in argument. Language is shown to be *contentio* in essence; there is nothing disinterested or general about it; its end as its origin is to move, persuade, possess. Hopkins leads us back to an aural situation (or its simulacrum) where meaning and invocation coincide. Everything depends on the right "pitch," or verbal cast.

But this is still an imperfect description of Hopkins' purpose. It fails to indicate the resistance met by the *ictus* of his voice. For it is no mean endeavor to make the voice "selve" or to attain what, by a characteristic metaphor, he calls "pitch of self." Resistance comes not only from the conventional sublimity of the Parnassian mode but also from the very nature of language. The substitution of "gash" for "gush" at the end of "The Windhover" (where embers "Fall, gall themselves, and gash gold-vermillion"), or semantic rhymes like "tread" and "trade" in "God's Grandeur," evoke the tendency of semantic distinctions to fall back into a phonemic ground of identity. There is, in other words, a linguistic indifference against which language contends, and contends successfully by diacritical or differential means. It is no wonder, therefore, that Hopkins' mannerisms extrovert the diacritical basis of meaning and so appear to be linguistic rather than rhetorical in nature. Such favorite devices as tmesis[3] contain a virtuoso element (cf. the splitting of notes or words in music) and suggest the precarious emergence of the individualizing feature out of the ground of phonemic similarity. Hopkins' heavy line, and the heavy sonnet as a whole (his most distinctive contribution to genre), re-enact this emergence and submergence pattern on a larger scale by the doggerel thickness of their phonemic material: "Our tale, O our oracle! Let life, waned, ah let life wind / Off her once skeined stained veined variety. . . ."

"Diacritical" may need more explanation. It is best to offer this in the form of an example and to consider the following phrase in description of the coming of night: *her earliest stars, earl-stars, stars principal* . . . ("Spelt from Sybil's Leaves"). A rhetorical analysis will not show more than an extended pun. A diacritical analysis, however, works on the basis of homophones to show how linguistic individuation occurs. The point about Hopkins' description is not the homophones or internal rhymes

---

[3] "Wind-lilylocks-laced"; "the O-seal-that-so feature"; "Forth Christ from the cupboard fetched." Words that (roughly) go together are separated by the interpolation of other words.

but the creatively tenuous process of disjunction. Hopkins separates "earl-stars" from "earliest stars" by natural elision or a modification of juncture and stress. Two syllables are elided: h̄er, which leans to ēar of "earliest," and ēst which already partially merged with "stars." Eliding all but the stressed syllables produces the cleanly shock of *earl-stars,* as if this phrase had been born of the first by a movement mimicking the "fire-featuring" procession of the actual stars. The elements that give meaning to the line are essentially vocalic: elision, juncture, stress.

Even a nontechnical reading can perceive the individuating stress and juncture progression of her/ear(l)iest/stars/earl-stars/stars. . . . The addition to this of "principal" is magically right: the word is itself an individuum, odd and learned, with a syllabic weight that compensates for sounds previously elided. Above all, it is a word independent of the preceding phonemic series, as if sprung loose or "selved" by it. Yet, like a joker or linguistic subplot, it repeats and justifies this series. Prince: principalis=earl:early.

The diacritical method might also be applied to the thorny problem of Hopkins' sprung rhythm. I cannot summarize here the controversy surrounding Hopkins' presumed innovation. But the essential feature of sprung rhythm, which he calls counterpoint and defines as "the super-inducing or mounting of a new rhythm upon the old," is structurally analogous to his linear mounting or juxtaposition of phonemically similar phrases differentiated by juncture or stress. This is seen by transcribing the end of "Spelt from Sybil's Leaves" so that its standard or ground-rhythm contrasts visibly with its mounted rhythm:

$$\text{standard: } \overset{\prime}{\text{thoughts}} \quad \text{against} \quad \overset{\prime}{\text{thoughts}} \quad \text{in} \quad \overset{\prime}{\text{groans}} \quad \overset{\prime}{\text{grind}}$$
$$\text{mounted: } \overset{\prime}{\text{thoughts}} \quad \overset{\prime}{\text{against}} \quad \text{thoughts} \quad \overset{\prime}{\text{in}} \quad \text{groans} \quad \overset{\prime}{\text{grind}}$$

We will not always find so perfect a counterpoint, but the principle remains the same for imperfect cases. Stress is here revealed as a diaeresis on the level of rhythm, and the stress sign as a diacritical mark. A recessive part of the phrase is featured or selved. But this featuring, this counterpointing, may also have an important intralinear function. In trying to get from "against" to "in" to "grind," "thoughts" and "groans" obtrude strongly, not only because of standard stress, but also because of an intralinear pull which assimilates the first "thoughts" to the second, and "groans" to "grind." The mounted rhythm, in other words, serves here to prevent intralinear mergings as well as discriminating cross-linear homophones ("thóughts" in the standard line vis-à-vis "thoughts" in the mounted).

That sprung rhythm is only one form of the diacritical tendency is confirmed by such coinages as "black, white; right wrong" in the same poem. Here the reversal or counterpoint is not metrical in nature. Though patterned, probably, on the analogy of the reversed metrical foot, the phrase is a semantic chiasmus forcing the rhyme words too close together and so destroying rhyme by imbalance. A wobble-rhythm is created comparable to the sensation that ensues on looking at a visual puzzle where now the white and now the dark squares stand out. Stress, pitch of self, the *principium individuationis* emerges from within a chiming of words that founds opposition of sense on identity of sound.

It almost seems as if transcendence for Hopkins came from a struggle of like with like. The end of the struggle being individuation, neutral elements of style, like unstressed elements in perception, disappear. The poem is justified as Jacob was justified, who wrestled with the angel, man to man, and attained his proper name (Genesis 32). The *like* or enemy-friend with whom Hopkins contends is language, nature, beauty, or even (as in "Carrion Comfort") God. Imitation begins with a direct grappling as the heart is caught by its like—say, the windhover. It grapples with the creature's drawing power. "Being draws-home to Being" is how Hopkins translates a passage from Parmenides: he is drawn to the falcon in the same way as the latter is itself "dapple-dawn-drawn." (Hyphens tend to be tension marks in Hopkins, and similar to diacritical signs in that they prevent words or syllables from collapsing into one another.) Hopkins' verse, with its verbal runs, lives by such attraction to Being, or to what he calls, anticipating the method of ordinary language philosophy, "the flush and foredrawn" (fore-drawn=predicate). Thus "being" is opposed to "individuation." But as whatever is completely one with itself *and* manifest, it is also the very ground of individuation.

Duns Scotus helps Hopkins to solve this paradox, but we do not really need him any more than we do Parmenides. The structure of Hopkins' transcendence is sufficiently defined in his poems. There is what we have named the lesser *imitatio,* a constraining of like by like, or nature drawing the heart of man in order to be realized and worded (see Romans 8:18 and "Ribblesdale"). Man receives nature's beauty, or wrestles to equal her patience, by what Gaston Bachelard has called the imagination of matter. But Christ, or the greater *imitatio,* puts a stress on man's imagination that transcends any "instress" of nature's. This is because divine stress again demands likeness: whatever disparity there is between human and divine, man can become Christ just as God in Christ became man. The possibility of likeness (a dangerous ideal, since it must either utterly exalt or annihilate selfhood) is the agony: "O which one, is it each one?"

Hopkins' pattern of transcendence is not uniform: his passage from the lesser to the greater *imitatio* can be variously achieved. In "The Windhover" we find an abrupt montage of one on the other, the example of Christ usurping, counterpointing, and even figurally completing that of the kestrel. But in "That Nature is a Heraclitean Fire and of the Comfort of the Resurrection" the transition is discursive and docrinal. Christian doctrine, however, is itself uncertain as to what is carried over from one state to the other. That is probably why the sonnet has two codas: the first suggests a radical discontinuity based on St. Paul's "We shall be utterly changed"—but this is a hard comfort; the second reminds us that man "puts on" Christ by means of purification rather than by utter change. Of the properties enumerated by Hopkins in the next to last line, a single one remains in the risen body but one that was originally there:

> In a flash, at a trumpet crash,
> I am all at once what Christ is, since he was what I am, and
> This Jack, joke, poor potsherd, patch, matchwood, immortal diamond
>   Is immortal diamond.

Hopkins' singling out and reweighting of "immortal diamond" suggests the coincidence of individuation and purification. He is neither a poet of total immanence nor of radical transcendence. Imitation of Christ is the means whereby the principle of self is purified and the body redeemed. We return to the faith exemplified by the nun in "The Wreck of the Deutschland": man is great enough for God to condescend to, and there will be a redemption in the flesh. This is *Christian* hybris, but the amount of service it enjoins is incalculable. "As if his true vocation . . . were endless imitation."

Hopkins is limited by the fact that, though his concept of vocation is as deep as Browning's, he could not fully associate it with poetry. "Felix Randall," where the obituary and reflective mood is continually broken by "strain of address," shows what may be achieved when the vocations of poet and priest unite. But "Henry Purcell," despite virtuoso flashes of diction and thought inspired by the subject, remains an abstract admiration-piece beset by religious scruple. It was no Romantic who said that "To follow Poetry as one ought, one must forget father and mother, and cleave to it alone" (Alexander Pope). Hopkins' defects are often traceable to his scrupling view of the poet's vocation. The parochialism, the punctilio in matters of craft, the unresolved experimentation, the mixing of linguistic orders and effects, the hypostatizing of and indulging in "beauty" (perhaps Pateresque, but suggesting a man who thinks he is secure enough to indulge mentally before turning away)—these betray a genius that will not risk itself beyond clearly marked virtuoso effects. Hopkins is certainly a great virtuoso in the tradition of Crashaw, and if he has not left us a "Music's Duell" we do have "The Leaden Echo and the Golden Echo." (Even as virtuoso he must still be compared to Swinburne.) Yet while nature and art are rivals in his poetry, between art and religion there cannot be an authentic challenge, only an uncertain progress from lesser to greater *imitatio*.

To judge is to compare; and it is useful to pursue the comparison with Crashaw and Browning. In one respect Hopkins surpasses both. His imagination is more directly and substantially engaged with air, earth, water, fire. He is our pre-Socratic among poets. It is also more directly engaged with the materiality of language as a fifth element. He not only loads every rift with ore but discovers unsuspected rifts to fill. Language, through him, is again part of the body of things, if not its very quintessence.

In a further respect he is at least their equal. Crashaw's style, with its audacities of wit, paradox, and point, was involved in a religious purpose, and supported the Counter Reformation against the developing plain style of Protestant England. Hopkins' poetry revives the pointed style in the lyric. Bridges complained of his *Marianism* where he could equally well have complained of his *Marinism*. But the great difference between the two Catholic poets is first of all historical, in that one had to revive what the other had merely to exploit (the pointed style); and secondly, that Hopkins is consciously *English* where Crashaw is "catholic" or "universal," and if he must be typed nationally, Italian. Despite rhetoric, despite artifices of stress, Hopkins insists on the colloquial element. "I can't help being a little amused," Coventry Patmore writes to him, "by your claiming for your style the extreme of popular character." Patmore is right in being amused, or bemused: where Hopkins is the most colloquial, he is often the most hermetic. He does not always escape a cultic attitude toward language.

Browning, too, sought a more rugged lyricism, which Hopkins interprets in snobbish if acute terms. "He has got a great deal of what came in with Kingsley and the Broad Church school, a way of talking (and making people talk) with the air and spirit of a man bouncing up from table with his mouth full of bread and cheese and saying that he meant to stand no blasted nonsense." Whether or not the religious cause is fundamental, each poet introduces a new density of diction and structure into the lyric. Browning does it primarily by the dramatic method, by speaking through characters caught in a moment which is the equivalent of the fruitful or characteristic moment prescribed for the visual arts. Like Hopkins, therefore, he destroys the picturesque by cramming it, by forcing its fulfilment. The Parnassian style, as we saw, was related to the picturesque, and Hopkins seems to develop his lyric structures out of the Pre-Raphaelite dream-vision. In his early "A Vision of the Mermaids" and "St. Dorothea" he may be struggling with such poems as Christina Rossetti's "The Convent Threshold" and Dante Gabriel Rossetti's "The Blessed Damozel," poems in which the poet stands at a lower level than the vision, or irrevocably, pathetically, distanced. Yet Hopkins, perhaps inspired by Pindar, evolves a more participating and less picturesque stance, one that allows a precarious communion. In both Hopkins and Browning the lyric moves away from simple reflection or reminiscence. The dreamer is lifted into the dream, the past into the present. Imitation is project more than retrospect.

With one thing more, but that essential, Hopkins might have surpassed Browning the modern Protestant, and Crashaw the militant Catholic. Through Pindar he approached a truly athletic conception of poetry. Yet he again stopped short at the critical point: admiring what Pindar achieved in diction and structure, he dissociated these accomplishments from Pindar's remarkable consciousness of himself and of poetic vocation. Poetry, for Pindar, is as divine as the feat he celebrates, yet is distinguished from other divine gifts by its human function. The athletic games are sublimated war games, but the game of poetry, equally skilled, may civilize the gods. Hopkins' view of poetic art is, in comparison, at once too serious and too light: too serious, because the game is not played out as a game, and too light because the poet's imitation is always subordinated to the priest's *imitatio*. We can see a similar difference between Hopkins and Crashaw: Crashaw alone has the courage of a *jongleur* or court-jester before God. The license of his art is truly extraordinary, while Hopkins shrinks from every audacity other than prosodic or lexical. There is no need to document the latter's prudishness: Patmore, who shared Hopkins' faith in the final redemption of the senses, is the truer follower of Crashaw:

> In season due, on His sweet-fearful bed,
> Rock'd by an earthquake, curtain'd by eclipse,

Thou shar'd'st the spousal rapture of the sharp spear's head
And thy bliss pale
Wrought for our boon what Eve's did for our bale.

                                                    (*The Unknown Eros*)

One can imagine Hopkins' own pallor at this. "That's telling secrets," as he once said to Patmore.

Even Browning, his tedious optimism and roughhousing aside, understands that poetry is a sacred game and that the game alone can justify the poet. Contentious and self-justifying, Browning's people direct their will at a hidden God. The poet is their advocate, caught in the same condition, and refuses to give the game away. He demands, yet does not preempt, judgment. His poetry builds up a sacrifice for which the consecrating fire must come from us or from above. Hopkins, though the purer talent, often appears narrow and idiosyncratic when placed beside him. We never forget, in Hopkins' poetry, that it is a priest speaking, and one more Roman than the Romans in his scruples as to what his religious order might allow. He does not even dare to follow where Ignatian meditation leads. Overcome by a "course of loathing and hopelessness which I have so often felt before, which made me fear madness, and led me to give up the practice of meditation," he can do no more (he says) than repeat: *Justus es, Domine, et rectum judicium tuum*. However authentic a suffering speaks in this, it is a passive suffering. Here is where vision or prophecy or scandal might have begun: where within his vocation a new vocation might have been born. Hopkins' acceptance of the Rule was so absolute that it did not permit him to be more than a pawn or servant in the sacred game he intuited. "Sheer plod makes plough down sillion shine." That shining remains his justification, when, in his poetry, he is challenged by an image of divine mastery akin to brute beauty, and when, so challenged, he becomes for a moment *magister ludi*.

A Note on the Essays

The criteria of selection were that essays should be critical, as well as informative, and that they should deal chiefly with the poetry, and then with the poetry as a whole rather than with one aspect of it. An exception was made for Romano Guardini's note on "The Windhover," but otherwise no article dealing exclusively with a single poem was included. It is in the nature of anthologies that not all essays of importance can be honored, and I regret that nothing seemed extractable from such books as W. H. Gardner's. Items of further interest are, however, listed in the bibliography. The selected articles are arranged as follows:

Part I contains those whose main purpose is evaluative, Part II those treating the poetry in relation to Hopkins' thought and religious situation, Part III focuses on affinities between Hopkins and other writers and on his language-consciousness in its broadest aspect. I have tried to juxtapose essays of very different persuasions: thus Yvor Winter's comparison of Hopkins and Bridges to the detriment of the former is followed by John Wain comparing the two poets to the detriment of the latter, and H. M. McLuhan's emphasis on the analogical vision in Hopkins is followed by J. Hillis Miller's exposition of univocity of being in its relation to Hopkins' poetry.

I

Gerard Manley Hopkins

by F. R. Leavis

Gerard Manley Hopkins died in 1889. He was one of the most remarkable technical inventors who ever wrote, and he was a major poet. Had he received the attention that was his due the history of English poetry from the 'nineties onward would have been very different. But that is a fanciful proposition: it would be extravagant to suppose that he would have received such attention even had his poems been generally accessible. Even now that they have been so for a dozen years, we see that it is possible for respected critics, writing about them with the consciousness of authority, to exhibit conspicuously in public a complete and complacent obtuseness, and yet arouse no remark: that is the measure of Hopkins' originality. It is, however, difficult not to believe that if the poems had been current they would have fertilized some young talent, and we should not now be contemplating the futility of the Georgian attempt to regenerate English poetry. But they were not published as a body until 1918. To explain how thirty years of potential influence were thus lost is a delicate undertaking; it is best left, perhaps, to the poet's biographer, Father Lahey[1]:

> The staunch love and the highest literary appreciation of him who was admittedly the best custodian of the poems, prevented Dr. Bridges from flooding an unappreciative and uncomprehending literary public with the rays of so original a source of pure poetry, so that he bided his time and with careful discrimination slowly educated his future readers with selec-

[1] G. F. Lahey, S.J., *Gerard Manley Hopkins* (London: Oxford University Press, 1930), p. 16.

tions given to anthologies. After almost thirty years of patient waiting he published the slender volume of poems to which were added his own notes, the creative criticism of a delicate poetic sensibility.

These notes continue the education of the reader by laying down firmly the limits within which the poet is to be approved, and do the poet the further service of discounting adverse criticism by insisting on it. In the following[2] Dr. Bridges raises radical issues:

> Apart, I say, from such faults of taste ["occasional affectation in metaphor," "perverted Marianism," etc.], which few as they numerically are yet affect my liking and more repel my sympathy than do all the rude shocks of his purely artistic wantonness—apart from these there are definite faults of style which a reader must have courage to face, and must in some measure condone before he can discover the great beauties. For these blemishes in the poet's style are of such quality and magnitude as to deny him even a hearing from those who love a continuous literary decorum and are grown to be intolerant of its absence. And it is well to be clear that there is no pretence to reverse the condemnation of those faults, for which the poet has duly suffered. The extravagances are and will remain what they were. Nor can credit be gained from pointing them out: yet, to put readers at their ease, I will here define them: they may be called Oddity and Obscurity; and since the first may provoke laughter when a writer is serious (and this poet is always serious), while the latter must prevent him from being understood (and this poet has always something to say), it may be assumed that they were not a part of his intention.

A great deal is too readily assumed here: it is possible to put readers of Hopkins too much at their ease. The "obscurity" is, in a sense to be explained later, intended. The "oddity," as Dr. Bridges goes on to show, Hopkins was aware of; but he felt that too big a price might be paid for the approval of "those who love a continuous literary decorum." What Dr. Bridges calls "blemishes" are essential to Hopkins's aim and achievement; it is difficult to understand how the attitude implicit in this description of them can go with an interest in his work. Dr. Bridges quotes from the poet's letters:

> "No doubt my poetry errs on the side of oddness. I hope in time to have a more balanced and Miltonic style. But as air, melody, is what strikes me most of all in music and design in painting, so design, pattern, or what I am in the habit of calling *inscape,* is what I above all aim at in poetry. Now it is the virtue of design, pattern, or inscape to be distinctive and it

[2] *Poems of Gerard Manley Hopkins,* second edition (London: Oxford University Press, 1930), p. 96. (The references that follow are all to the second edition.)

is the vice of distinctiveness to become queer. This vice I cannot have escapèd." And again two months later: "Moreover the oddness may make them repulsive at first and yet Lang might have liked them on a second reading. Indeed, when, on somebody returning me the *Eurydice*, I opened and read some lines, as one commonly reads whether prose or verse, with the eyes, so to say, only, it struck me aghast with a kind of raw nakedness and unmitigated violence I was unprepared for: but take breath and read it with the ears, as I always wish to be read, and my verse becomes all right."

But that "love of a continuous literary decorum" stood in the way. Such a decorum, like Good Form, has its uses; but both become cramping absurdities when erected into ultimate ends. That Hopkins' experiments should not have been obviously reasonable and obviously justified by a considerable measure of success shows how badly they were needed. He aimed to get out of his words as much as possible unhampered by the rules of grammar, syntax and common usage. But to the late Dr. Bridges, as to so many people, these rules were ends in themselves. He complains that in Hopkins one often has to determine the grammar by the meaning, "whereas the grammar should expose and enforce the meaning, not have to be determined by the meaning."—"Should": one is reminded of *les jeunes* who discuss whether Mr. Eliot's methods in *The Waste Land* are "legitimate" or not, when the only question worth discussing is, Do they work?

But it is only fair to Dr. Bridges to admit that it is not the indecorum alone that he objects to:

Here, then, is another source of the poet's obscurity; that in aiming at condensation he neglects the need that there is for care in the placing of words that are grammatically ambiguous. English swarms with words that have one identical form for substantive, adjective and verb; and such a word should never be so placed as to allow of any doubt as to what part of speech it is used for; because such ambiguity or momentary uncertainty destroys the force of the sentence. Now our author not only neglects this essential propriety but he would seem even to welcome and seek artistic effect in the consequent confusion; and he will sometimes so arrange such words that a reader looking for a verb may find that he has two or three ambiguous monosyllables from which to select, and must be in doubt as to which promises best to give any meaning that he can welcome; and then, after his choice is made, he may be left with some homeless monosyllable still on his hands. Nor is our author apparently sensitive to the irrelevant suggestions that our numerous homophones cause; and he will provoke further ambiguities or obscurities by straining the meaning of these unfortunate words.

This criticism assumes that poetry ought to be immediately comprehensible. But Hopkins felt no obligation to subscribe to that particular
notion of Good Form. "Writers," says Dr. Bridges, "who carelessly rely
on their elliptical speech forms to govern the elaborate sentences of
their literary composition little know what conscious effort of interpretation they often impose on their readers. But it was not carelessness
in Gerard Hopkins. . . ."—Nor can Hopkins have been unaware that
he imposed a conscious effort of interpretation upon his readers. It is
true that he felt that his critics exaggerated the difficulty of his verse:
"The sonnet (I say it snorting) aims at being intelligible." [3] Or rather,
he felt that with an effort that might be fairly demanded he *could* be
understood, and that it was not at intrinsic difficulties alone that they
were boggling. For he must deliberately have contemplated leaving the
reader in more than momentary uncertainty: he had positive uses for
ambiguity, and he presumed to expect from the reader prolonged and
repeated intellectual effort. A great many people who fancy themselves
interested in poetry resent such an expectation: very few are prepared
to make any effort at all. I have heard it announced in a cultivated
drawing room that the choruses from Gilbert Murray's Euripides are
some of the finest poetry in the language. But Hopkins is very unlike
his contemporary, Swinburne. Hopkins is really difficult, and the difficulty is essential. If we could deceive ourselves into believing that we
were reading easily, his purpose would be defeated; for every word in
one of his important poems is doing a great deal more work than almost
any word in a poem of Robert Bridges. If (as Mr. I. A. Richards pointed
out[4] in what appears to have been the first intelligent critique of
Hopkins) we were allowed to slip easily over the page, the extremely
complex response called for would not have a chance to develop. The
final, adequate reading will not be a matter of arduous struggle (though
a sense of tension and resistance is usually an essential part of the effect),
but it will have been made possible by previous intellectual effort, the
condition of various subtle and complex organizations.

Hopkins, as Dr. Bridges points out, did not take to obscurity and
oddity because of any incapacity for the conventional forms. He prac-
tised verse-training from an early age, and wrote prize poems while at
school. These are remarkably accomplished, but, in the relation that
they exhibit to Keats, Shelley, Byron, and Tennyson, normal products

[3] *Poems of Gerard Manley Hopkins*, ed. cit., p. 118. Cf. "O, once explained, how clear
it all is!" p. 115.
[4] *The Dial*, September 1926.

of the period. Having, while at Oxford, become a Catholic, he entered
the Order of Jesus, and gave up poetry for some time:

> What (verses) I had written I burnt before I became a Jesuit (*i.e.* 1868)
> and resolved to write no more, as not belonging to my profession, unless it
> were by the wish of my superiors; so for seven years I wrote nothing but
> two or three little presentation pieces which occasion called for. But when
> in the winter of '75 the *Deutschland* was wrecked in the mouth of the
> Thames and five Franciscan nuns, exiles from Germany by the Falck Laws,
> aboard of her were drowned I was affected by the account and happening
> to say so to my rector he said that he wished some one would write a poem
> on the subject. On this hint I set to work and, though my hand was out
> at first, produced one. I had long had haunting my ear the echo of a new
> rhythm which now I realised on paper. . . . I do not say the idea is alto-
> gether new . . . but no one has professedly used it and made it the prin-
> ciple throughout, that I know of. . . . However, I had to mark the stresses
> . . . and a great many more oddnesses could but dismay an editor's eye, so
> that when I offered it to our magazine, *The Month* . . . they dared not
> print it.[5]

Hopkins went on with his experiments, sending his poems for criticism
to his friends Robert Bridges and Canon Dixon. His friends, it appears,
stood unwearyingly to the defence of a continuous literary decorum. But
Hopkins knew what he was trying to do, and without encouragement,
in this complete isolation, kept on his path. He was a man of rare character as well as intelligence. He writes[6] in reply to one can guess what
kind of suggestion: "The effect of studying masterpieces is to make me
admire and do otherwise. So it must be on every original artist to some
degree, on me to a marked degree. Perhaps then more reading would
only *refine my singularity*, which is not what you want."—Self-sureness
of that kind (it was justified) is genius.

Hopkins's originality was radical and uncompromising: there was, as
he owns, some excuse for the dismay of his first readers. He could not
himself, as the *Author's Preface* shows, be reconciled to his originality
without subterfuge. His prosodic account in terms of Logaoedic Rhythm,
Counterpoint Rhythm, Sprung Rhythm, Rocking Feet and Outriders
will help no one to read his verse—unless by giving the sense of being
helped: it merely shows how subtle and hard to escape is the power of
habits and preconceptions. The prescription he gives when warm from
reading his verse—"take breath and read it with the ears, as I always

---

[5] *Poems of Gerard Manley Hopkins*, p. 102.
[6] *Ibid.*, p. 118.

wish to be read, and my verse becomes all right"—is a great deal more to the point, and if we add "and with the brains and the body" it suffices.

This is a measure of the genuineness of his originality.[7] For the peculiarities of his technique appeal for sanction to the spirit of the language: his innovations accentuate and develop bents it exhibits in living use and, above all, in the writings of the greatest master who ever used it. Hopkins might have said about each one of his technical idiosyncrasies what he says about the rhythm of *The Wreck of the Deutschland:* the idea was not altogether new, but no one had professedly used it and made it a principle throughout as he had. Paradoxical as it may sound to say so, his strength was that he brought poetry much closer to living speech. How badly some such regeneration was needed may be judged from the inability of critics avowedly interested in him, as Bridges and Dixon were, to appreciate his significance: the habits and conventions he defeated were so strong. They are strong still: Mr. Charles Williams, the editor of the second edition of the *Poems,* concludes in his *Critical Introduction* that the "poet to whom we should most relate Gerard Hopkins" is Milton. Now if one were seeking to define the significance of Hopkins by contraries, Milton is the poet to whom one would have recourse: the relation is an antithesis. But, alas! Mr. Williams leaves no room to suppose that he means that.

The way in which Hopkins uses the English language (that is the primary order of consideration; "consciousness of the universe" [8] is an unprofitable abstraction apart from it) contrasts him with Milton and associates him with Shakespeare. There is no essential characteristic of his technique of which it might not be said that it is a matter of "using professedly" and "making a principle" of something that may be found in Shakespeare:

> . . . the world-without-end hour[9]
>
> . . . bloody, bawdy villain!
>
> Remorseless, treacherous, lecherous kindless villain! [10]

---

[7] "The poem which is absolutely original is absolutely bad; it is, in the bad sense, 'subjective' with no relation to the world to which it appeals.

"Originality, in other words, is by no means a simple idea in the criticism of poetry. True originality is merely development."—T. S. Eliot, Introduction to *Selected Poems: Exra Pound,* p. x.

[8] "The simultaneous consciousness of a controlled universe, and yet of division, conflict, and crises within that universe, is hardly so poignantly expressed in any other English poets than those two."—*Poems of Gerard Manley Hopkins,* Introduction, p. xiv.

[9] *Sonnet* 57.

[10] *Hamlet,* II, ii.

... cabin'd, cribb'd, confined [11]

> what thou wouldst highly,
> That wouldst thou holily.[12]

If it were done when 'tis done, then 'twere well
It were done quickly: if the assassination
Could trammel up the consequence, and catch
With his surcease success; that but this blow
Might be the be-all and the end-all here,
But here, upon this bank and shoal of time,
We'd jump the life to come.[13]

—This last passage takes us beyond technical devices, found in embr
in Shakespeare. Indeed, it would be a mistake to insist too much
these (they could be exemplified indefinitely); it might distract attenti
from the more essential likeness illustrated by the passage as a who
Hopkins' imagery, and his way of using the body and movement of t
language, are like Shakespeare's.

O the mind, mind has mountains; cliffs of fall
Frightful, sheer, no-man-fathomed. Hold them cheap
May who ne'er hung there. Nor does long our small
Durance deal with that steep or deep.[14]

—That is Shakespearian, but quite un-Miltonic. And this ("what's n
meet" being made to suggest at the same time "not what's meet") hand
grammar and syntax in the spirit of Hopkins:

In a rebellion,
When what's not meet, but what must be, was law,
Then were they chosen: in a better hour,
Let what is meet be said it must be meet,
And throw their power in the dust.[15]

If we look for a parallel to a characteristic Shakespearian rendering
the very movement of consciousness—

My thought, whose murder yet is but fantastical,
Shakes so my single state of man, that function
Is smother'd in surmise, and nothing is,
But what is not [16]

[11] *Macbeth*, III. iv.
[12] *Macbeth*, I. v.
[13] *Macbeth*, I. vii.
[14] *Poems of Gerard Manley Hopkins*, p. 62.
[15] *Coriolanus*, III. i.
[16] *Macbeth*, I. iii.

—we shall find it easily in Hopkins:

> Only what word
> Wisest my heart breeds dark heaven's baffling ban
> Bars or hell's spell thwarts. This to hoard unheard,
> Heard unheeded, leaves me a lonely began.[17]

It is not that he derives from Shakespeare (Shakespeare, we have often been told, is a dangerous model). We cannot doubt that he knew his Shakespeare well, but if he profited he was able to do so because of his own direct interest in the English language as a living thing. The bent of his genius was so strong that we are forced to believe that his experimenting would have taken much the same lines even if there had been no Shakespeare. The similarities arise out of a similar exploitation of the resources and potentialities of the language. Hopkins belongs with Shakespeare, Donne, Eliot and the later Yeats as opposed to Spenser, Milton and Tennyson. He departs very widely from current idiom (as Shakespeare did), but nevertheless current idiom is, as it were, the presiding spirit in his dialect, and he uses his medium not as a literary but as a spoken one. That is the significance of his repeated demand to be tested by reading aloud: "read it with the ears, as I always wish to be read, and my verse becomes all right." [18] It is not merely the rhythm that he has in mind:

> I laughed outright and often, but very sardonically, to think you and the Canon could not construe my last sonnet; that he had to write to you for a crib. It is plain I must go no further on this road: if you and he cannot understand me who will? Yet, declaimed, the strange constructions would be dramatic and effective.[19]

It is not only the constructions that gain, and "dramatic" has a further sense here than perhaps Hopkins intended. His words and phrases are actions as well as sounds, ideas and images, and must, as I have said, be read with the body as well as with the eye: that is the force of his concern to be read aloud. He indicates now and then in notes the kind of thing he is doing. "Here comes a violent but effective hyperbaton or suspension, in which the action of the mind mimics that of the labourer—surveys his lot, low but free from care; then by a sudden strong act throws it over the shoulder or tosses it away as a light mat-

---

[17] *Poems of Gerard Manley Hopkins*, p. 65.
[18] *Poems of Gerard Manley Hopkins*, p. 97.
[19] *Ibid.*, p. 114.

ter." [20]—Effects of this order may be found on any page of his work.
Even more significant is a note on a word in *The Leaden Echo and the
Golden Echo*. It is the more interesting in that Mr. Sturge Moore paid
this poem some attention in a recent number of *The Criterion*.[21] The
poem opens:

> How to keep—is there ány any, is there none such,
> 　nowhere known some, bow or brooch or braid
> 　or brace, láce, latch or catch or key to keep
> Back beauty, keep it, beauty, beauty, beauty, . . .
> 　from vanishing away?

Hopkins notes:[22] "*Back* is not pretty, but it gives that feeling of physical
constraint which I want." This suggests fairly the spirit of his dealings
with the English language. How alien to English poetry that spirit had
become is illustrated by Mr. Sturge Moore, a critic and verse-writer
formed in the last century, who, writing on *Style and Beauty in Literature,* offers to improve Hopkins in this way:

> How to keep beauty? is there any way?
> Is there nowhere any means to have it stay?
> Will no bow or brooch or braid,
> Brace or lace
> Latch or catch
> Or key to lock the door lend aid
> Before beauty vanishes away?

There is no need to quote further. No reader of *The Criterion,* apparently, protested. Mr. Sturge Moore remarks at the end that he has re-
tained most of Hopkins's felicities, while discarding "his most ludicrous
redundancies." He has discarded also "back" and everything it represents; words as he uses them have no body. He has discarded, not merely
a certain amount of music, but with the emotional crescendo and dimin-
uendo, the plangent rise and fall, all the action and substance of the
verse.

Not that *The Leaden Echo and the Golden Echo* is one of the poems
in which the poet's greatness manifests itself. Remarkable as it is, if it

---

[20] *Poems of Gerard Manley Hopkins,* p. 115. For an analogous effect, cf.:
> 'On a huge hill,
> Cragged, and steep, Truth stands, and hee that will
> Reach her, about must, and about must goe;
> And what the hills suddennes resists, winne so;'
> 　　　　　　　　　Donne, *Satyre* III.

[21] *Criterion,* July 1930.
[22] *Poems of Gerard Manley Hopkins,* p. 113.

were fully representative of Hopkins, he would not demand much space in this study. In this kind of work he is elaborating and mastering his technical devices for more important purposes. It is not as mere musical effects (if such were possible in poetry)—melody, harmony, counterpoint —that these devices are important; they are capable of use for expressing complexities of feeling, the movement of consciousness, difficult and urgent states of mind. Take for instance the kind of word-play, the pattern and progression of verbal echo, alliteration, rime and assonance represented in the opening verse:

> How to kéep—is there ány any, is there none such,
>   nowhere known some, bow or brooch or braid
>   or brace, láce, latch or catch or key to keep
> Back beauty . . .

—That need not be (indeed, is not) a mere musical trick, any more than conventional end-rime need be. Such devices may be used, as good poets use end-rime, to increase the expectancy involved in rhythm and change its direction, to control movement, to give words new associations and bring diverse ideas and emotions together, to intensify the sense of inevitability—in short, to get new, precise and complex responses out of words.

Of course, to be something convincingly more than word-play, to escape the limiting description, "music," these devices must have adequate work to do. The theme of *The Leaden Echo and the Golden Echo* does not offer very much resistance, and if this poem represented the height of Hopkins' achievement Mr. Middleton Murry's judgment [23] would not be immediately absurd: "If one were to seek in English the lyrical poem to which Hopkins' definition ["The roll, the rise, the carol, the creation"] could be most fittingly applied, one would find Shelley's *Skylark*. A technical progression onwards from the *Skylark* is accordingly the main line of Hopkins' poetical evolution." But if one looks at *The Wreck of the Deutschland*, which, says Bridges, "stands logically as well as chronologically in the front of his book, like a great dragon to forbid all entrance," it becomes plain that Hopkins has no relation to Shelley or to any nineteenth-century poet. This poem was his first ambitious experiment, and it is the more interesting in that his technical resources are deployed in it at great length: the association of inner, spiritual,

---

[23] Middleton Murry, *Aspects of Literature*, (London: William Collins & Sons, Ltd., 1921) p. 55. It is only fair to say that Mr. Murry's essay was written in the circumstances of weekly journalism. In those circumstances to have written seriously and at length on Hopkins must go on the credit side of a critic's account. *Aspects of Literature* contains some of the best criticism of modern poetry that has appeared.

emotional stress with physical reverberations, nervous and muscular
tensions that characterizes his best verse is here explicitly elaborated in
an account of the storm which is at the same time an account of an
inner drama. The wreck he describes is both occasion and symbol. He
realizes it so vividly that he is in it; and it is at the same time in him:

> I did say yes
> O at lightning and lashed rod;
> Thou heardst me truer than tongue confess
> Thy terror, O Christ, O God;
> Thou knowest the walls, altar and hour and night:
> The swoon of a heart that the sweep and the hurl of thee trod
> Hard down with a horror of height:
> And the midriff astrain with leaning of, laced with fire of stress.

He takes the actual wreck as the type of the worldly disaster that brings
conviction, supernatural assurance, to the soul:

> Stroke and a stress that stars and storms deliver,
> That guilt is hushed by, hearts are flushed by, and melt

—and identifies such experience mystically with Christ's Passion. In
an audacious image he identifies the sudden overwhelming conviction,
the insight, the illumination to the effect of a sloe bursting in the mouth:

> The dense and driven Passion, and frightful sweat;
> Thence the discharge of it, there its swelling to be,
> Though felt before, though in high flood yet—
> What none would have known of it, only the heart, being hard at
> bay,
> Is out with it! Oh,
> We lash with the best or worst
> Word last! How a lush-kept plush-capped sloe
> Will, mouthed to flesh-burst,
> Gush!—flush the man, the being with it, sour or sweet,
> Brim, in a flash, full!—Hither then, last or first,
> To hero of Calvary, Christ's feet—
> Never ask if meaning it, wanting it, warned of it—men go.

The conceit is Metaphysical, but the technique is pure Hopkins. It
would be difficult to produce a more elaborate pattern of alliteration,
echo, assonance and internal-rime, but we do not feel of any element
(except, perhaps, "lush-kept plush-capped") that it is there for the sake
of pattern. Even of "lush-kept plush-capped" it might be said that by a
kind of verbal suggestion (two different expressions sounding so like) it
contributes to the sense of mystical identification that the passage is con-

cerned to evoke—identification of "the stress felt" with the Passion; [it]
helps also the metaphorical identification of the experience with the
bursting of the sloe. Of the pattern generally it may be said that it issues
out of and expresses emotional intensities in the same kind of way as
"cabin'd, cribb'd, confined" and

> bloody, bawdy villain!
> Remorseless, treacherous, lecherous, kindless villain!

and

> . . . trammel up the consequence, and catch
> With his surcease success.

Particularly it may be pointed out how the words stressed by the pattern
justify their salience.

> Is out with it! Oh,
> We lash with the best or worst
> Word last!

—"lash" (the highly stressed "out" carries on from the previous line)
both suggests the inevitability (a lashing out on the stimulus of pain)
of the response at this supreme testing moment ("last"), and gives the
response a physical urgency. The moment is ripe ("lush"): and "lush"
applied to "sloe" also suggests the paradoxical poignancy ("sour or
sweet"?) of the revelation. In "fleshburst" we have both the physical disaster "that storms deliver" and Calvary. The progression—"gush,"
"flush," "flash," "full"—is as much a matter of sense as sound: "gush"
describes the overwhelming onset of the experience, "flush" the immediate bewildering immersion; "flash"—it becomes illumination; "full" suggests "cup."

Such an analysis is clumsy and inadequate: it is merely a means of
indicating the kind of function that the more obvious technical devices
serve. What Hopkins does here in this sustained and elaborated way he
does in concentration in *The Windhover* and *Spelt from Sibyl's Leaves.*

Imagery that reminds us still more readily of the Metaphysical conceit (the characteristic Hopkins pattern is less insistent here) occurs in
the fourth stanza:

> I am soft sift
> In an hourglass—at the wall
> Fast, but mined with a motion, a drift,
> And it crowds and it combs to the fall;
> I steady as a water in a well, to a poise, to a pane,

> But roped with, always, all the way down from the tall
> Fells or flanks of the voel, a vein
> Of the gospel proffer, a pressure, a principle, Christ's gift.

—The superb metaphor in the first part of the stanza offers no difficulty. It conveys perfectly the inner sinking and dissolution, and then (with a subtle shift from sand to water) the steadying and recovery. The imagery in the last three lines is more complex, but, when (from the notes) we know that "voel" is Welsh for "bare hill," not too difficult. The note adds: "the meaning, obscured by *roped,* is that the well is fed by trickles of water within the flanks of the mountains." This brief elucidation is a useful foil to the strength of Hopkins' imagery. The "obscured" should imply no adverse criticism: the metaphorical "roped" may make the original passage less immediately intelligible than Bridges' summary, but it also makes the mountain-rill something far more suggestive of power than a trickle, something capable of exerting pressure; it also suggests, illogically but not incompatibly (it is often the business of metaphor to reconcile opposed impulses, bents or emotions), that the "pressure," the "principle," can draw upwards. Nothing approaching this imagery in subtlety and strength can be found in any other poet of the nineteenth century.

Hopkins' technique justifies itself equally in the description of the storm in the second part of the poem—justifies itself obviously. Indeed, Bridges' "dragon" exaggerates the general difficulty: a great deal of the poem is as inviting to the anthologist as the first stanza, which he printed in *The Spirit of Man.* The first stanza of the second part, for instance, is even less refractory to "the grand style of our poetry":

> "Some find me a sword; some
> The flange and the rail; flame,
> Fang, or flood" goes Death on drum,
> And storms bugle his fame.
> But wé dream we are rooted in earth—Dust!
> Flesh falls within sight of us, we, though our flower the same,
> Wave with the meadow, forget that there must
> The sour scythe cringe, and the blear share come.

(The last line has six stresses.)

But remarkable as *The Wreck of the Deutschland* is it does not put his technical skill to the utmost stretch. This skill is most unmistakably that of a great poet when it is at the service of a more immediately personal urgency, when it expresses not religious exaltation, but inner debate. *The Windhover* is a poem of this kind. Since not only Mr.

Richards, in the essay[24] already mentioned, but Mr. Empson also, in *Seven Types of Ambiguity*,[25] have dealt admirably with this poem, there is no need to analyse it here. Mr. Empson's book is one that nobody interested in English poetry can afford not to have read. It is an implicit commentary on Bridges' complaint that "ambiguity or momentary uncertainty destroys the force of the sentence" [26] and imposes on the reader a "conscious effort of interpretation." [27] The kind of ambiguity that Mr. Empson finds to be the essence of *The Windhover* is suggested here: "Thus in the first three lines of the sestet we seem to have a clear case of the Freudian use of opposites, where two things thought of as incompatible, but desired intensely by different systems of judgments, are spoken of simultaneously by words applying to both; both desires are thus given a transient and exhausting satisfaction, and the two systems of judgment are forced into open conflict before the reader." It is in place at this point to observe that Hopkins' genius was as much a matter of rare character, intelligence, and sincerity as of technical skill: indeed, in his great poetry the distinction disappears; the technical triumph is a triumph of spirit.

The inner friction expressed in the equivocal burden of *The Windhover* comes out more explicitly in *Spelt from Sibyl's Leaves,* which, if it represents a less difficult undertaking, is more indubitably a complete success. It is one of the finest things that he ever did, and since it exhibits and magnificently justifies most of the peculiarities of his technique, I will (though Mr. Richards has analysed it) venture a brief commentary:

> Earnest, earthless, equal, attuneable, | vaulty, voluminous, . . . stupendous
> Evening strains to be tíme's vást, | womb-of-all, home-of-all, hearse-of-all night.
> Her fond yellow hornlight wound to the west, | her wild hollow hoarlight hung to the height
> Waste; her earliest stars, earl-stars, | stárs principal, overbend us,
> Fíre-féaturing heaven. For earth | her being has unbound, her dapple is at an end, as-
> tray or aswarm, all throughther, in throngs; | self ín self steepèd and páshed—qúite
> Disremembering, dísmémbering | áll now. Heart, you round me right

²⁴ See p. 165.
²⁵ W. Empson, *Seven Types of Ambiguity* (London: Chatto & Windus, Ltd.), p. 248 ff.
²⁶ *Poems of Gerard Manley Hopkins,* p. 98.
²⁷ *Ibid.,* p. 97.

With: óur évening is over us; óur night | whélms, whélms, ánd will
   end us.

Only the bleak-leaved boughs dragonish | damask the tool-smooth
   bleak light; black,

Ever so black on it. Our tale, O óur oracle! | Lét life, wáned, ah
   lét life wind

Off hér once skéined stained, véined varíety | upon, áll on twó
   spools; párt, pen, páck

Now her áll in twó flocks, twó folds—black, white; | right, wrong;
   reckon but, reck but, mind

But thése two; wáre of a wórld where bút these | twó tell, each off
   the óther; of a rack

Where, selfwrung, selfstrung, sheathe- and shelterless, | thóughts
   agáinst thoughts ín groans grínd.

The poem opens with evening deepening into night. We are not
merely told that evening "strains," we feel evening straining, to become
night, enveloping everything, in the movement, the progression of alliteration, assonance and rime. This progression is associated with, and
hardly distinguishable from, the development of meaning in the sequence
of adjectives: evening is first sweetly solemn, serene, etherealizing and
harmonizing, then becomes less tranquillizing and more awful, and
finally ends in the blackness of night.

Her fond yellow hornlight wound to the west, her wild hollow
   hoarlight hung to the height
Waste. . . .

—The "yellow hornlight" is, of course, the setting moon; "fond"—
tender, soft, sympathetic, clinging as if reluctant to go, the slow gentle
sinking being felt in the movement and modulation of the verse. The
"hoarlight" is the cold, hard starlight, "wild" and "hollow"—remote,
inhuman, a kind of emptiness in the hollow vault—in contrast to the
"fond yellow" moonlight. The verse-movement itself, with the inevitable
rest upon "height," seems to hang. The "dapple" of earth, the rich
coloured variety that Hopkins loved so much (cf. *Pied Beauty*[28]—"Glory
be to God for dappled things") has gone, merged ("throughther"—each
through other) into neutrality. That he is not concerned with "pure description" the introduction of "self" intimates, together with the unex-
pected strength of "steepèd and páshed" and "dismembering."

He suddenly realizes the whole thing as a parable, not meditatively

⚹ *Poems of Gerard Manley Hopkins*, p. 30.

worked out, but immediate: he sees the outward symbol and the significance as one, in a kind of metaphor. It is Blake's *Sun-flower* rather
than Matthew Arnold's *Yes: in the sea of life enisled.*

> Heart, you round me right
> With: Óur évening is over us; oúr night whélms

—the heavy stress that his rhythm enables him to put upon "our"
brings home the poignant realization. His heart "rounds" him, i.e.
whispers (as in the ballads), and "rounds upon him" with, the thought
that he has sacrificed the "dapple" of existence for the stark dichotomy
of right and wrong.

> Only the beak-leaved boughs dragonish | damask the tool-smooth
>   bleak light; black,
> Ever so black on it.

—The trees are no longer the beautiful, refreshing things of daylight;
they have turned fantastically strange, hard and cruel, "beak-leaved"
suggesting the cold, hard light, steely like the gleam of polished tools,
against which they appear as a kind of damascene-work ("damask") on
a blade. Then follows the anguished surrender to the realization:

> . . . Oúr tale, O oúr oracle! | Lét life, wáned, ah lét life wind
> Off hér one skéined stained véined varíety | upon, áll on twó
>   spools; párt, pen, páck
> Now her áll in twó flocks, twó folds—black, white; | right,
>   wrong. . . .

—The run of alliterations, rimes and assonances suggests the irre-
sistible poignancy of the realization. The poem ends with a terrible
effect as of unsheathed nerves grinding upon one another. The grinding
might at first be taken to be merely that of "right" against "wrong," the
inner conflict of spirit and flesh, and the pain that which the believer
knows he must face, the simple pain of renunciation. Yet we are aware
of a more subtle anguish and a more desperate plight. And if we look
closely, we find that Hopkins is explicit about it:

> black, white; right, wrong . . . .

—The first draft had "wrong, right," but he deliberately, and significantly, reversed the order. If he were merely "ware of a world where
but these two tell," his torment would be less cruel. But his consciousness is more complex; his absolutes waver and change places, and he is
left in terrible doubt.

In comparison with such a poem of Hopkins' as this, any other poetry of the nineteenth century is seen to be using only a very small part of the resources of the English language. His words seem to have substance, and to be made of a great variety of stuffs. Their potencies are correspondingly greater for subtle and delicate communication. The intellectual and spiritual anaemia of Victorian poetry is indistinguishable from its lack of body. Hopkins is a very different poet from Dante, but a remark that Mr. Eliot throws out[29] in the discussion of Dante has a bearing here: "that Hell, though a state, is a state which can only be thought of, and perhaps only experienced, by the projection of sensory images; and that the resurrection of the body has perhaps a deeper meaning than we understand." The critical implications of this (they can be generalized and discussed apart from any theological context) deserves pondering. They relate to another remark of Mr. Eliot's that has been quoted already and applies also to Hopkins: in his verse "the intellect is at the tip of the senses." And along with the qualities indicated by this phrase goes a remarkable control of tempo and modulation.

The poems of Hopkins that stand in best hope of general acceptance (after *Margaret*) are the group of intensely personal sonnets that he wrote towards the end of his life. *The Windhover* and *Spelt from Sibyl's Leaves* are in sonnet form, but the late sonnets are immediately recognizable as such. Moreover they lack anything in the nature of

The roll, the rise, the carol, the creation,

for the pressure of personal anguish was too strong; and consequently they do not present so formidable an appearance as where the Hopkins technique is more copiously elaborated. As Bridges put it,[30] when Hopkins died "he was beginning to concentrate the force of all his luxuriant experiments in rhythm and diction, and castigate his art into a more reserved style." The austerity was rather, perhaps, the effect of that cruel inner friction expressed in *The Windhover* and *Spelt from Sibyl's Leaves*. In spite of the terrible import of these poems there is still a certain magnificent buoyancy in the handling of the technical problems. But when he wrote those last sonnets, Hopkins had no buoyancy left. They are the more interesting from the point of view of this study in that they bring out more plainly the relation of his medium to speech. More obviously here than in the more canorous poems the ruling spirit is that of living idiom; we can hear the speaking voice:

[29] *Dante* (London: Faber & Faber, 1929), p. 32.
[30] *Poems of Gerard Manley Hopkins*, p. 99.

I wake and feel the fell of dark, not day.
What hours, O what black hoürs we have spent
This night! what sights you, heart, saẃ; ways you went!
And more must, in yet longer light's delay.
  With witness I speak this. But where I say
Hours I mean years, mean life. And my lament
Is cries countless, cries like dead letters sent
To dearest him that lives alas! away.

Yet this is characteristic Hopkins in its methods of compression and its elimination of all inessential words. There is the familiar use of assonance: "feel" becomes "fell," i.e. feeling becomes an obsessing sense of the overwhelming darkness (the adjectival homonym is felt in "fell," which is therefore the smothering coat of a fell beast); and the sequence "night," "sights," "light's" suggest the obsessing horror of the night.

There are a few difficulties; notably, for instance, in the sestet of the sonnet (47) that begins: *My own heart let me have more pity on.* This is admirably dealt with in *A Survey of Modernist Poetry*[31] by Laura Riding and Robert Graves (p. 90 ff.). But the difficulty will mainly be, not to get the sense, but to realize the full effect intended, to get the "oddities" into focus. Some of the effects are extremely subtle and original. One of the most remarkable has already been quoted:

                    Only what word
   Wisest my heart breeds dark heaven's baffling ban
   Bars or hell's spell thwarts. This to hoard unheard,
   Heard unheeded, leaves me a lonely began.

This conveys the very process of frustration, the very realizing of failure. No poet with a respect for literary decorum could have accepted that "began" even if it had come; but it is magnificently justified. The passage, with all its compression, achieved by characteristic means, suggests the speaking voice using modern idiom: "word wisest" has nothing in common with ordinary poetic inversion. And it would be hard to illustrate better the difference between Hopkins' use of alliteration and assonance and Swinburne's: in Hopkins they serve to call the maximum attention to each word.

Another particularly remarkable effect is the close of the sonnet called *Carrion Comfort*:

              That night, that year
   Of now done darkness I wretch lay wrestling with (my God!) my
   God.

---

[31] This is a very uneven book. The authors, for instance, discuss Hopkins and E. E. Cummings with equal gravity.

This, as the sonnet is read through, is completely successful: it represents fairly the control, the sureness of touch, and the perfection of essential decorum that accompany Hopkins' audacities.

Yet training in the other decorum may cause a great deal of boggling. For example, the sonnet *The Candle Indoors* (not one of the "terrible" ones) begins:

> Some candle clear burns somewhere I come by,
> I muse at how its being puts blissful back
> With yellowy moisture mild night's blear-all black,
> Or to-fro tender trambeams truckle at the eye.

Of the last line the editor of the second edition of the *Poems* remarks:

> It is perfectly possible to smile at the line, but hardly possible to laugh; or only sympathetically, as at the wilder images of the metaphysicals, the extremer rhetoric of Marlowe, the more sedate elegances of Pope, the more prosaic moralities of the Victorians, or the more morbid pedestrianisms of Thomas Hardy. Such things are the accidents of genius seriously engaged upon its own business, and not so apt as the observer to see how funny it looks.

And yet, once the meaning has been taken, there should be nothing funny about the line. The image is so just, the expression of it, far from producing any accidental effect, so inevitable and adequate, that we hardly see the words as such; the image replaces them. Hopkins is describing the lines of light (caused, I believe, by the eyelashes) that, in the circumstances specified, converge upon the eye like so many sets of tram-rails. But "tram" unqualified would suggest something too solid, so he adds "tender"; and "truckle" conveys perfectly the obsequious way in which they follow every motion of the eyes and of the eyelids.

Bridges, again, boggled at the second couplet of *Margaret*, and, in printing this poem (probably Hopkins' best-known) in *The Spirit of Man*, left it out. I have heard him commended for the improvement. The sonnet addressed to him perhaps he may be excused for venturing to correct. It opens (as printed by him and Mr. Williams):

> The fine delight that fathers thought; the strong
> Spur, live and lancing like the blowpipe flame,
> Breathes once and, quenchèd faster than it came,
> Leaves yet the mind a mother of immortal song.
> Nine months she then, nay years, nine years she long
> Within her wears, bears, cares and moulds the same:

—Bridges notes: "In line 6 the word *moulds* was substituted by me for *combs* of original, when the sonnet was published by Miles; and I leave

it, having no doubt that G. M. H. would have made some such altera-
tion." Others will have considerable doubt. To use so weak a word as
"moulds" in this place is most unlike Hopkins. The objection to
"combs" seems to be based on nothing better than a narrow conception of metaphor—the same misconception that prompts editors to
emend the "To-morrow and to-morrow and to-morrow" passage in *Macbeth*: ". . . having regard to the turn of thought and the necessary continuity of metaphors, I am convinced that Shakespeare's epithet was
dusky." [32] Good metaphor need not be a matter of consistently worked
out analogy or point-for-point parallel; and the shift represented by
"combs" imposes itself as "right" on the unprejudiced sensibility, and
is very characteristic of Hopkins. Perhaps the term *prolepsis*, suitably
invoked, would suffice to settle any qualms.

The strength and subtlety of his imagery are proof of his genius. But
Victorian critics were not familiar with such qualities in the verse of
their time. The acceptance of Hopkins would alone have been enough
to reconstitute their poetic criteria. But he was not published in 1889.
He is now felt to be a contemporary, and his influence is likely to be
great. It will not necessarily manifest itself in imitation of the more
obvious of his technical peculiarities (these, plainly, may be dangerous
toys); but no one can come from studying his work without an extended
notion of the resources of English. And a technique so much concerned
with inner division, friction, and psychological complexities in general
has a special bearing on the problems of contemporary poetry.

He is likely to prove, for our time and the future, the only influential
poet of the Victorian age, and he seems to me the greatest.

[32] *Macbeth: The Arden Shakespeare*, p. 141.

Gerard Manley Hopkins

by Yvor Winters

It is my intention to begin by comparing three poems, a sonnet by John Donne, a short poem by Robert Bridges, and a sonnet by Gerard Hopkins, and to compare them with reference to a particular theory of poetry. The poems by Donne and Bridges conform to this theory and illustrate it perfectly; the poem by Hopkins deviates sharply and I believe suffers as a result. Hopkins provides an excellent example of deviation, however, for two reasons: in the first place, though his deviation is serious, it is not crude or ridiculous and thus differs from the deviations of many romantic poets before and after, even poets of genius; and in the second place, his gift for language, as far as his procedure will allow it to emerge, appears almost as great as that of Donne or Bridges, so that we may examine with a minimum of distraction the consequences of the deviation itself. The poems of Donne and Bridges deal with closely related themes, under different figures derived from different views of human history; the theme of Hopkins may be similar but is inadequately defined and one cannot be sure.

The theory of poetry may be summarized briefly as follows. A poem is a statement in words, and about a human experience, and it will be successful in so far as it realizes the possibilities of that kind of statement. This sentence may seem childishly obvious, but it states facts of which we must never lose sight if we are to understand poetry, and facts of which sight is very commonly lost. When we are discussing poetry, we should not beguile ourselves with analogies drawn from music, sculpture, architecture, or engineering; a poem is not a symphony, neither is it a structure made of bricks. Words are primarily conceptual: the words *grief, tree, poetry, God,* represent concepts; they may communicate some feeling and remembered sensory impression as well, and they may be

made to communicate a great deal of these, but they will do it by virtue
of their conceptual identity, and in so far as this identity is impaired
they will communicate less of these and communicate them with less
force and precision. It is the business of the poet, then, to make a statement in words about an experience; the statement must be in some sense
and in a fair measure acceptable rationally; and the feeling communi-
cated should be proper to the rational understanding of the experience.

Poetry has something, however, though relatively little, in common
with music; namely, rhythm. Rhythm, with the other elements of sound
which may be combined with it—in poetry these other elements are
relatively few and simple—is to some extent expressive of emotion, and
it may be used to modify the emotional content of language. The value
of rhythm is not primarily in its power to intensify emotion, though it
has this power; it is rather in its power to modulate and define emotion,
so that a finer adjustment of emotion to thought may be possible.

The poem thus differs from the statement of the philosopher or scien-
tist in that it is a fairly complete judgment of an experience: it is not
merely a rational statement, but it communicates as well the feeling
which the particular rational understanding ought to motivate. It differs
from the statement of the writer of imaginative prose, in that the poet's
language is more precise and more flexible and hence can accomplish
more in little space and accomplish it better. But with the development
of romantic theory in the eighteenth, nineteenth, and twentieth centuries,
there has been an increasing tendency to suppress the rational in poetry
and as far as may be to isolate the emotional. This tendency makes at
best for an incomplete poetry and makes at worst for a very confused
poetry.

My first poem is by John Donne:

> Thou hast made me, and shall thy work decay?
> Repair me now, for now mine end doth haste,
> I run to death, and death meets me as fast,
> And all my pleasures are like yesterday;
> I dare not move my dim eyes any way,
> Despair behind and death before doth cast
> Such terror, and my feeble flesh doth waste
> By sin in it, which it toward hell doth weigh;
> Only thou art above, and when toward thee
> By thy leave I can look, I rise again;
> But our old subtle foe so tempteth me,
> That not one hour myself I can sustain;
> Thy Grace may wing me to prevent his art,
> And thou like Adamant draw mine iron heart.

This poem is simple in conception: the poet looks forward a little way to death and backward on the sins of his life; he is oppressed with his helplessness and prays for God's grace that he may love God, repent, and be saved. The situation is a general one: we have an orthodox theological definition of a predicament in which every man is supposed to share; yet the poet knows it to be his own predicament, and the theological proposition becomes a personal experience. The language is plain, but is exact and powerful.

My second poem, *Low Barometer,* is by Robert Bridges:

> The southwind strengthens to a gale,
> Across the moon the clouds fly fast,
> The house is smitten as with a flail,
> The chimney shudders to the blast.
>
> On such a night, when Air has loosed
> Its guardian grasp on blood and brain,
> Old terrors then of god or ghost
> Creep from their caves to life again;
>
> And Reason kens he herits in
> A haunted house. Tenants unknown
> Assert their squalid lease of sin
> With earlier title than his own.
>
> Unbodied presences, the pack'd
> Pollution and Remorse of Time,
> Slipped from oblivion reënact
> The horrors of unhoused crime.
>
> Some men would quell the thing with prayer
> Whose sightless footsteps pad the floor,
> Whose fearful trespass mounts the stair
> Or bursts the lock'd forbidden door.
>
> Some have seen corpses long interr'd
> Escape from hallowing control,
> Pale charnel forms—nay ev'n have heard
> The shrilling of a troubled soul,
>
> That wanders till the dawn hath cross'd
> The dolorous dark, or Earth hath wound
> Closer her storm-spredd cloke, and thrust
> The baleful phantoms underground.

The theme of this poem, as I have said, is similar to the theme of the sonnet by Donne. Donne sees man as fallen from Grace and evicted from paradise, and as capable of salvation only through a return of Grace as an aid to his own imperfect ability; though he does not say so in this poem, his system depends in part on the right use of Reason, though Reason without Grace is insufficient, and the poem is a prayer for Grace. Bridges sees man as risen from brutality and as governed precariously by Reason. Both poets deal with man's unequal struggle with his lower nature, and with what we may call either literally or figuratively the effect of Original Sin. Bridges, like Donne, feels the need for supernatural aid in addition to Reason; unlike Donne, he cannot state this need directly and in theological language, for he is not a Christian, but he implies it in his figurative use of Air: ". . . when Air has loosed/ Its guardian grasp on blood and brain." Through the figure of the storm, he indicates supernatural violence; as a result of the storm, the steady force of the air, like the pressure of water on submarine life, is relaxed, and man's nature is unbalanced, and man sees corpses "Escape from hallowing control"; Reason is overwhelmed by the ancient and powerful demonic forces in its fleshly habitation. This poem, like Donne's, deals with a common predicament; unlike Donne's, the poem does not profess to deal with a personal experience. Both poems deal with the experience in the most general of terms: Donne's despair, death, and sin could hardly be more general, but they are definite, for they have a body of theology behind them, and we know what they include and why Donne feels as he does; Bridges, without such a theological system for direct reference, must limit his statement further:

> Unbodied presences, the pack'd
> Pollution and Remorse of Time,
> Slipped from oblivion reënact
> The horrors of unhouseled crime.

These lines are the culmination of his account of sin as the subhuman, the archaic, and the chaotic; he is forced to greater particularity here than Donne, and he achieves greater power, but the statement is nevertheless general and very inclusive. What I wish to call to the attention at present is this: that though both poems are generalized, they are precise; that there is a great difference between generalization and uncertainty.

Let us now consider the sonnet by Hopkins:

> No worst, there is none. Pitched past pitch of grief,
> More pangs will, schooled at forepangs, wilder wring.
> Comforter, where, is your comforting?
> Mary, mother of us, where is your relief?

My cries heave, herds-long; huddle in a main, a chief
Woe, world-sorrow; on an age-old anvil wince and sing—
Then lull, then leave off. Fury had shrieked 'No ling-
  ering! Let me be fell: force I must be brief.'

O the mind, mind has mountains: cliffs of fall
Frightful, sheer, no-man-fathomed. Hold them cheap
May who ne'er hung there. Nor does long our small
Durance deal with that steep or deep. Here! creep,
Wretch, under a comfort serves in a whirlwind: all
Life death does end and each day dies with sleep.

This poem differs from the two preceding in that it deals primarily with
a particular and personal experience; the difficulty consists in the fact
that there is so little generalization that we can feel no certainty regarding the nature of the experience beyond the fact that it has generated a
desperate emotion. This is not a poem about the effects of violent emotion in general; it is a poem about a particular violent emotion experienced by the poet. The nearest thing to a statement of motive occurs in
the first line and a half of the sestet; but what are these mountains of
the mind? One does not enquire because one holds them cheap, but because one has hung on so many oneself, so various in their respective
terrors, that one is perplexed to assign a particular motive. One is inclined to ask: "What do you know of these matters? Why are you so
secretive? And above all, why are you so self-righteous in your secretive-
ness?" Hopkins' modern admirers have often assumed that the poem
deals with a struggle to maintain what they consider an irrational and
unwholesome faith, that it deals with the self-inflicted torture of the religious. There is nothing in the poem either to prove or to disprove the
idea of such a struggle. The emotion might result from such a struggle,
might result as in Donne's sonnet from a sense of sin either general or
particular or both and for the need of Grace, from the contemplation
of any of several metaphysical propositions, from the death of a friend,
from betrayal by a friend, from the desperation of personal loneliness,
from a mixture of some of these, or from something else. We have passed
beyond the limits of generalization; we are in the realm of uncertainty;
and the mind cannot organize itself to share Hopkins' experience with
any real feeling of security.

It is interesting to observe the manner in which he achieves a part of
the precision he needs, a small part which is managed with such skill
that it gives a brief illusion of a great part, in the use of metaphor. Take,
for example, his most brilliant phrase: "on an age-old anvil wince and
sing—." The anvil is presumably God's discipline, and on it lies the poet

as a piece of metal. The two verbs, the first with its sense of human suffering combined with metallic vibration, the second with its sense of metallic vibration combined perhaps with human triumph, make the metal suffer as metal under the hammer, and the suffering metal is terribly vivid. We suffer with the metal under the blow, and we forget that the literal metal does not suffer, that metal and blow are figurative, and that the human half of the figure is incomplete. Thus the poet conveys emotion for a moment, and conveys it with an illusion of motivation but with no real motivation. If the mountains of the mind were adequately identified, Hopkins' figure would have a power comparable to that of Donne's last line; but Donne's line has meaning, and Hopkins' figure the illusion of meaning.

The meter of the poem contributes to the difficulty, or at least emphasizes it. Hopkins' published explanation of his meter is incomplete and contradictory, and will help us only a little to understand his work. I will consider it in some detail presently, but for the moment I would like to give my own definition of sprung rhythm, which agrees only in part with that of Hopkins, and then proceed to an examination of the meter of the present sonnet. Sprung rhythm occurs when two stresses come together by means other than the normal inversion of a foot; it occurs freely in accentual meter and in syllabic meter; it may occur as a variant in standard English meter as a result of the dropping of an unaccented syllable with the resultant creation of a monosyllabic foot, or as a result of the equally heavy accentuation of both syllables of a foot. For example, when Barnabe Googe writes in an iambic pentameter poem: "Fair face show friends when riches do abound," the first two feet are sprung. It is most profitable, I think, to approach the sonnet under consideration as a variant on iambic pentameter, using Hopkins' remarks as occasional guides. I shall offer a scansion of the poem, with alternative readings of certain lines, and shall then comment on the scansion:

1. No worst/ there is/ none. Pitched/ past pitch/ of grief/,

   No worst/

2. More pangs/ will, schooled/ at fore/pangs wild/er wring/.

3. Comfort/er where/ where is/ your com/forting/?

4. Mary/, mother/ of us/ where is/ your relief/?

5. My críes/ heave, hérds/-long; húd/dle in a maín/, a chíef/

   (My) cries heave/ hérds-long/; húddle/ in a maín/, a chíef/

6. Wóe, world sór/(row); on an áge/-old án/vil wínce/ and síng/—

   Wóe, world sór/row; on an áge/-

7. Then lúll/, then leáve/ off. Fú/ry had shriekéd/ "No líng/-

8. ering/! Lét me/ be féll/: fórce I/ must be bríef/."

9. O the mínd/, mínd/ has móunt/ains: clíffs/ of fáll/

10. Fríghtful/, shéer/, nó-man-fáth/omed. Hóld/ them chéap/

11. Máy who/ ne'er húng/ there. Nór/ does lóng/ our smáll/

    Máy who ne'er/ húng there/. Nór does/ lóng/ our smáll/

12. Dúrance/ déal with/ thát steép/ or deép/. Hére! Créep/,

13. Wrétch, un/der a cóm/fort sérves/ in a whírl/wind: áll/

14. Life deáth/ does énd/ and eách/ day díes/ with sleép/.

The first line is normal, unless we read the first foot as reversed; in either version it defines the pattern. In the second line, the first two feet are reversed, and the last three are normal; the reversal of the second foot is unusual, as Hopkins says in his preface, and is the first indication of the violence to follow. In the third line the first and third feet are reversed and the rest normal, this being a more ordinary arrangement. The fourth line is composed of four reversed feet and a normal trisyllabic foot, the first four feet giving us what Hopkins calls counterpoint, or a heard rhythm running counter to the remembered norm. The fifth line may be scanned in either of two ways: as composed of four iambic feet (the first three and the fifth), with the fourth foot reduced to three syllables by the elision of *huddle* and *in;* or with *My* regarded as extra-metrical, a violent procedure from the standpoint of the ordinary metrist, but defensible in Hopkins's system of lines which are "rove over," and thereafter three reversed feet, a normal trisyllabic foot, and a normal dissyllabic. The two readings may be regarded as a

case of counterpoint, perhaps, the first giving the theoretic norm and
the second the heard rhythm. In regard to this and other elisions, real
or possible, in Hopkins, one may suggest that Hopkins may have had a
notion comparable to that of Bridges, whereby elision takes place for the
eye and so pays its respects to regularity but does not take place for the
ear: his elisions, or possible elisions, in any event, are usually preferable
if seen but not heard. The sixth line contains seven inescapable accents, and so eliminates any possibility that the poem be scanned as
regular accentual meter. I should be inclined to call the first three syllables, all of which are accented, a single sprung foot, of the same sort
employed by Googe in dissyllabic units when he wrote, "Fair face show
friends." I am acquainted with no poet save Hopkins who has used a
sprung foot of three syllables, but the sprung foot of two syllables, employed as a variation on standard English meter, is fairly common in
the sixteenth century. The second syllable of *sorrow* may then be regarded as extrametrical, the position of the extrametrical syllable before
the caesura instead of at the line-end being natural enough in a system
in which the line-end need not involve a pause and in which the
caesural break may be heavy, that is in a system of lines which are
"rove-over," as I have said; or *sorrow* may be elided with *on;* thereafter
we have a normal trisyllabic foot followed by three normal dissyllabics.
The seventh line is simple except for the termination in mid-word, a
procedure justified by Hopkins' theory and successful use of "rove-over"
rhythm, and for which classical—and even, in a measure, Miltonic—
precedent can be found if it is wanted; the fourth foot of this line is a
normal trisyllabic, the others are normal dissyllabics. The eighth line
contains an inverted foot in the difficult second position and another in
the fourth, and for the rest contains two normal dissyllabics and a final
normal trisyllabic, and thus brings the octet back more or less obviously
to the iambic pentameter pattern.

In the ninth line, we have a trisyllabic, a monosyllabic, and three dissyllabics, the accents falling normally. The monosyllabic foot, as a method
of achieving sprung rhythm, has, like the sprung dissyllabic, its precedents in the sixteenth century. It occurs in some of the seven-syllable
couplets of Greene: the reader may examine specimens of both, if he is
curious, in *The Oxford Book of Sixteenth Century Verse.* In line ten we
have an inverted dissyllabic, a monosyllabic, an inverted trisyllabic, and
two normal dissyllabics. In the eleventh line we may read five dissyllabics,
the first only being inverted; or we may read an inverted trisyllabic followed by two inverted dissyllabics, a monosyllabic, and a normal dissyllabic; the first reading giving the theoretic norm and the second the

heard rhythm, with another example of Hopkins' counterpoint as the result. The twelfth line consists of two inverted dissyllabics, a sprung dissyllabic, a normal dissyllabic, and a sprung dissyllabic, to give us another line of seven accents. The thirteen line consists of an inverted dissyllabic, a normal trisyllabic, a normal dissyllabic, a normal trisyllabic, and a normal dissyllabic. The last line consists of five normal dissyllabics, although the long syllables in the first and fourth feet almost give the illusion of sprung feet: this line returns to the original pattern, yet echoes some of the more violent variations.

The poem, then, is not written in syllabic meter, for the number of syllables varies from line to line; if it is an attempt at accentual meter, it is irregular, for two lines contain extra accents. But it can be described, and without undue trouble, as a variant on standard English meter, a variant both learned and perverse but in which the rhythm is successfully maintained, in which the perversity is equalled by the skill.

Skill to what purpose, however? The rhythm is fascinating in itself, but it does not exist in itself, it exists in the poem. It is a rhythm based on the principle of violent struggle with its governing measure, and it contributes to the violence of feeling in the total poem. But it is this very violence which makes us question the motive, and I think one may add that the violence is in some degree the result of the inadequacy of the motive. When Bridges writes:

> Unbodied presences, the pack'd
> Pollution and Remorse of Time,
> Slipped from oblivion reënact
> The horrors of unhouseled crime,

he is making a statement about human nature which is true and important; the concept and all its implications are clear; and he can make his statement quietly, for he knows that we should recognize its importance and be moved appropriately. I do not mean that the importance of the concept absolves him from the necessity of deliberately communicating the appropriate emotion, and in this passage the emotional weight of the language is great; I mean that his statement has the dignity of conviction. Hopkins has no such generating concept, or at least offers none; since he cannot move us by telling us why he himself is moved, he must try to move us by belaboring his emotion. He says, in effect: "Share my fearful emotion, for the human mind is subject to fearful emotions." But why should we wish to share an emotion so ill sponsored? Nothing could be more rash. We cannot avoid sharing a part of it, for Hopkins has both skill and genius; but we cannot avoid being confused by the experience and suspecting in it a fine shade of the ludicrous. Who is this man to lead us so far and blindfold into violence? This kind of thing is a violation of our integrity; it is somewhat beneath the dignity of man.

There seems to be some agreement to the effect that Hopkins' commonest method of constructing a poem is to describe a landscape or a part of one and then to provide an application which is usually religious. Arthur Mizener, in an essay devoted very largely to this aspect of Hopkins, writes:

> The basic structure of Hopkins' lyrics is a description followed by a comment, an application. They are, for all their intensity, poems of reflection, in the best sense of the word rhetorical rather than dramatic. Occasionally he indulged in the kind of naked symbolism by which the lion, for instance, becomes God's strength and conducts himself accordingly, without regard for the natural habits of lions. At best this practice made for the fantastic kind of poetry we associate with Crashaw. . . .[1]

H. M. McLuhan, in an essay in which interpretation is often carried so far from the actual text as to approach pure fantasy, recognizes the same structure, but regards it as an essential property of a certain kind of religious mind:

> Hopkins looks at external nature as a Scripture exactly as Philo Judaeus, St. Paul, and the Church Fathers had done. . . . Hopkins habitually shifts his gaze from the order and perspectives of nature to the analagous but grander scenery of the moral and intellectual order. . . . Or the book of nature provides parallel passages with the supernatural revelations of Scripture.[2]

McLuhan illustrates these remarks with quotations which I omit. Mizener is perhaps a little apologetic about the method, but is not greatly disturbed by it; McLuhan seems to regard it as a major virtue. Neither appears to discern certain important difficulties inherent in it.

I will try to illustrate certain of these dangers, beginning with some of the more striking examples and proceeding to the milder ones. I will quote the opening lines of a famous sonnet:

> The world is charged with the grandeur of God.
>   It will flame out like shining from shook foil;
>   It gathers to a greatness, like the ooze of oil
>   Crushed. . . .

---

[1] *Gerard Manley Hopkins,* by the Kenyon Critics (New York: New Directions, 1945), p. 103.

[2] *Ibid.,* p. 19.

The first line offers a major concept, in impressive phrasing. Instead of developing the concept, as a concept, however, in the manner of a poet of the Renaissance, Hopkins proceeds to illustrate it with two descriptive figures. In the first of these we are confronted with the kind of ambiguity which occurs so often in Hopkins: if we assume that the second line is grammatically correct, then *foil* is a quantitative word and refers to tin-foil or to gold-leaf, or to something of that nature, and we have what amounts, in effect, to an image of a mad man (or at least of a remark-ably eccentric man) brandishing a metal bouquet; if the foil in question, however, is a fencing foil, then the grammar is defective, for the article is omitted.[3] This particular defect is not an uncommon form of poetic license, especially in Hopkins, and Hopkins takes much greater liberties elsewhere; but the image is indeterminate. In the next image there is a curious inaccuracy of natural description: "crushed" (or spilled) oil does not "gather" to a greatness, it spreads; or if Hopkins is referring to the gathering of oil from the crushing of olives, he is not only incomplete but is again inexact in his grammar. Aside from the difficulties just men-tioned, which I suppose will appear trivial to many, but which never-theless seem to me to introduce an element of shoddiness into the style, both of these figures are almost grotesquely trivial as illustrations of the first line; as so often happens, Hopkins is unable to rise to his occasion, and he relies on violent assertiveness and violent rhythm to carry him over his chasms.

The Starlight Night devotes the octet to ecstatic description of a natural scene. In the first line of the sestet, we have the interjection:

Buy then! bid them!—What?—Prayer, patience, alms, vows.

Then we have two more lines of description, and in the last three lines a statement to the effect that the universe described is the home of "Christ and his mother and all his hallows." It is a curious poem. The description is sometimes extremely brilliant and is interesting everywhere save in the sestet. Yet the real theme of the poem is to be found in the first line of the sestet, and nothing is done with it. A devotional poet of the Renaissance, dealing with "prayer, patience, alms, vows," would have had a good deal to say of each and of what each meant in terms of daily life and toward salvation. The reader who wishes to orient himself, might begin by rereading Ben Jonson's *To Heaven,* John Donne's *Thou*

[*] We learn from a note on page 226 of Gardner (*Poems of Gerard Manley Hopkins,* third edition) that Hopkins had shaken goldfoil in mind. We do not learn how it was shaken. The ambiguity is still in the text of the poem, however, and the essential weakness of the image remains.

hast made me, Greville's *Down in the depth of mine iniquity,* and
Herbert's *Church Monuments.* In no other literary period, I think, save
our own, would a poet who was both a priest and a genuinely devout
man have thought that he had dealt seriously with his love for Christ
and his duty toward him by writing an excited description of a landscape: this kind of thing belongs to the nineteenth and twentieth centuries, to the period of self-expression and the abnegation of reason. The
impressiveness of the landscape described in this poem provides a more
nearly adequate motivation for the feeling asserted than one can find in
many other poems similarly constructed: Hopkins' method in general is
to employ the landscape as the immediate motive for a feeling which is
too great for it, and then to append the perfunctory moral as a kind of
theoretic justification. A few additional poems in which this formula
occurs more or less obviously are the following: *Spring, The Sea and the
Skylark, The Windhover, Pied Beauty, Hurrahing in Harvest,* and *Duns
Scotus's Oxford.* One could add to this list, but these will serve for illustration; and I shall discuss only two of these.

Duns Scotus's Oxford offers an octet devoted to a description of the
Oxford landscape, with especial reference to the mingling of city and
country and the regrettable domination of the city. The sestet then provides the personal reference:

> Yet ah! this air I gather and I release
> He lived on; these weeds and waters, these walls are what
> He haunted who of all men most sways my spirit to peace;
>
> Of realty the rarest veinëd unraveler; a not
> Rivalled insight, be rival Italy or Greece;
> Who fired France for Mary without spot.

This is the climax and the point of the poem, yet it is obviously very
weak. We are told that Scotus is the one "who of all men most sways
my spirit to peace"; yet we are not told how he does it nor why. We are
told that he is "of realty the rarest veinëd unraveler; a not/ Rivalled insight," yet these are empty epithets, and the subject of the poem, properly
speaking, is merely mentioned sentimentally and is not defined or developed. It is as if one should say: "This is a magnificent landscape," or
"this is a great man," or "this is the most beautiful woman I have ever
seen." What we have is a stereotyped assertion, which we are supposed to
take seriously, but which we cannot take seriously for lack of definition
and perceptual evidence. This is not the method of Donne, or of Herbert.
These poets discuss the subject and omit or pass lightly over the incidentals. Hopkins all but ignores the subject and is at his best in dealing

fragmentarily with the incidentals: the "towery city and branchy between towers," and the like. The incidentals are sometimes, as in this line, charming, but they are minor, and they are not incorporated into a well organized poem, even a minor one, but are parts, rather, of a disorganized poem which pretends to be more than it is.

The Windhover has been named repeatedly as Hopkins' best poem. Hopkins considered it to be such, and his admirers have followed him in this opinion, and some of them have carried it much farther than Hopkins did. McLuhan, for example, says:

> *The Windhover* could never have become the richly complex poem it is if Hopkins had not tested and explored all its themes beforehand, in other poems. There is no other poem of comparable length in English, or perhaps in any language, which surpasses its richness and intensity or realized artistic organization. There are two or three sonnets of Shakespeare . . . which might be put with Donne's "At the round earth's" for comparison and contrast with this sonnet. But they are not comparable with the range of experience and multiplicity of integrated perception which is found in *The Windhover.*[4]

The Windhover begins with the much discussed description of the bird in flight; if one can keep himself disentangled from perverse theories of scansion while reading it, it is a fine description, but in itself it is merely description, that is, an example of the simplest subject matter available to the poet. As description it can be equalled and even surpassed by a great many passages in Coleridge, Wordsworth, Keats, Hardy, and perhaps others. Hardy's nighthawk, for example, is rendered more clearly and concisely as regards the bird itself; it is free from the pathetic fallacy which occurs in Hopkins' reading of his own ecstasy into an action which for the bird was merely a routine matter of business; and it is not required at any point in the poem to carry a symbolic burden too great for it. I offer Hardy's nighthawk, from the poem entitled *Afterwards*:

> If it be in the dusk when, like an eyelid's soundless blink,
> The dewfall hawk comes crossing the shades to alight
> Upon the wind-warped upland thorn. . . .

The epithet *dewfall* contributes to the sense of the time of day and suggests the soundless and mysterious appearance of the bird: it does this quite as effectively as Hopkins' *dapple-dawn-drawn* achieves its particular ends, more economically, and perhaps with greater originality. The simile in the first line contributes to both of the same effects. Every de-

[4] *Gerard Manley Hopkins,* by the Kenyon Critics, p. 27.

tail in the description reinforces every other. There is no vaguely excited and actual inefficient description such as Hopkins' *morning's minion, kingdom of daylight's dauphin.*

The unexplained ecstasy which hangs over the octet is supposedly explained in the sestet:

> Brute beauty and valour and act, oh, air, pride, plume, here
> Buckle! AND the fire that breaks from thee then, a billion
> Times told lovelier, more dangerous, O my chevalier!
>
> No wonder of it: sheer plod makes plough down sillion
> Shine, and blue-bleak embers, ah my dear,
> Fall, gall themselves, and gash gold-vermilion.

Before we can discover the degree and kind of success which appear in these lines, however, we must discover the meaning of the words. The first difficulty inheres in the word *buckle;* the second in the identity of the chevalier; and the third in the meaning of the phrase *makes plough down sillion/ Shine.*

John Pick, in *Gerard Manley Hopkins, Priest and Poet,* has this to say, after discussing the beauty described in the octet:

> But here is a beauty far, far greater. And the sestet is devoted to a revela-
> tion of a beauty beyond this beauty, a beauty which is "a billion times
> told lovelier, more dangerous" than the purely natural and triumphant
> flight. And whence comes this achievement which is more than achieve-
> ment, this mastery which is more than mastery?
>   It is in the act of "buckling," when the windhover swoops down, when
> its flight is crumpled, when "brute beauty and valour and act, oh, air, pride,
> plume" in an act of self-immolation send off a fire far greater than any
> natural beauty. . . . Nor is this to be wondered at, for this is true even in
> humble little things—is true of everything: the sheen of common earth
> shines out when the plough breaks it into furrows; and fire breaks from
> fire only in the moment of its own destruction. . . . Here is Christ upon
> the Cross and Hopkins the *alter Christus.* Beautiful was Christ's public life,
> but "a billion times told lovelier" was His self-immolation on the Cross,
> His sacrifice transmuted by the Fire of Love into something far greater than
> any mere natural beauty. More beautiful than any natural achievement
> was Hopkins' own humble and plodding continuance of the ethic of re-
> demption through his own mystical self-destruction, his own humble fol-
> lowing of Christ to the very Cross of Calvary. And the beauty of Christ and
> the beauty of the Jesuit to eyes that see more than this world is the beauty
> of their dying to live.[5]

[5] John Pick, *Gerard Manley Hopkins, Priest and Poet* (New York: Oxford University Press, 1942), p. 71.

Pick selects one of several possible meanings for *buckle:* for him the word means to collapse, as if we should say, "The wings of the plane buckled and it crashed." He finds support for his general interpretation in the writings of Loyola, which Hopkins as a Jesuit had studied carefully, and from scattered passages in Hopkins' other writings. But we have no right to suppose that any poem by Hopkins is a gloss on Loyola or on anything else unless there is clear evidence in the text, and there is no such evidence here. The falcon's wings do not buckle, in this sense, when he dives: they are retracted close to the body, or else are raised directly above the body, and are under perfect control; the dive, or the drop, of the falcon is one of the most remarkable physical facts observable in brute nature. Furthermore, the dive or the drop is not an act of self-sacrifice, it is an attack on the bird's prey. If Pick's interpretation is right, then the poem is badly conceived from start to finish; but it would be unfair to Hopkins to read into his poem a meaning for which the poem offers no evidence and which, once it is there, ruins the poem.

Pick apparently takes the expression *O my chevalier!* as being addressed to Christ, but there is no real evidence of this either. Christ is not mentioned in the poem. The poem is dedicated *To Christ our Lord,* but this does not mean that the poem is addressed to Christ. When a man dedicates a novel to a friend, he does not imply that the novel is addressed to his friend or is about him—he is merely offering a gift: since Hopkins regarded this as his best poem, he may merely have offered it to Christ in homage. On the other hand, it is possible that Hopkins meant to imply address in the dedication; there is no way of being sure. The difficulty in the second tercet is a minor one, in the sense that it does not affect the interpretation of the poem, but it is troublesome with respect to the particular image. The question is this: does Hopkins mean to say that the sheer plodding of the plowman makes the plow shine as it goes down the furrow, or does he mean to say that the plowed down earth is made to shine? If the first meaning is correct, then *plough* is a noun and should have an article; if the second meaning is correct, then *plough* is a past participle incorrectly spelled for the sake of euphony. The first of these licenses, though awkward, is common, not only in Hopkins but in other poets; the second would be violent and unlikely in any other poet, but is plausible enough in Hopkins. Pick believes that the earth shines and not the plow; but the passage has been taken in both ways by various critics.

McLuhan is at least as adventurous as Pick in his departures from the text. He writes:

To a member of a militant order whose founder was a Spanish soldier or chevalier, the feudal character of the opening imagery is quite natural. "Minion," "dauphin," "valour," "plume," and "buckle" alike evoke the world of dedicated knighthood and shining panoply of armor. Thus the mounted chevalier flashing off exploit as he "rung upon the rein" enables Hopkins later to reverse the situation with great dramatic effect in "sheer plod makes plough down sillion Shine." The paradox consists in the fact that Hopkins as lowly plowman following a horse flashes off infinitely more exploit than Hopkins the imagined chevalier.

More central still to the dramatic movement is the way in which the chevalier images of the octet are concentrated in "here Buckle!" Buckling is the traditional gesture of the knight preparing his armor for action. A buckler is the bright shield of defense bearing insignia, flashing defiance. . . . I have already said that "here" means in the "obedient and humble heart" and that "Buckle" means that the "brute beauty" of the bird as the mirror of God's grandeur is to be transferred or flashed to the "heart in hiding," just as the burnished surface of the plow in action is hidden in the earth. The high-spirited but obedient heart of man is "a billion times" better a mirror of Christ the chevalier than is the mirror of the external world. . . .[6]

McLuhan supports his interpretation at some length by quoting passages from other poems which suggest the theme which he has here in mind; my objection to his interpretation is simply that he departs too appallingly far from the actual text of the poem in hand. It is worth noting in passing that he agrees with Pick in the meaning of *chevalier,* and that, although he seems here to accept the other meaning of the plow image, he yet accepts both meanings of this latter in the course of his essay.

Miss Ruggles, although she believes that the plow shines rather than the earth, offers a more direct and simple explanation of the other phrases, and she gives us an interpretation which we can find justified, more or less, in the text. She says:

His imagination is caught and lifted as the small spiralling creature, magnificent in his instinctive performance, hovers at the very crux of its mastery, poised almost stationary against the opposing tide of wind.

Brute beauty and valour and act, oh, air, pride, plume, here Buckle!

This is the ultimate assertion, the carrying out of selfhood—

Op. cit., pp. 22-23.

> AND the fire that breaks from thee then, a billion
> Times told lovelier, more dangerous, O my chevalier!

It is in the act of buckling, when every sinew and chord of the identity thrills, at grips with its appointed function, that the beauty of the self flares brightest.

> No wonder of it: shéer plód makes plough down sillion
> Shine, and blue-bleak embers, ah my dear,
> Fall, gall themselves, and gash gold-vermilion.

The crude plough gleams in the moment of its contact with the resistful soil. Embers, foredoomed to crumble, can glow in this obscure enactment as fiercely as the flame.[7]

Miss Ruggles interprets the poem in terms of the concept of haecceity, inscape, or selfhood, which so obsesses Hopkins, and so keeps the poem closer to the bird which it apparently describes. For her, *buckle* means to concentrate all one's powers, as when we say: "He buckled to his work." And for her, the chevalier is the bird itself. She, also, is able to support her interpretation through other passages in Hopkins. In terms of her interpretation, we have a conclusion in the second tercet which merely points out that much less impressive actions give off their own fire: the first, the plodding effort of the plowman, which is humble but active; the second, the passive action of the coals when they fall and light up; so that it is no wonder that the striking action of the bird should give off a superior fire.

With this interpretation in mind, we may return to McLuhan for a moment. McLuhan assumes that Hopkins is developing a single chivalric image until he gets to the last tercet and abandons it, but the skate image interrupts this, and even McLuhan makes no effort to translate it into chivalric terms; it is the usual procedure of Hopkins, moreover, to hurl miscellaneous images at his subject from all sides, rather than to develop one of them fully. There is no reason to accept McLuhan's interpretation of *buckle,* therefore, unless it draws the whole poem together, which it fails to do. McLuhan believes that the plowman is figuratively Hopkins, but the poem does not say so; McLuhan says that the figurative plowman "flashes off infinitely more exploit than Hopkins the imagined chevalier," but the poem says that it is no wonder that the bird at the height of his achievement should flash light when a mere plowman can do it in a small way. McLuhan says that "here" means "in the obedient

[7] Eleanor Ruggles, *Gerard Manley Hopkins* (New York: W. W. Norton Co., Inc., 1944), p. 156.

and humble heart," but Hopkins says nothing about obedience and
humility, and of his heart he says "my heart in hiding," which on the
face of it seems to mean "my heart within me," or "my heart unob-
served."

Miss Ruggles takes another step in her interpretation, which brings
her closer to Pick and to McLuhan, though still leaves her far behind
them. She says:

> The beauty and valor of the winging falcon are Christ's own beauty and
> valor in an unthinking and finite form. Thus in a sense, the windhover is
> Christ. Christ is the windhover.

The poem does not say this, and the dedication does not necessarily
imply it, but this interpretation would be in line with Hopkins' thought
and with his practice in other poems; it would offer, moreover, some
explanation of the violent rhapsody of the first tercet. This brings us to
the crucial weakness of the poem, however; for if Miss Ruggles is right
at this point, as I suspect she is, then the poem falls short of its theme
in just about the same fashion as does the poem on Duns Scotus. To
describe a bird, however beautifully, and to imply that Christ is like him
but greater, is to do very little toward indicating the greatness of Christ.

Let me illustrate this objection with an account of my own experience.
For more than thirty years I have bred and exhibited Airedales in a
small way, and I have owned some very fine ones. At the present time I
own a young dog who seems to me exceptionally beautiful, especially
when he is in motion. No less than Hopkins' falcon, he is one of God's
little creatures; he is probably a much better specimen of his kind and
better adapted to his peculiar ends, and if one is sufficiently scholarly
and sufficiently perceptive, one will be aware of this probability; in addition, I am fairly certain that his moral character is more admirable than
that of the bird. Yet it would never occur to me to write a poem describing his beauty and then stating that the beauty of Christ was similar but
merely greater. To do so would seem to me ludicrous, and to many it
would seem blasphemous. Yet there is no essential difference between my
dog and Hopkins' bird; the bird has the advantage merely of the Romantic and sentimental feeling attached to birds as symbols of the free and
unrestrained spirit, a feeling derived very largely from Shelley's *Skylark*
and from a handful of similar—and similarly bad—poems of the past
century and a half. Hopkins' poem employs a mechanical and a very
easy formula. His image resembles the image of the anvil in *No worst,
there is none,* in which we get the physical embodiment of the meaning,
without the meaning, or with too small a part of it. To defend this sort

of thing with pretentious remarks about the "sacramental view of nature" is merely foolish, no matter how numerous, pious, and ancient the precedents which one may be in a position to cite.

Even if we leave Christ out of it and confine the poem to the bird, we find much the same difficulty in the first tercet: the light that flashes from the bird when he buckles is "a billion times told lovelier, more dangerous" than it was before; but the degree and kind are the important things, and one is not given them. We are left where we were left with the "rarest-veined unraveller, a not rivalled insight," in *Duns Scotus's Oxford*.

I would like to add one minor suggestion in post-script. I am no great philologist, myself, but in my casual reading of the more obvious dictionaries I have observed that the word *buckle,* in Scots and in northern English, sometimes means *to marry.* In this sense, the word would function as well as it would in any other sense. I am not aware that Hopkins ever made a notation of this meaning of the word, though he may have done so; but we know that Hopkins was inordinately fascinated with folk locutions and examined them endlessly, and this interest strikes me as being quite as relevant to the poem as his training in Loyola or his interest in Duns Scotus's theory of haecceity. What the word actually means in the poem, I confess I do not know. The reader may proceed from this point as he sees fit.

What should the verdict be on such a poem? As I have shown, the metrical intentions of the poet are more than uncertain and are probably unsound; but one can make out fairly well with the rhythm if one simply reads the poem as it seems to be written. The crucial statement of the poem, regardless of the interpretation which one accepts, appears to occur in the second and third lines of the first tercet, yet this statement is merely an *assertion* of importance and of excitement, it is not an explanation and description. The sestet contains three expressions which have led to various interpretations and of which no interpretation is certain. As to *buckle,* Pick's interpretation (like my own as well), has grammar on its side; for if McLuhan is right, the expression should be *buckle on,* and if Miss Ruggles is right, it is *buckle to,* and each of these calls for an object. But grammar is worth very little as a criterion in dealing with Hopkins; he violates grammar as he sees fit, and the interpreter can seldom call it to witness. He violates grammar as he sees fit, mainly to gain results which he considers more valuable than grammar: striking epithets and striking phonic effects. But the phonic effects are frequently overwrought and badly wrought, and the epithets, when they do not overwhelm the subject with an assortment of ill-adjusted details, are likely to be incomprehensible because of the way in which they have been attained. The first tercet fails to define its subject; the second tercet is more nearly comprehensible, but in itself is not very effective, especially with regard to the embers: the function of the embers in the total theme seems clear enough, at least in Miss Ruggles' terms, but the embers as embers, as "inscape," are described in language which is coarse and imperceptive. The language is violent, and it continues both the tone of strong emotion and the rhythm which seem to have been established, but it offers a poor perception of embers as such. The description of the bird in the octet is impressive in the main, though I believe that it has been overrated. The bird is apparently used to symbolize the perfection of Christ, but the haecceity of the bird and the haecceity of Christ are very different matters indeed, and of the haecceity of Christ we are told precisely nothing in the poem. Unless Christ is symbolized, however, or unless something far greater than the bird is symbolized, then the ecstatic tone of the poem is not justified; and in fact it is not justified if Christ is symbolized, for it could be justified only by an indication of those qualities of Christ which would serve the purpose. The poem is romantic both in its overwrought emotionalism and in its carelessness. It is not the greatest sonnet ever written, nor even the best poem in Hopkins; it is a poem of real, but minor and imperfect virtues, and that is all.

An Idiom of Desperation

by John Wain

. . . To have taken nothing whatsoever from his literary environment, Hopkins would have had to be a freak, and no one is suggesting he was that. Naturally he used some of the same materials as the others, but the structures he built with them are completely different. Compare him with any English poet living in his day, and the differences are far stronger than the resemblances. Since demonstration saves a world of argument, let me read you a poem by Bridges and then one by Hopkins.

London Snow

When men were all asleep the snow came flying,
  In large white flakes falling on the city brown,
Stealthily and perpetually settling and loosely lying,
  Hushing the latest traffic of the drowsy town;
Deadening, muffling, stifling its murmurs failing;
Lazily and incessantly floating down and down:
  Silently sifting and veiling road, roof and railing;
Hiding difference, making unevenness even,
Into angles and crevices softly drifting and sailing.
  All night it fell, and when full inches seven
It lay in the depth of its uncompacted lightness,
The clouds blew off from a high and frosty heaven;
  And all woke earlier for the unaccustomed brightness
Of the winter dawning, the strange unheavenly glare:
The eye marvelled—marvelled at the dazzling whiteness:
  The ear hearkened to the stillness of the solemn air;
No sound of wheel rumbling nor of foot falling,
And the busy morning cries came thin and spare.
  Then boys I heard, as they went to school, calling,

They gathered up the crystal manna to freeze
Their tongues with tasting, their hands with snowballing,
  Or rioted in a drift, plunging up to the knees;
Or peering up from under the white-mossed wonder,
"O look at the trees!" they cried, "O look at the trees!"
  With lessened load a few carts creak and blunder,
Following along the white deserted way,
A country company long dispersed asunder:
  When now already the sun, in pale display
Standing by Paul's high dome, spread forth below
His sparkling beams, and awoke the stir of the day.
  For now doors open, and war is waged with the snow;
And trains of sombre men, past tale of number,
Tread long brown paths, as toward their toil they go:
  But even for them awhile no cares encumber
Their minds diverted; the daily work is unspoken,
The daily thoughts of labour and sorrow slumber
At the sight of the beauty that greets them, for the charm they have broken.

Felix Randal

Felix Randal the farrier, O he is dead then? my duty all ended,
Who have watched his mould of man, big-boned and hardy-handsome
Pining, pining, till time when reason rambled in it and some
Fatal four disorders, fleshed there, all contended?

Sickness broke him. Impatient he cursed at first, but mended
Being anointed and all; though a heavenlier heart began some
Months earlier, since I had our sweet reprieve and ransom
Tendered to him. Ah well, God rest him all road ever he offended!

This seeing the sick endears them to us, us too it endears.
My tongue had taught thee comfort, touch had quenched thy tears,
Thy tears that touched my heart, child, Felix, poor Felix Randal;

How far from then forethought of, all thy more boisterous years,
When thou at the random grim forge, powerful amidst peers,
Didst fettle for the great grey drayhorse his bright and battering sandal!

One thing that certainly becomes clear from taking those two poems together is the reason why the Hopkins-Bridges debate concerned itself so much with technique. It was the only ground on which they could even hope to meet. Bridges, all his life, considered himself—and, up to a point, was—an "experimental" poet. "London Snow," in its mild, unchallenging way, is experimental; it is an interesting use of *terza rima*, keeping very close to the movement of Italian verse and yet naturalizing the metre very successfully so that it never sounds un-English. It is a skillful and sensitive performance, and, as with all Bridges' better poems, an apprentice could learn a good deal about writing from studying it carefully. Many subsequent poets do, in fact, show signs of having learnt from Bridges, perhaps unconsciously; a line such as

A country company long dispersed asunder

has something of a parental relationship to the rhythms of, say, a poet like John Crowe Ransom:

The little cousin is dead, by foul subtraction.

Of the experimental nature of the Hopkins sonnet there is no need of demonstration. Both poems explore possibilities of rhythm, but "Felix Randal" breaks new ground in a number of other directions. Notably in diction: the poem reflects Hopkins' belief that the language of poetry should stay close to ordinary speech, and—equally clearly—his realization that poetry is not conversation and so can be heightened and rhetorical without falling into artificiality. These two principles, working together, give the poem its contrapuntal flavour: "all road" is a Northernism for "in whatever way," and would not come naturally from Hopkins *in propria persona;* it seems natural because the poem is saturated with the earthy and demotic presence of the smith himself; whereas a colloquialism like "This seeing the sick endears them to us" would be quite normal in educated speech and does, in fact, occur in one of Hopkins' letters to Bridges ("This going to Birmingham throws out the trains," August 28, 1866). The language of "London Snow," by comparison, has no pipe-line to living, informal speech; it is out of books, and the effect, though elegant, is dead. "Full inches seven," for example, is an irredeemably bookish phrase, as different from "full seven inches" as if it were from another language—which, in fact, it is.

Not to dwell on these *minutiae,* the striking contrast between the two poems can be summed up by saying that Hopkins has life, waywardness, density, action, where Bridges gives us nothing but a picturesque scene conveyed by a neat arrangement of syllables. Although Hopkins' poem is much shorter, it *says* far more. Consider the "I," for instance. Bridges has an "I," but his is merely a quiescent watcher and listener; the "I" of the Hopkins poem is vividly reacting and participating. He is as much the subject as Felix Randal—they share the first line, in fact. Because Felix Randal is dead, the priest's duty is all ended. Yet the relationship that came into being during those months of sickness cannot be cancelled; it stays in the priest's life as a permanent thing. Without any hint of egoism, the priest muses on the whole story as it affects him as well as the man under his spiritual care. For he, the comforter, was also comforted; the fact that he has been some use to the dying man gives him renewed faith in himself. The quiet pride of

My tongue had taught thee comfort, touch had quenched thy tears

has a beautifully delicate blend of pity and humility with pride in achievement. There is a sensitivity here that makes Bridges—and, to be fair, most other poets—seem crude and oversimplified. It is all done so lightly and with such stylistic modesty; the word "touch," for instance, in the line just quoted, is immediately echoed in the next line ("Thy tears that touched my heart"), carrying the idea of a mutual, two-way relationship delicately into the reader's mind: *touch . . . tears . . . tears . . . touched*—the words play their own music within the orchestration of the poem.

If we cast about for anything in Victorian verse that resembles the work of Hopkins in boldness and originality, we shall find that the most serious candidates are the nonsense poets. For it was in the work of Dodgson and Lear that the English imagination, dammed up by institutional respectability and rationalistic good manners, burst out into the open. The extent to which the "official" literature of the twentieth century has derived from, and paid tribute to, the unofficial literature of the nineteenth is a striking testimony to this. When he goes into the nursery, the Victorian poet is free to forget his social responsibilities and say what is in his mind. And Dodgson and Lear do say, horrifyingly, what is in their minds, and it turns out to be nightmare, guilt, privation, dread. The literature of the twentieth century is sometimes called morbid because of its preoccupation with violence and terror. But at least the twentieth-century writer owns up to what he is doing. He sees a world full of trouble and he writes about that trouble. He does not play practical jokes on himself by dressing up as a comic uncle to amuse the children and then crying his despair from behind the jolly smile of a cardboard mask.

There was an Old Man who screamed out
Whenever they knocked him about,

one of Lear's whimsical limericks begins. A modern writer might well begin a poem in this way, but he would not pretend that he was doing it to amuse the children.

Nothing, in truth, brings out the difference between the Victorian age and our own so much as this sublime unconsciousness of theirs, this universal agreement to take everything at face value. For our part we have become extremely wary of talking about a "private language," since psychoanalysis has demonstrated that apparently nonsensical figments of dream and fantasy can relate to a pattern that is much the same for everyone; to the Victorians, fantasy was valuable chiefly as a kind of universal amnesty, a white flag which, once it was hoisted, gave immunity from any kind of critical retribution.

And what things they were prepared to say, what experiments they were willing to try, once the white flag was safely playing in the breeze! . . . Certainly there is no oppressive rationality here. Rimbaud, writing to Desseny in 1871, declared that the poet became a visionary by means of what he called "un long, immense et raisonné dérèglement de tous les sens." No conventional English poet was likely to derange his senses, even in the interests of becoming a seer. But the nonsense writers, in their own fashion, undertook just this.

And this is where we rejoin Hopkins. Alone among the English poets, he is willing to try anything, to desert logic, to wrench language, to treat the individual word as a mystery and a challenge. To him, the iron curtain between "sense" and "nonsense" does not exist.[1]

> The blue wheat-acre is underneath
> And the braided ear breaks out of the sheath,
> And ear in milk, lush the sash,
> And crush-silk poppies aflash,
> The blood-gush blade-gash
> Flame-rash rudred
> Bud shelling or broad-shed
> Tatter-tassel-tangled and dingle-a-danglèd
> Dandy-hung dainty head.

In short, what Baudelaire and Verlaine accomplished by vice and squalor, Hopkins accomplished by being a priest. In either case it was a means of living outside the ordinary social enclosures.[2] The pressure to conform, to stand well with the community, was as absent from his life as it was from Rimbaud's. Or from Father Brown's. Chesterton's detective, who sees with superhuman clarity because his eyes have the brightness of candour, is a vulgarization of the type represented in real life by

---

[1] There is an interesting unpublished thesis on the nonsense poets and Hopkins by a student of Amherst College, Massachusetts: "Gerard Manley Hopkins, The Winning Innocent," by David A. Sonstroem, May 1958.

[2] Cf. E. H. W. Meyerstein's remark in a letter to R. M. Dawkins (October 26, 1928): "If I thought I could write a good poem, or a good anything, by putting myself beyond the social pale, I sometimes think I would do it."

Hopkins. Away from the printed page, a man with that candour and perception does not become a detective: he becomes a poet. Father Brown travesties one side of Hopkins where Sherlock Holmes travesties another —the fruitful meditation on detail. Hopkins sat down to write poetry because he wanted to tell the truth, and he had truths to tell that could not be conveyed except in a new language.

It is therefore easy to see why, when Hopkins' poems were first published in 1918, the "modernist" poets and critics of that day should have seen him as one of themselves, unaccountably born out of his time. He had anticipated almost their entire program. Above all, his work is founded on the two chief principles which have underlain all modern poetic theory: irreducibility and simultaneity.

These two principles are too well known to need much comment here. If there is one point over which poets, and their attendant critics, have reached general agreement in the last sixty years, it is that a poem is irreducible. "Poems do not mean, but be." "It means what it says." The unwillingness of many recent poets, particularly poets of the Symbolist wing, to provide "explanations" of their work is rooted in a deep suspicion of the discursive. And this suspicion is as old as the industrial and scientific phase of man's history. It was already strongly developed at the beginning of the nineteenth century. When Coleridge remarked that the symbol "always partakes of the reality which it renders intelligible," he was saying that symbols were irreducible—and no one, I think, would hesitate to take the next step and say that if the symbol is autonomous, so is any work of the imagination. Yeats admired Blake for being "the first writer of modern times to preach the indissoluble marriage of all great art with symbol," and went on to describe the symbol as "the only possible expression of some invisible essence, a transparent lamp about a spiritual flame." The early nineteenth-century attitude has been neatly formulated by a French scholar of English literature, M. Albert Gérard.

> In romantic doctrine, the work of art, like the poetic experience which it expresses, owes its value as synthesis to a concert of the faculties which is orchestrated by the imagination. All the faculties (sensory, emotional, intellectual, imaginative and moral) contribute to the elaboration of the work of art. They are all necessary for uniting the particular with the universal, the concrete with the ideal, the cognitive with the emotional, and for embodying the parent idea into organic sensuous forms which are both highly individualised and capable of touching the heart of the reader.

I think we may accept that as a statement of the central theory that obtained during the heyday of European romanticism. As the nineteenth century lengthened out, the theory was not so much altered as sharpened, interpreted more stringently and applied more rigidly. By the end of the century, the characteristic poet—in France, at any rate—would probably have distrusted that phrase about "embodying the parent idea" in "organic sensuous forms." To take a preexisting "idea" and "embody" it is precisely what he was against. "It cannot be too strongly stated," says Laforgue, "that a poem is not the expression of a feeling the poet had before he began to write." The poem, in fact, calls into being the feeling it expresses. And with this assertion we reach the ultimate frontier. Irreducibility is now total. Literature takes its place among the other arts, acknowledging a closer relationship with them than had been traditionally allowed. After all, everyone had always realized that music and painting were irreducible. A man who went to a gallery and saw a painting did not imagine that he could go home and tell his wife what it was like, except in the vaguest terms; nor did anyone try to convey a tune from one head to another by means of words. Words do not describe colours or sounds; and what the poetic theory of the late nineteenth century maintained was that words do not describe poems either. It was in an essay on painting ("The School of Giorgione") that Pater made his remark, "All art constantly aspires to the condition of music." This, and similar slogans, have now and then been dangerous to the best interests of literature, in that they have helped to give rise to the unfortunate subtradition of Symbolism which has held that vague and undisciplined "suggestion" is all a poet need concern himself with. There has been a tendency, among the weaker brethren, to assume that, if it was desirable for poetry to resemble music, one could make poems by simply putting together a string of melodious and evocative words. How far this is from the "transparent lamp about a spiritual flame," the "symbol [which] partakes of the reality which it renders intelligible," I need not underline.

Along with irreducibility, simultaneity. There is perhaps no logical reason why these two concepts should have gone together, but, historically, they certainly have done. When Poe made his famous declaration that the long poem was a contradiction in terms, he was writing in an age when the long poem was both respectable and popular; today, it is the deadest of all forms; the characteristic "long poem" of our time has usually turned out, like Pound's Cantos, to be a new form relying heavily on collage, juxtaposition, and cinematographic changes of focus. "Poetry," during the last sixty years, has meant something compressed, something that the reader, once he has gained an initial familiarity with it, can comprehend instantaneously, as he takes in a picture.

The implication for the student of Hopkins is clear. When Hopkins

tried to explain to Bridges what he meant by "inscape," he was in reality
pouring into that monumentally deaf eardrum the doctrines of irreducibility and simultaneity. The notion of inscape arose in his mind in
response to a need, as we see from the Journal entry for May 6, 1866.

> Grey. A little time ago on much such another day noticed Trinity
> gardens. Much distinctness, charm, and suggestiveness abt. the match of
> white grey sky, solid smooth lawn, firs and yews, dark trees, below, and
> chestnuts and other brighter-hued trees above, the young green having
> a fresh, moist opaque look and there being in the whole picture an absence
> of projection, and apprehension of colour. On such a day also last Friday
> week boated with H. Dugmore to Godstow, but the warm greyness of the
> day, the river, the spring green, and the cuckoo wanted a canon by wh.
> to harmonize and round them in—e.g. one of feeling.

Some five years later the theory of inscape as simultaneity is fully developed, as we see in the famous "bluebell" passage (May 9, 1871).

> . . . The bluebells in your hand baffle you with their inscape, made to
> every sense: if you draw your fingers through them they are lodged and
> struggle/ with a shock of wet heads; the long stalks rub and click and
> flatten to a fan on one another like your fingers themselves would when
> you passed the palms hard across one another, making a brittle rub and
> jostle like the noise of a hurdle strained by leaning against; then there is
> the faint honey smell and in the mouth the sweet gum when you bite
> them. But this is easy, it is the eye they baffle. They give one a fancy of
> pan-pipes and of some wind instrument with stops—a trombone perhaps.
> The overhung necks—for growing they are little more than a staff with a
> simple crook but in water, where they stiffen, they take stronger turns,
> in the head like sheephooks or, when more waved throughout, like the
> waves riding through a whip that is being smacked—what with these over-
> hung necks and what with the crisped ruffled bells dropping mostly on
> one side and the gloss these have at their footstalks they have an air of the
> knights at chess. Then the knot or "knoop" of buds some shut, some just
> gaping, which makes the pencil of the whole spike, should be noticed:
> the inscape of the flower most finely carried out in the siding of the axes,
> each striking a greater and greater slant, is finished in these clustered buds,
> which for the most part are not straightened but rise to the end like a
> tongue and this and their tapering and a little flattening they have, make
> them look like the heads of snakes.

There is a certain fluidity about Hopkins's use of "inscape" and its
companion term "instress"; perhaps the most helpful explanation is that
given by the late W. H. Gardner: ". . . *instress* is not only the unifying
force *in* the object; it connotes also the impulse *from* the "inscape" which

acts on the senses and, through them, actualizes the inscape in the mind of the beholder (or rather 'perceiver,' for inscape may be perceived through all the senses at once)."

In that last sentence Gardner touches upon a facet of "inscape" that has been unduly neglected. The whole change from outer to inner landscape, which has characterized all modern art, was accompanied by another change: from an art sequential and linear to an art simultaneous and multidimensional. Mr. H. M. McLuhan has recently pointed out that the four centuries during which the printing press dominated Western civilization resulted in a sensibility attuned to the linear and the selective. Since the eye can only focus on what is directly in front of it, whereas the ear can receive sounds from any angle, the effect of the new media which in the last fifty years have arisen to challenge the printing press can be seen as an encouragement to the multidimensional. Mr. McLuhan sees traces of this new sensibility everywhere in the recent history of the arts; he suggests, for instance, a link between the Symbolist poem, with its dense structure of materials that seem on the surface to be incongruous, and the layout of a newspaper page, once the telegraph had made possible the simultaneous unrelated presentation of news from all over the world. Essentially, the telegraph was an aural medium, though its method of communication was visual; it began the shift towards simultaneity which has now been completed by radio, cinema, and electronics. I personally find Mr. McLuhan convincing when he says that the sensibility of the artist jumped with this change while that of the average man stayed where it was. It seems to me that much of the "obscurity" with which all modern art has been charged is in fact nothing more than simultaneity. Hopkinsian "inscape" leads on to the "image" of the Imagists, which Ezra Pound defined as "that which presents an intellectual and emotional complex in an instant of time." Going back, one finds distinct evidences of the same impulse to simultaneity, to instantaneous inclusiveness within the image, in Baudelaire.

> Je crois que le charme infini et mystérieux qui gît dans la contemplation d'un navire, et surtout d'un navire en mouvement, tient, dans le premier cas, à la régularité et à la symétrie, qui sont un des besoins primordiaux de l'esprit humain, au même degré que la complication et l'harmonie,— et, dans le second cas, à la multiplication successive et à la génération de toutes les courbes et figures imaginaires opérées dans l'espace par les éléments réels de l'objet.
>
> L'idée poétique qui se dégage de cette opération du mouvement dans les lignes est l'hypothèse d'un être vaste, immense, compliqué, mais eurythmi-

que, d'un animal plein de génie, souffrant et soupirant tous les soupirs et
toutes les ambitions humaines. (*Fusées*, xxii.)

Like Baudelaire, Hopkins was interested in painting; indeed, as in the
case of so many French poets (and so few English!) at about that time,
he gives the impression of being able to nourish his poetry directly from
his studies in the other arts, because he does not rigorously separate them.
The Hopkins who pushed forward beyond Victorian taste in the direction of modern poetics also pushed backward beyond it in his love for the
music of Purcell. The Hopkins who was isolated, who had "made writing
so difficult," who had to endure being patronized and misunderstood by
Patmore and Bridges, had in fact found a place for himself at the most
sensitive point in the development of a new awareness.

This is nowhere more clearly seen than in his attitude towards language. The Hopkinsian idiom involves a continual effort to give words
the solidity, the completeness of dimension, that one associates with
physical things. (We might contrast him, in this respect, with a poet like
Swinburne, whose words are always, and inescapably, merely *words*.) In
his notebooks Hopkins often writes as if words were natural objects—
which, in a sense, they are. If he heard a Lancashire gardener use an un-
familiar dialect word, he would treasure it up and, as often as not, use it
in a poem. This explains why he could so consistently censure the literary archaism of Bridges, arguing for a poetry based on living speech, and
yet stud his work with expressions likely to baffle the reader. If he heard
a word on the lips of a living man, it was alive; if it were merely copied
from book to book, it was "culture." All words, to him, were *objets
trouvés;* he botanized among them and collected specimens for study.
"Every word," he wrote in his notebook on February 9, 1868, "may be
considered as the contraction or coinciding point of its definitions."
Over half a century separates that sentence from Mr. Empson's *Seven
Types of Ambiguity:* yet it might well have been printed on the title-
page. Hopkins, though it was not within the scope of his life's work to
demonstrate his discovery in detailed literary essays, had anticipated
that whole modern critical preoccupation with density and plurisignifi-
cance in the poetic language. It was all part of his impulse towards en-
richment, towards the recognition of the solidity of dimension that lay
behind the flatly presented object. Naturally this links him at certain
points with the common or garden synaesthesia of the time, as in the
passage which Gardner quoted from the Notebooks: "But this sober
grey darkness and pale light was happily broken through by the orange
of the pealing of Mitton bells." But beside this, set another fragment

from the Notebooks, also quoted by Gardner but with no relevant comment. "I saw the inscape . . . freshly, as if my eye were still growing." At such a moment Hopkins' imagination is not only that of a painter and a poet; it is performing one of the chief functions for which we now use the cinema and television—that of presenting an image which moves and takes form while it is focused. The eye grows as it sees: in other words, it magnifies, travels, takes on depth of focus. Nothing stands still in a Hopkins poem. Everything is captured within the one simultaneity, but it is a simultaneity of endlessly apprehended movement.

Let me demonstrate briefly how the characteristic Hopkinsian procedures work out in a specific poem, the sonnet "Andromeda."

> Now Time's Andromeda on this rock rude,
> With not her either beauty's equal or
> Her injury's, looks off by both horns of shore,
> Her flower, her piece of being, doomed dragon's food.
>
> Time past she has been attempted and pursued
> By many blows and banes; but now hears roar
> A wilder beast from West than all were, more
> Rife in her wrongs, more lawless, and more lewd.
>
> Her Perseus linger and leave her to her extremes?—
> Pillowy air he treads a time and hangs
> His thoughts on her, forsaken that she seems,
>
> All while her patience, morselled into pangs,
> Mounts; then to alight disarming, no one dreams,
> With Gorgon's gear and barebill, thongs and fangs.

There are many things that might be said about this poem; but I must stick to essentials. And the first essential is, what is it *about?* The orthodox commentator, working within a pre-Hopkinsian tradition, has no doubt that some cut-and-dried answer can be found. To him, the poem is a code message, to be "cracked" and its matter extracted. Thus Dr. Gardner unhesitatingly glossed: "Line 1, *Time's Andromeda* (symbol), the Church." No nonsense here about irreducibility! Similarly a more recent critic, Mr. Alan Heuser, describes the poem as "a public sonnet on the political situation of the Church. . . . 'Time's Andromeda' was the Roman Church militant in England ('on this rock rude') persecuted in the past, now threatened from the West with industrial mob-rule ('A wilder beast.')." It is all refreshingly simple. The only problem that remains is why Hopkins bothered to write a poem. If all he wanted to convey was that the Church was in a difficult position in 1879, but still had a mighty rescuer to look to, surely he might have said so straight

out? Personally, I would rather get my illumination from that rejoinder
of Rimbaud's. "It means what it says." Hopkins is giving us a picture,
and a picture is irreducible. What does the picture show? A girl, fast
bound, on a rocky promontory, menaced by a dragon; a rescuer close at
hand; a scene of urgent peril and yet also of patience and courage.

> All while her patience, morselled into pangs,
> Mounts.

"Mounts," there, is a good example of the way the grammar of the poem
is constructed so as to lead into itself, as it were. Obviously the formal
syntax requires that "mounts" refers back to "her patience"; yet as we
read or hear the poem, the verb also leans forward on to Perseus, hovering for an instant before swooping down to the attack. In the same way,

> Pillowy air he treads a time and hangs
> His thoughts on her

gives us a verb that radiates both ways; formally, "hangs" is transitive;
Perseus hangs his thoughts on Andromeda; yet the ear picks up the line
with a strong half-conscious suggestion that it is Perseus who hangs, who
is poised, as he treads the pillowy air.

The whole grammar of the poem is orchestrated in the interests of
simultaneity. The concluding lines, for instance, do not say, "Then
Perseus alighted, disarming the thongs and fangs with the Gorgon's gear
and barebill." Nor even, "Soon he will alight." Nor even, "Wouldn't it
be wonderful if he were to alight?" No, what Hopkins says is,

> then to alight disarming, no one dreams,
> With Gorgon's gear and barebill, thongs and fangs.

The lack of a main verb describing Perseus' action is not evasion. The
poem is not trying to avoid making a statement. On the contrary, it is
making an extremely precise statement of a certain kind. And in the
same way, it is not saying that Andromeda "is" the Church, or that
Perseus "is" Christ. Mr. Heuser is doubtful about Gardner's identification
of Perseus with Christ, and points out that Hopkins elsewhere "interpreted the earth and the constellation Draco, in terms of the woman and
the dragon of the Apocalypse (Revelation xii)—which would make the
constellation Perseus equivalent to St. Michael." So that by Perseus "St.
Michael (or Christ 'steaded' in St. Michael) seems to be intended. Another
possibility for Perseus is St. George of England." The indecision here,
the impossibility of lighting on one definite identification, is a good example of the trivial kind of puzzle that awaits those who treat poems as
code messages. Surely we need to be more simple-minded in one way,

less so in another. Hopkins was a priest. His life was given to piety.
Furthermore, he seems to have been without a trace of that self-lacerating,
masochistic kind of Roman Catholicism that one finds in, say, the novels
of Graham Greene. To him, Christ really was a rescuer.

> Thou art lightning and love, I found it, a winter and warm;
>   Father and fondler of the heart thou has wrung:
> Hast thy dark descending and art most merciful then.

Hence, when Hopkins feels the story of Perseus and Andromeda strongly
enough in his blood to write a poem about it, he is not constructing an
allegory in which this "stands for" that. He is conveying a sense of the
situation in all its implications. The idea of rescue was central to his
sensibility as it was to his theology. Perseus is an interesting figure to
Hopkins because, like Christ, he was a rescuer; also like Christ, he was
freshly come from another encounter with the powers of darkness. Christ's
victory over Satan, followed by the Redemption of man, is paralleled by
Perseus's defeat of the Gorgons and rescue of Andromeda. But if anyone
wishes to bring St. George in, or St. Michael, there is room for them. In
a poem about rescue there is room for the idea of any noble rescuer. If
we will just let the poem alone, leave it to stand in its own solidity, without trying to peel off specific meanings and argue about their correctness,
we shall find that it will speak to us as music, painting, or sculpture do.

In conclusion, I have nothing left to do but to add a word in justification of my title. Hopkins, I have been saying, was a completely successful
poet; his work, despite its occasional eccentricities, was right in all its
major decisions; he is the needle that points to the true north. So why
speak of desperation?

The answer is that the desperation was in the loneliness. Only someone
who was completely alone could have produced an art that takes so little
and gives so much. For Hopkins, the struggle of creation must have been
agonizing; and the incomprehension which met his work must often have
numbed his entire being. The price he paid for being the greatest of the
Victorian poets was a heavy one. His isolation removed him from the
hubbub of the market-place and enabled him to listen in silence to the
messages which came from the real spirit of his age. Yet the deep-seated
inability to trade in that market-place also involved him in disappoint-
ment, humiliation, and weariness. He had no sense of a public. Perhaps
if he had, it might have corrupted him as a poet. He had to be free of the
need for any give-and-take with the ordinary Victorian reader. "Hopkins'
poems," writes Mr. Austin Warren, "intend, ideally, an audience never
actually extant, composed of literarily alert countrymen and linguistically

adept, folk-concerned scholars." The "audience never actually extant," or never in one place at one time—that was the price he had to pay. It was the same in his sermons, perhaps the most beautiful since the seventeenth century. On the page, they fill us with admiration, not only of their formal beauty, but of their goodness and humility. And yet, after all, a sermon belongs to the category of "applied" literature. It is designed for a definite purpose. And, by all accounts, Hopkins' lack of contact with an audience, his failure to judge public tone, was a constant difficulty and discouragement in his life as a priest. We can smile at the story of his telling a fashionable Farm Street congregation that the Church was like a milch cow wandering through the world and offering grace to humanity by means of her full udders. But Farm Street was not amused. Nor, by all accounts, was he more successful with his congregations of working men and their wives. Hopkins could speak memorably *of* Felix Randal and Harry Ploughman, but not successfully *to* them. And when his superiors made the decision to employ him mainly in teaching duties, he seems to have been painfully conscientious, but not very much more.

All these discomfitures and disappointments bore too heavily on one always brave, but never robust or resilient. "I think that my fits of sadness, though they do not affect my judgment, resemble madness. Change is my only relief, and that I can seldom get." He died at forty-five, exhausted, and with no idea that his verse had done more than make a few scratches on the granite wall of conventional taste.

The rest is history. During the years when Hopkins' poems lay buried, the English poetic mind slowly began to turn in the direction he had indicated, like a plant growing towards the light: by the time he was published, most of his innovations could be paralleled in the work of men who had never read him. Resistance went on, of course, and with it derision. As late as 1936 Mr. G. M. Young could declare, speaking of Hopkins as a metrical innovator, "the root of his error lay in an ignorance of the subject so profound that it was not aware that there was anything to know." But then Hopkins was accustomed to this kind of reaction in his own lifetime, and would not have been surprised to see it carried on for forty years after his death. He managed without approbation and encouragement, and he does not need our praise now. The source of his poetic energy and inventiveness was within himself. He invented a language, and wrote in it, for the one valid reason: because he had things inside him that he must communicate. To study him is to realize the truth of Cocteau's great epigram: "If the poet has a dream, it is not of becoming famous, but of being believed."

The Oddities of Genius

by Robert Bridges

Mannerism

Apart from questions of taste—and if these poems were to be arraigned for errors of what may be called taste, they might be convicted of occasional affectation in metaphor, as where the hills are "as a stallion stalwart, very-violet-sweet," or of some perversion of human feeling, as, for instance, the nostrils' relish of incense "along the sanctuary side," or "the Holy Ghost with warm breast and with ah! bright wings," these and a few such examples are mostly efforts to force emotion into theological or sectarian channels, as in "the comfortless unconfessed" and the unpoetic line "His mystery must be instressed stressed," or, again, the exaggerated Marianism of some pieces, or the naked encounter of sensualism and asceticism which hurts the "Golden Echo."—

Apart, I say, from such faults of taste, which few as they numerically are yet affect my liking and more repel my sympathy than do all the rude shocks of his purely artistic wantonness—apart from these there are definite faults of style which a reader must have courage to face, and must in some measure condone before he can discover the great beauties. For these blemishes in the poet's style are of such quality and magnitude as to deny him even a hearing from those who love a continuous literary decorum and are grown to be intolerant of its absence. And it is well to be clear that there is no pretence to reverse the condemnation of those faults, for which the poet has duly suffered. The extravagances are and will remain what they were. Nor can credit be gained from pointing them out: yet, to put readers at their ease, I will here define them: they may be called Oddity and Obscurity; and since the first may provoke laughter when a writer is serious (and this poet is always serious), while the latter must prevent him from being understood (and this poet has always something to say), it may be assumed that they were not a part of his intention. Something of what he thought on this subject may be seen in the following extracts from his letters. In Feb. 1879, he wrote: "All therefore that I think of doing is to keep my verses together in one place—at present I have not even correct copies—, that, if anyone should like, they might be published after my death. And that again is unlikely, as well as remote. . . . No doubt my poetry errs on the side of oddness. I hope in time to have a more balanced and Miltonic style. But as air, melody, is what strikes me most of all in music and design in painting, so design, pattern, or what I am in the habit of calling *inscape* is what I above all aim at in poetry. Now it is the virtue of design, pattern, or inscape to be distinctive and it is the vice of distinctiveness to become queer. This vice I cannot have escaped." And again two months later: "Moreover the oddness may make them repulsive at first and yet Lang might have liked them on a second reading. Indeed when, on somebody returning me the *Eurydice,* I opened and read some lines, as one commonly reads whether prose or verse, with the eyes, so to say, only, it struck me aghast with a kind of raw nakedness and unmitigated violence I was unprepared for: but take breath and read it with the ears, as I always wish to be read, and my verse becomes all right."

Obscurity

As regards Oddity then, it is plain that the poet was himself fully alive to it, but he was not sufficiently aware of his obscurity, and he could not understand why his friends found his sentences so difficult: he would never have believed that, among all the ellipses and liberties of his grammar, the one chief cause is his habitual omission of the relative pronoun; and yet this is so, and the examination of a simple example or two may serve a general purpose.

This grammatical liberty, though it is a common convenience in conversation and has therefore its proper place in good writing, is apt to confuse the parts of speech, and to reduce a normal sequence of words to mere jargon. Writers who carelessly rely on their elliptical speech-forms to govern the elaborate sentences of their literary composition little know what a conscious effort of interpretation they often impose on their readers. But it was not carelessness in Gerard Hopkins: he had full skill and practice and scholarship in conventional forms, and it is easy to see that he banished these purely constructional syllables from his verse because they took up room which he thought he could not afford them:

he needed in his scheme all his space for his poetical words, and he wished those to crowd out every merely grammatical colourless or toneless element; and so when he had got into the habit of doing without these relative pronouns—though he must, I suppose, have supplied them in his thought,—he abuses the licence beyond precedent, as when he writes "O Hero savest!" for "O Hero that savest!."

Another example of this will discover another cause of obscurity: the line

> Squander the hell-rook ranks sally to molest him

means "Scatter the ranks that sally to molest him": but since the words *squander* and *sally* occupy similar positions in the two sections of the verse, and are enforced by a similar accentuation, the second verb deprived of its pronoun will follow the first and appear as an imperative; and there is nothing to prevent its being so taken but the contradiction that it makes in the meaning; whereas the grammar should expose and enforce the meaning, not have to be determined by the meaning. Moreover, there is no way of enunciating this line which will avoid the confusion; because if, knowing that *sally* should not have the same intonation as *squander,* the reader mitigates the accent, and in doing so lessens or obliterates the caesural pause which exposes its accent, then *ranks* becomes a genitive and *sally* a substantive.

Here, then, is another source of the poet's obscurity; that in aiming at condensation he neglects the need that there is for care in the placing of words that are grammatically ambiguous. English swarms with words that have one identical form for substantive, adjective, and verb; and such a word should never be so placed as to allow of any doubt as to what part of speech it is used for; because such ambiguity or momentary uncertainty destroys the force of the sentence. Now our author not only neglects this essential propriety but he would seem even to welcome and seek artistic effect in the consequent confusion; and he will sometimes so arrange such words that a reader looking for a verb may find that he has two or three ambiguous monosyllables from which to select, and must be in doubt as to which promises best to give any meaning that he can welcome; and then, after his choice is made, he may be left with some homeless monosyllable still on his hands. Nor is our author apparently sensitive to the irrelevant suggestions that our numerous homophones cause; and he will provoke further ambiguities or obscurities by straining the meaning of these unfortunate words.

Rhymes

Finally, the rhymes where they are peculiar are often repellent, and so far from adding charm to the verse that they appear as obstacles. This must not blind one from recognizing that Gerard Hopkins, where he is simple and straightforward in his rhyme is a master of it—there are many instances,—but when he indulges in freaks, his childishness is incredible. His intention in such places is that the verses should be recited as running on without pause, and the rhyme occurring in their midst should be like a phonetic accident, merely satisfying the prescribed form. But his phonetic rhymes are often indefensible on his own principle. The rhyme to *communion* in "The Bugler" is hideous, and the suspicion that the poet thought it ingenious is appalling: *eternal,* in "The Eurydice," does not correspond with *burn all,* and in "Felix Randal" *and some* and *handsome* is as truly an eye-rhyme as the *love* and *prove* which he despised and abjured;—and it is more distressing, because the old-fashioned conventional eye-rhymes are accepted as such without speech-adaptation, and to many ears are a pleasant relief from the fixed jingle of the perfect rhyme; whereas his false ear-rhymes ask to have their slight but indispensable differences obliterated in the reading, and thus they expose their defect, which is of a disagreeable and vulgar or even comic quality. He did not escape full criticism and ample ridicule for such things in his lifetime; and in '83 he wrote: "Some of my rhymes I regret, but they are past changing, grubs in amber: there are only a few of these; others are unassailable; some others again there are which malignity may munch at but the Muses love."

Euphony and Emphasis

Now these are bad faults, and, as I said, a reader, if he is to get any enjoyment from the author's genius, must be somewhat tolerant of them; and they have a real relation to the means whereby the very forcible and original effects of beauty are produced. There is nothing stranger in these poems than the mixture of passages of extreme delicacy and exquisite diction with passages where, in a jungle of rough root-words, emphasis seems to oust euphony; and both these qualities, emphasis and euphony, appear in their extreme forms. It was an idiosyncrasy of this student's mind to push everything to its logical extreme, and take pleasure in a paradoxical result; as may be seen in his prosody where a simple theory seems to be used only as a basis for unexampled liberty. He was flattered when I called him περιττότατος, and saw the humour of it—and one would expect to find in his work the force of emphatic condensation and the magic of melodious expression, both in their extreme forms. Now since those who study style in itself must allow a proper place to the emphatic expression, this experiment, which supplies as novel examples of success as of failure, should be full of interest; and such interest will promote tolerance.

The fragment, on a piece of music, No. 67,[1] is the draft of what appears to be an attempt to explain how an artist has not free-will in his creation. He works out his own nature instinctively as he happens to be made, and is irresponsible for the result. It is lamentable that Gerard Hopkins died when, to judge by his latest work, he was beginning to concentrate the force of all his luxuriant experiments in rhythm and diction, and castigate his art into a more reserved style. Few will read the terrible posthumous sonnets without such high admiration and respect for his poetical power as must lead them to search out the rare masterly beauties that distinguish his work.

[1] No. 110 in *Poems of Gerard Manley Hopkins*, third edition.

II

Aesthetic-Theological Thoughts
on "The Windhover"

by Romano Guardini

Of his poem "The Windhover," composed in 1877, Hopkins himself said that it was the best thing he had ever written. But the poem is not easy to understand and has given rise to many interpretations. The interpretation that follows in no way wishes to compete with these, for its author is not acquainted with the secondary materials. His analysis arose from a firsthand encounter with the poem and does no more than give the fruits of that encounter. It is not scholarship, then, but one reader's effort to come nearer to a work of art that moved him no less by its expertise than by its profundity.

The fixed form of the sonnet is, in "The Windhover," filled with a very concentrated subject matter. This consists of but two figures: a falcon in the expanse of morning and a ploughshare in the furrow. The two are related, however, to a third and more essential theme. Without changing their identity they mediate this theme, become transparent for it, and make us feel its existence through theirs. The dedication "To Christ Our Lord" orients us further toward it.

In the quatrains of the sonnet a series of images drawn from widely disparate areas of experience make the falcon vividly present. These images are not developed independently but, rather, coalesce. A technique reminiscent of Rilke's *Duino Elegies* makes each one participate

"Aesthetic-Theological Thoughts on 'The Windhover,'" by Romano Guardini. (Translated from the German by Geoffrey Hartman and Christopher Levenson.) This appeared as "Aesthetisch-Theologische Gedanken zu Hopkins' Gedicht 'Der Sturmfalke'" in *Sprache—Dichtung—Deutung* (Würzburg: Werkbund Verlag, 1962). Reprinted by permission of the author and the publisher.

momentarily in the phenomenon they clarify: the splendor of that flight
in the dawn's effulgence. The bird is "morning's minion" and "daylight's
dauphin." He "rides" on the air, which rolls "level" and "steady" underneath him; thus, implicitly, the image of a ship travelling on the swell of
a gently rolling sea is brought into play. The bird appears next as a
young horse trotting in a wide circle on the trainer's line. The wing
turned toward the center of the circle is seen at first as the line, then
immediately as a wimple fluttering in the breeze. The flight's arc ex-
pands, and now for the precision and dexterity of motion the picture
of a skate's heel gliding across ice is introduced. The image changes once
more, and, as if in attack, the "hurl and gliding" runs up against the "big
wind" and rebuffs it.

Nature appears to the poet in the fullness of its presence; a nature,
however, in motion from within and which changes, even transforms, itself to become fully what it is: "the achieve of, the mastery of the thing!"
is the observer's cry on seeing it revealed and consummate. The curious
neuter "of the thing" relieves the figure of the bird of any assumption
of familiarity. The bird becomes something strange, a new encounter
takes place, its archetype or *inscape* as Hopkins terms it—the inner form,
the sense of a thing mediated by sensation—radiates from it toward the
Platonist (for that essentially is what Hopkins was).

Everything is reality brought to its highest pitch. The light-drenched
atmosphere of dawn, the powerful flight, the vigor of the bird's circling
—Nature verges on ecstatic self-transcendence. . . . The Greeks said
that whatever fulfils itself becomes divine, its *theion* appears. Hopkins
goes further. The ecstasy here described (the word ecstasy is actually
used for the falcon) differs from mythical versions in that nature does
not remain self-contained but answers a higher power that strives to
reveal itself through nature. The observer's feeling also responds to it:
"My heart in hiding/Stirred for a bird." The deeply excited beating of
his heart is itself a kind of ecstasy, a being caught up in the process of
revelation. Yet what revelation specifically?

First of all that of the essential, self-manifested Idea of a thing, to
which a Platonist would tend to be sensitive. But within this Hopkins
senses a further Idea which cannot be interpreted from the world as we
know it. It stirs him to presentiments yet remains confined till God's
Word should release and name it. A reference to that Word is provided,
as we have said, by the dedication "To Christ Our Lord" under the
poem's title. The dedication suggests that after the "inscape" or *eidos*
has, in Nature's perfection-ecstasy, made itself manifest to the Platonist,
then is the Christian made aware of the form through which the ground

of all *eide* is proclaimed, namely Christ, the Logos, "through whom all
was made that was made": so through the beauty of "daylight's dauphin"
the glory of the Son.

But now abruptly, without formal transition and as if precipitously—
one might almost say as in the precipitous dive of a bird of prey—there
appears in the two tercets the realm that stands over against the heights:
earth, field and furrow.

A greatness that even now had captured the imagination by its freedom and magnificence is, as it were, dethroned: "Brute beauty and
valour and act, oh, air, pride, plume"—all these are invoked—"here/
Buckle!" However the word "buckle" may be explicated, it includes the
meaning that what was before free in the heights, surrounded by light,
unlimited . . . must now yield to or become a thing that dwells in the
lower darkness, constricted, care-worn, yet in truth, greater. The Being
of which the poem had all the time spoken is now directly addressed with
the old-fashioned ceremonial "thee." From him "breaks" the fire, and
the sufferer becomes a "chevalier."

One thinks quite naturally of St. Paul's word according to which he
who formerly lived in the divine light, through the Incarnation
"emptied himself, taking the form of a servant" (Philippians 2.7). Once
like a falcon, he is now like a serf bound to the plough. . . . In such
darkness of servitude, however, a brilliance of being reveals itself which
is "a billion/ Times . . . lovelier, more dangerous" than that of the
free bird. The adjective "dangerous" forces the contrast to the point of
paradox. Hopkins uses it to express intensely what he feels in Nature:
the untamed, primeval "wildnerness" element. The adjective removes
from his experience everything that might have been sentimental or
pathetic and leads into the cry "O my chevalier!" For it is an elemental
force which is subjected by divine command to such rigorous service.

In all this, no cause for surprise ("No wonder of it"). It is self-evident
and cannot be otherwise. For consider the ploughshare: it labors here
below and furrows the soil but for this very reason is whetted so sharply
that it shines. Though motioned by "sheer plod," by will and effort
rather than by an organic freedom, its effect is beauty.

But now we encounter a difficulty: part of the "evidence" of the whole
is that "blue-bleak embers . . . Fall, gall themselves" yet also that they
"gash gold-vermilion." It is not obvious to what in the manifest experience of the poet these images may be attached. One can perhaps take
them thus: the ashes are something on top of iron, like rust. As the result of a blow they fall off but in so doing become hot and incandescent.
But here a different image, from the latent revelation, intrudes: that of

the suffering Christ whose wounds gape blood-red in the struggle for redemption yet gleam like gold because of His secret glory. This might also explain the tone of deep love in "ah, my dear"—words from the realm of mysticism.

Should the sudden interpolation of this image surprise, it is useful to remember that Hopkins not only, as his writings and sketches prove, was struck constantly and anew by the power of natural forms, but that he also spent a considerable part of his time in religious meditation. This created a wellspring of vital representations directed toward the reality of his faith and which permeated all his thoughts and daily activities.

The Analogical Mirrors

by Herbert Marshall McLuhan

Hopkins is full of pitfalls for the unwary. There is a double difficulty: his Catholic beliefs and experience on one hand; his individual
use of the resources of English on the other, to say nothing of his irrelevant theory of prosody. The non-Catholic reader—especially the non-
Christian reader—is timid or hostile in the presence of Hopkins' faith
and doctrine. He is beset with "mnemonic irrelevance" and stirred to a
thousand acts of undemanded vigilance and depreciation which inevitably distort the pattern and texture of the poems.

For the Catholic reader Hopkins has, understandably, a great deal of
prestige value. Long accustomed to a defensive position behind a
minority culture, English and American Catholics have developed multiple mental squints. Involuntarily their sensibilities have been nourished
and ordered by a century or more of an alien literary and artistic activity
which, *faute de mieux,* they still approach askance. However, their intellectual distrust in the presence of, say, the emotional chaos of Shelley or
Browning has not in the least prevented the assimilation of the vision
of those poets. (One might add that it has not in the least prevented
them from hailing as "Catholic poetry" the febrile immaturities of
Francis Thompson and Joyce Kilmer.)

Thus there was no Catholic magazine which would accept any poem
of Hopkins in his lifetime. With Bloomsbury's sudden acclaim of Hopkins as a major poet, however, Catholics were caught off-guard. They
hastened to enshrine but not to understand him. Somewhat inconse-
quentially they have begun to feel at home in the present world of art
because "their" poet is a big gun on the literary front. That is the catch.
The Catholic reader comes to Hopkins with a mechanism of sensibility
which came off the line in 1850. His sensibility has been unmodified by
the impact of Baudelaire, Laforgue, Pound or Eliot. Bloomsbury was at

"The Analogical Mirrors" by Herbert Marshall McLuhan. First published in *The
Kenyon Review* (1944). Reprinted by permission of *The Kenyon Review* and the
author.

least readied for Hopkins by these and *The Seafarer*. But the Catholic assumes his proprietary manner on the strength of doctrinal affinity alone. With equal justification the professors of Anglo-Saxon might have staked out an exclusive claim in Hopkins. Insentience or modesty has prevented them so far; or is it simply that they are incapable of seeing that the work of Hopkins is almost the sole civilized fruit of their brain-starved plodding?

Before there can be any basis for Catholic complacency in the presence of Hopkins we must explain our tardy recognition of him. Again, if Catholic doctrine made Hopkins a major poet, why aren't there more like him? All, I think, that need be said of this peculiarly Catholic pitfall is that some knowledge (the more the better) of Catholic doctrines and Scotist philosophy is needed for the full elucidation, though not for the immediate enjoyment, of Hopkins. Such knowledge, however, will never reveal his poetic excellence. The Catholic reader has the advantage only in that he is disposed to give Hopkins a chance. And, of course, he is not inclined to urp, with Bridges, when Hopkins speaks of the Virgin or the Trinity. The problem, in short, is much the same as that of reading, say, Dante or John Donne. The ancillary scholarly effort should, but seldom does, keep ever sharply focussed the stereoscopic gaze at the work itself.

Before looking at "The Windhover," as our chosen text, let us consider the crux of Hopkins' sensibility—"inscape." It is the "fineness, proportion of feature" mastering the recalcitrance of matter which he saw everywhere in the world. It is the ontological secret:

> It is the forgèd feature finds me; it is the rehearsal
> Of own, of abrupt self there so thrusts on, so throngs the ear.
> ("Henry Purcell")

Hopkins finds this Euclid peeping from the chaos of matter alike in the veins of a violet, and "roped" sides of a mountain, or the bright shoe on the anvil. (Note the precise yet witty implications of "forged feature" in this connection.) That Hopkins should take the further step of greeting Christ at such moments of natural perception should cause even the non-Catholic reader very little inconvenience, for the poet is making no pantheistic claims whatever:

> Since, tho' he is under the world's splendour and wonder,
> His mystery must be instressed, stressed.
> ("The Wreck of the Deutschland")

Hopkins is not a nature mystic at all, nor a religious mystic, either, but an analogist. By stress and instress, by intensity and precision of perception, by analogical analysis and meditation he achieves all his effects. His is literally a sacramental view of the world since what of God is there he does not perceive nor experience but takes on faith. It may sound at first strange to hear that Hopkins is not a mystic but an analogist. That he does not lay claim to a perception of natural facts hidden from ordinary men is evident in every line of description he ever wrote. As for religious experience, it is the same. Nowhere in his work does he draw on an experience which is beyond the range of any thoughtful and sensitive Catholic who meditates on his Faith. Let the authoritative statement of Jacques Maritain clarify this matter at once. He begins a chapter on "Expérience Mystique et Philosophie" this way:

> Nous entendrons ici le mot "expérience mystique," que cela soit convenu une fois pour toutes, non pas en un sens plus ou moins vague (extensible à toutes sortes de faits plus ou moins mystérieux ou préternaturels, ou même à la simple religiosité), mais au sens de *connaissance expérimentale* des profondeurs de Dieu, ou de *passion des choses divines,* menant l'âme, par une suite d'états et de transformations, jusqu'à éprouver au fond d'elle-même le toucher de la déité, et à "sentir la vie de Dieu." *Les Degrés Du Savoir* (Paris, 1935), pp. 489-490.

But there is nothing of this in Hopkins. He deals sensitively with the commonplaces of Catholic dogma in the order of Faith, and he records a vigorous sensuous life in the order of nature. Since for the agnostic no precision is possible in these matters, and all distinctions are nugatory, he will continue to call both Blake and Hopkins "mystical."

Hopkins looks at external nature as a Scripture exactly as Philo Judaeus, St. Paul and the Church Fathers had done. Their views, which have never ceased to be current, though their prevalence has fluctuated, are summarily expressed by the conventional patristic divine, Jeremy Taylor:

> Thus when (God) made the beauteous frame of heaven and earth, he rejoyced in it, and glorified himself, because it was the glasse in which he beheld his wisdom, and Almighty power: . . . For if God is glorified in the Sunne and Moon, in the rare fabric of the honeycombs, in the discipline of Bees, in the œconomy of Pismires, in the little houses of birds, in the curiosity of an eye, God being pleased to delight in those little images and reflexes of himself from those pretty mirrours, which like a crevice in a wall thorow a narrow perspective transmit the species of a vast excellency: much rather shall God be pleased to behold himself in the glasses of our obedience. . . .

Hopkins habitually shifts his gaze from the order and perspectives of nature to the analogous but grander scenery of the moral and intellectual order. And he does this methodically:

> . . . O the mind, mind has mountains; cliffs of fall
> Frightful, sheer, no-man-fathomed.
>> ("No worst, there is none")

Or the book of nature provides parallel passages with the supernatural revelations of Scripture:

> . . . For Christ plays in ten thousand places,
> Lovely in limbs and lovely in eyes not his
> To the Father through the features of men's faces.
>> ("As Kingfishers Catch Fire")

As the microcosm of man is a nobler, a more perfect mirror of God's beauty and grandeur, so Christ, as Taylor goes on to say in the same place, "was the image of the Divinity . . . designed from eternal ages to represent as in a double mirrour, not onely the glories of God to himself, but also to all the world; and he glorified God by the instrument of obedience, in which God beheld his own dominion. . . ." Hopkins freely employs these three traditional mirrors (physical, moral, divine) of God's beauty and grandeur, using them sometimes simply ("Pied Beauty"), doubly ("The Caged Skylark"), or triply ("The Wreck of the Deutschland"). Naturally, these combinations admit of infinite variations since the particulars reflected in each "mirror" can be chosen from a great store.

"The Windhover" exploits all three mirrors of God's grandeur.

> I caught this morning morning's minion, king-
>> dom of daylight's dauphin, dapple-dawn-drawn Falcon, in his
>> riding
>> Of the rolling level underneath him steady air, and striding
> High there, how he rung upon the rein of a wimpling wing
> In his ecstasy! then off, off forth on swing,
>> As a skate's heel sweeps smooth on a bow-bend: the hurl and
>> gliding
>> Rebuffed the big wind. My heart in hiding
> Stirred for a bird,—the achieve of, the mastery of the thing!
>
> Brute beauty and valour and act, oh, air, pride, plume, here
>> Buckle! AND the fire that breaks from thee then, a billion
> Times told lovelier, more dangerous, O my chevalier!

No wonder of it: shéer plód makes plough down sillion
Shine, and blue-bleak embers, ah my dear,
    Fall, gall themselves, and gash gold-vermilion.

The bird "literally" mirrors the physical order of subrational "valour
and act." But, analogously, as "kingdom of daylight's dauphin," it mirrors
Christ. As Hopkins transfers his gaze from the first mirror to the second,
we see that his own heart is also a hidden mirror (moral obedience) which
flashes to God the image not of "brute beauty and valour and act" but
a "fire" which is "a billion times told lovelier"—the chevalier image of
Christ. We can thus simply, and, I believe for the first time, fully explain
the function of "here Buckle!" Rhetorically, fire bursts from Hopkins as
he looks at the fiery falcon whose action mirrors the mastery of Christ
over the world. Now, he says, let us take this mirror (St. Paul's "armour")
and buckle it here in my hidden heart, raising the image of Christ in
the bird to the image of Christ in the obedience and humility of the
heart. Christ's fire will burst on and from the second mirror "a billion
times told lovelier" than from the falcon. This is the basic structure of
this image. The superstructure of its ambiguity will be shown later on.
Hopkins would even seem to have this mirror mechanism in the fore-
front of his mind as he compares his obedient day-by-day plodding to
the homely ploughshare whose polished surface is hidden in the earth
("my heart in hiding") but which imparts a sheen even to the mud and
dirt which it turns up. (Compare with this "sheer plod" image "the jading
and jar of the cart"—"Deutschland," stanza 27.)

To have seen the dialectic or mechanism of the poem is not, however,
to have seen anything of what constitutes its dramatic action. In other
words, we have yet to see that it is a poem at all. There is a logical movement which has been indicated. There is also dramatic surprise achieved
by a striking peripateia. This happens when the ecstatic hyperboles of
the octet are yet rendered trite by the merely homely images of the sestet.
Moreover, while the sestet is in a lower key, befitting the change to the
theme of humble obedience, it is more intense, fuller of compressed implication. Hopkins has Spiritual humility act out its easy victory over
"brute beauty and valour and act." Yet this victory is not won by crushing "brute beauty" but by catching it to the hidden heart which reflects
it back to God.

The assonance and alliteration in the first three lines perform just the
opposite of their usual functions in Hopkins' verse—the opposite of
"gall" and "gash" in the last line, for example. Here, in conjunction
with the even phrasing, they convey the delicate poise, the hovering
emphasis of the falcon's movements. The falcon is seen as a chevalier, a

horseman glorying in the great power under him and the quick response to the rein as he sweeps "forth on swing." (The skate on ice image shifts the point of view only to stress the precision and sharply etched movements of the bird. Compare: "It is the forgèd feature finds me" in "Henry Purcell." "Dapple-dawn-drawn Falcon" also insists upon the etched quality of the scene. The bird is drawn to the light but it is also drawn, etched, against the dawn.)

To a member of a militant order whose founder was a Spanish soldier or chevalier, the feudal character of the opening imagery is quite natural. "Minion," "dauphin," "valour," "plume" and "buckle" alike evoke the world of dedicated knighthood and shining panoply of armor. Thus the mounted chevalier flashing off exploit as he "rung upon the rein" enables Hopkins later to reverse the situation with great dramatic effect in "sheer plod makes plow down sillion Shine." The paradox consists in the fact that Hopkins as lowly plowman following a horse flashes off infinitely more exploit than Hopkins the imagined chevalier.

More central still to the dramatic movement of the poem is the way in which the cavalier images of the octet are concentrated in "here/ Buckle!" Buckling is the traditional gesture of the knight preparing his armor for action. A buckler is the bright shield of defense bearing insignia, flashing defiance. (The relevance of the sense of "buckle" as "collapse" or "crumple" has often been debated in this context. It has been suggested that Hopkins, in shifting his point of view, here means that the sensuous beauty of the world is a feeble prop, that he is making a conventional renunciation of "mortal beauty" as dangerous to the spiritual life. But this is to ignore the dramatic development, to blur it with cliché. It ignores the excited emphasis of "here" at the end of the line and "Buckle!" at the beginning of the next. It is, of course, almost impossible not to accept these suggestions so long as the basic mirror images of his analogist vision are not grasped.) Whichever way one looks at this image the implication of shining brilliance, of enthusiastic gesture, is present. I have already said that "here" means "in the obedient and humble heart," and that "Buckle" means that the "brute beauty" of the bird as mirror of God's grandeur is to be transferred or flashed to the "heart in hiding," just as the burnished surface of the plow in action is hidden in the earth. The high-spirited but obedient heart of a man is a "billion/Times" better a mirror of Christ the chevalier than is the mirror of the external world. "AND the fire that breaks from thee then" (note how the eager stress on "AND" serves to flash attention intensely on what follows as being an inevitable result) is ambivalent in suggesting both the fire and ecstasy which the poet has felt as he watched the bird as well as the much greater fire which Christ will flash on him and from him, and which will flame out at the world. The mirror of man's moral life can "give beauty back to God," the beauty of God's world, and in so doing it becomes the mirror in which (by the imitation of Christ) God can flash out more brilliantly. ("Give beauty back," as in a mirror, is also the theme of "The Leaden Echo and the Golden Echo," as the title suggests.)

Once it is seen that the shining armor of the falcon's imitation of Christ's mastery is to be buckled in the hidden heart of the poet it is easy to find other passages in Hopkins which show that this image obsessed him. In the sonnet to St. Alphonsus Rodriguez there is the same running image of military brilliance and valor:

> But be the war within, the brand we wield
> Unseen, the heroic breast not outward-steeled,
> Earth hears no hurtle then from fiercest fray.

The whole sonnet is helpful to an understanding of "Windhover." But there is especial relevance in the second line:

> And those strokes that once gashed flesh or galled shield.

There is here a direct clue to the last lines of our poem.

> No wonder of it: shéer plód makes plough down sillion
> Shine, and blue-bleak embers, ah my dear,
> Fall, gall themselves, and gash gold-vermilion.

"Gall" and "gash" are in both places associated with shield and mirror and flesh—mortified or obedient flesh, of course. The underlying image in these last three lines is that of mortal *clay* transformed. It is made to shine and to fructify by the humble service of the plough (the obedient will). The "blue-bleak" earth provides the transition to the embers covered with clay-like ash. Just as "the fire that breaks from thee then" (after the mirror of mortal beauty has been buckled to the hidden heart) is not a fire produced by any direct action or valor, so the fire that breaks from the "blue-bleak embers" is not the effect of *ethos* but *pathos*, not of action but of suffering or patience. The true "achieve of, the mastery of the thing" from which flashes the most dangerous and daring exploit

> dates from day
> Of his going in Galilee
> Warm-laid grave of a womb-life grey;
> ("The Wreck of the Deutschland")

Here again is the image of the fire in the hidden heart which evokes the "blue-bleak embers," and, which, as some have suggested, leads on to the image of the vermilion side of Christ on the Cross.

One might even suggest that as the ash-covered coals gash gold-vermilion when touched by the poker (spear), so when Hopkins "kissed the rod, Hand rather" ("Carrion Comfort"), he becomes a mirror of Christ, flashing gold-vermilion:

> I kissed the rod,
> Hand rather, my heart lo! lapped strength,
> Stole joy, would laugh, chéer.
> Cheer whom though? the hero whose heaven-handling
> flung me, fóot tród
> Me? or me that fought him?

The *crucial* ambivalence which Hopkins stresses is owing to the double mirror image which he keeps always in mind. As a mirror of Christ he must imitate both the valor and also the obscure sufferings of Christ. He must overcome and be overcome at the same instant—at every instant. But this complexity does not exist in the mirror of mortal beauty, the "brute beauty and valour and act" which is a simple reflection of Christ's mastery but not of His suffering and love.

Familiarity with Hopkins soon reveals that each of his poems includes all the rest, such is the close-knit character of his sensibility. A relatively small number of themes and images—such is the intensity of his perception—permits him an infinitely varied orchestration. Thus it is really impossible to feel the full impact of "The Windhover" without awareness of the tentacles which its images stretch out into the other poems. To take once more the analogy of "sheer plod makes plough down sillion Shine," its paradox is brightly illuminated in the poem "That Nature is a Heraclitean Fire." Contemplating his "joyless days, dejection," "flesh fade, and mortal trash," he reflects that:

> This Jack, joke, poor potsherd, patch, matchwood, immortal
> diamond,
> Is immortal diamond.

This "Jack, joke" plodding behind the plough makes the trash and mud of earth shine like diamond, "wafting him out of it." And diamond flashing from the silicates of the soil is also, once again, the mirror of Christ in the hidden and humble heart of mortal clay.

Another aspect of this analogy of the plough grinding through the gritty soil is seen in the last line of "Spelt from Sybil's Leaves":

> Where, selfwrung, selfstrung, sheathe- and shelterless, thóughts
>   against thoughts in groans grínd.

This aspect of the plough and the soil is the more obviously dramatic
one—immortal beauty won from the harshest dullest toil, suffering and
discipline.

An inevitable dispersal of attention has accompanied the above elucidation of this poem. But then only an oral reading with all the freedom
and flexibility of spoken discussion can really point to the delicate in-
teraction, at each moment of the poem, of all its cumulative vitality of
logic, fancy, musical gesture.

"The Windhover" could never have become the richly complex poem
it is if Hopkins had not tested and explored all its themes beforehand, in
other poems. There is no other poem of comparable length in English,
or perhaps in any language, which surpasses its richness and intensity
or realized artistic organization. There are two or three sonnets of Shakespeare (for example, "They that have power to hurt" and "The expense
of spirit") which might be put with Donne's "At the round earth's" for
comparison and contrast with this sonnet. But they are not comparable
with the range of the experience and multiplicity of integrated perception which is found in "The Windhover."

The Univocal Chiming

by J. Hillis Miller

There is one possible mode of harmony and only one. By gradually extending the empire of this principle Hopkins puts the world together, escapes his isolation, and conquers that proximity to God for which he longs.

The poet's conversion to Catholicism does not give him overnight all that he wants. Even if he had permitted himself to write poetry just after his conversion, the decade of slow construction recorded in the journals, letters, and early papers would have been necessary to the explosion of "The Wreck of the Deutschland" and the great nature poems. The putting together of the all-embracing harmony which makes these poems possible is like certain of Hopkins' meticulous landscape drawings.[1] In these it is not a question of sketching rapidly a composition which is filled in with details later. Hopkins can work only through the gradual ordering of minute details, each one of which is another tiny area conquered from chaos and blankness. This habit of microscopic vision is a basic characteristic of his mind, and exists in tense opposition to his desire to have a vision of the whole.[2] Not with universals but with individuals must he begin, for he is confronted at the beginning with a world of unrelated particulars. Only at the very end will the harmony of the whole be revealed. In all realms this harmony is approached by the extension of a single sovereign principle.

"The Univocal Chiming" by J. Hillis Miller. From *The Disappearance of God: Five Nineteenth-Century Writers* (Cambridge, Mass.: Harvard University Press), pp. 276-317. Copyright © 1963 by the President and Fellows of Harvard College. Reprinted by permission of the publisher and the author. Retitled by the editor.
[1] See Humphry House and Graham Storey, eds., *The Journals and Papers of Gerard Manley Hopkins* (London: Oxford University Press, 1959), Plates 19, 23, 24; hereafter cited as "J."
[2] See, for example, the memories of Hopkins of an old lay brother who had been with him at Stonyhurst: "One of Hopkins's special delights, said the brother, was the path from the Seminary to the College. After a shower, he would run and crouch down to gaze at the crushed quartz glittering as the sun came out again. 'Ay, a strange yoong man,' said the old brother, 'crouching down that gate to stare at some wet sand. A fair natural 'e seemed to us, that Mr. 'opkins'" (J. 408).

This principle is *rhyme*. For Hopkins "any two things however unlike are in something like" [3] and insofar as any two things are like one another they may be said to rhyme. In Hopkins' analysis of selfhood it seemed that any two things would either be tuned to exactly the same pitch, and hence be in harmony, or would be so unlike one another that there could be no relation between them. In a universe of unique particulars all would be dissonance. But two strings not tuned to the same pitch may still be in resonance, as are middle C and the octave above, or as are C and G. Such notes are harmonic chimes of one another, bound together by a subtle mathematical relation in their vibrations. This relation may be found everywhere in the universe: in words which resemble one another without being identical, in trees or clouds which have similar but not identical patterns, and so on. The universe, even though no two things in it are exactly alike, is full of things which rhyme, and by extending the range of observed rhymings who knows how many things may ultimately be brought into harmony?

The principle of rhyme is first announced by Hopkins in an undergraduate essay of 1864 ("On the Signs of Health and Decay in the Arts" [J, 74-79]). There the comparison of two or more things is said to "include the principles of Dualism, Plurality, Repetition, Parallelism" (J, 74). In his dialogue "On the Origin of Beauty" (1865) Hopkins shows that all forms of beauty, in nature and in art, are different versions of the relation which holds between unlike things which are similar. This relation may be defined in its most general form by saying: "Likeness therefore implies unlikeness . . . , and unlikeness likeness" (J, 105). Therefore, says Hopkins, "all beauty may by a metaphor be called rhyme . . ." (J, 102).

Another motif recurs in Hopkins' undergraduate essays and in the dialogue on beauty. This is the opposition between *diatonism* and *chromatism*. Diatonism is any change in things, any difference between part and part, which is abrupt. Chromatism is change or difference which is sliding or transitional (J, 76, 84, 104). At times it seems that this is a mere neutral principle. Things may shade into one another, or exist as nodes of pattern or hue separated by a gulf. Each kind of change leads to its own characteristic form of beauty, the chromatic style of Newman or the diatonic style of Carlyle (J, 76).

Elsewhere Hopkins shows a distinct preference for diatonic beauty. The reason for this is related to his rejection of the Paterian philosophy of flux. In an early essay on "The Probable Future of Metaphysics"

[3] Christopher Devlin, ed., *The Sermons and Devotional Writings of Gerard Manley Hopkins* (London: Oxford University Press, 1959), p. 123; hereafter cited as "S."

(1867) Hopkins associates chromatism with the idea that the variety of beings in the world has developed spontaneously from the shapeless slime. In an evolutionary world species are not eternal types, like beads on a string. They are momentary and accidental coagulations of universal matter, developed without a break from the species below, and ready to flow at any time to a higher species in the perpetual stream of development. "To the prevalent philosophy and science," says Hopkins, "nature is a string all the differences in which are really chromatic but certain places in it have become accidentally fixed and the series of fixed points becomes an arbitrary scale" (J, 120). Such a view of nature is "a philosophy of flux," based on the ideas "of a continuity without fixed points, not to say *saltus* or breaks, of development in one chain of necessity, of species having no absolute types" (J, 120). Against this Hopkins puts his conviction that organization can only be imposed downward from a realm of predetermined types. He therefore opposes to evolutionary chromatism the diatonic philosophy which he calls in this essay "Platonism" or "Realism."

In Hopkins' choice of diatonism over chromatism more is at stake than the question of the direction from which the patterning force comes. In a chromatic world nature is a string, a series of infinitesimal points at all distances from one another. Each note, species, or color merges imperceptibly into its neighbor. All is "bleared, smeared"[4] and "self in self" is "steepèd and pashed" (P, 104) in the perpetual flux. As a result, rhyming is impossible, and in a world where rhyme is impossible no principle of ordering remains. The individuals do not have sufficiently sharp or permanent patterns to have a relation of chiming with one another, and the intervals between species or individuals are not fixed enough to establish a regular system of harmony.

Against this "prevalent philosophy of continuity or flux" Hopkins sets his version of Platonic realism. It is a version which is calculated to preserve the possibility of rhyme. Against the floating species of evolutionism Hopkins proposes the existence of inalterable types at definite intervals, intervals which have a mathematical relation providing for a grand system of harmony. Hopkins' later doctrine of inscape, his feeling for pattern, and for the relation between patterns, is implicit in this early description of a world of imperishable forms at fixed distances from one another in the scale of being:

> The new Realism will maintain that in musical strings the roots of chords, to use technical wording, are mathematically fixed and give a standard by

[4] *Poems of Gerard Manley Hopkins*, ed. W. H. Gardner, third edition (New York: Oxford University Press, 1948), p. 70; hereafter cited as "P."

which to fix all the notes of the appropriate scale: when points between
these are sounded the ear is annoyed by a solecism, or to analyse deeper,
the mind cannot grasp the notes of the scale and the intermediate sound in
one conception; so also there are certain forms which have a great hold on
the mind and are always reappearing and seem imperishable, such as the
designs of Greek vases and lyres, the cone upon Indian shawls, the honey-
suckle moulding, the fleur-de-lys, while every day we see designs both simple
and elaborate which do not live and are at once forgotten . . . It may be
maintainable then that species are fixed and to be fixed only at definite
distances in the string and that the developing principle will only act when
the precise conditions are fulfilled. (J, 120)

The principle of rhyme and a choice of diatonism over chromatism
permit Hopkins to reconstruct the world. Diatonism guarantees the
stability of patterns and of the intervals between patterns, and rhyme is
the name for the relation between two patterns which chime like notes
in a musical chord.

The etymological speculations of Hopkins' early diaries are the first
examples in his work of a reconstruction of the world through discovery
of rhymes.

Words seem a perfect example of the disorder of the world. The universe is a collection of unrelated things, and words are a collection of unrelated names for those things, or for their qualities and actions. The
best order that can be given to words is the arbitrary alphabetical
sequence of the dictionary.

But some words sound like one another. The basis of Hopkins' etymological hypotheses is the idea that if words are similar in sound they
will also be similar in meaning. Hopkins assumes that a group of words
of similar sound are variations of some *ur*-word and root meaning.
Among the earliest entries in his undergraduate diaries are lists of words
of similar sounds with comments on their similarity of meaning. Hopkins
already shows great virtuosity in finding out inner connections of word-
sounds and meanings:

Grind, gride, gird, grit, groat, grate, greet, κρούειν, *crush, crash*, κροτεῖν etc.
Original meaning to *strike, rub,* particularly *together.* (J, 5)

Crook, crank, kranke, crick, cranky. Original meaning crooked, not
straight or right, wrong, awry. (J, 5)

Drill, trill, thrill, nostril, nese-thirl (Wiclif etc.)
Common idea piercing. (J, 10)

Each word for Hopkins is a node or pattern of linguistic energy. It has its own unique tone, but it is at a fixed interval from other similar words and is therefore able to chime with them, both in sound and in meaning. He notes that the sequence *"flick," "fleck," "flake"* is like a chord of variations on the same sound and meaning, each change in vowel producing a different tone in the chord and a new nuance in meaning (J, 11). Here the sequence is produced by a variation in the vowel, but a variation in consonant can produce the same kind of sequence, as in "the connection between *flag* and *flabby . . . flick* and *flip, flog* and *flap, flop*" (J, 12).

As Alan Ward observes (J, 499), such word lists are miniature poems, or poems in the rough. Though Hopkins may have been confirmed in his feelings for the interrelations of words by his study of Greek poetry, Old English alliterative verse, and Welsh *cynghanedd,* it is only a step from *"skim, scum, squama, scale, keel"* (J, 12) or *"spuere, spit, spuma, spume, spoom, spawn, spittle, spatter, spot, sputter"* (J, 16) to such characteristic passages of "vowelling" in his poetry as "bow or brooch or braid or brace, láce, latch or catch or key to keep/Back beauty" (P, 96), or "Earnest, earthless, equal, attuneable,/vaulty, voluminous, . . . stupendous/Evening" (P, 104).

The fundamental method of Hopkins' poetry is to carry as far as it will go, into every aspect of his verse, the principle of rhyme. His early diaries show him interested in words in themselves, without reference to the grasp they give of the external world. This develops into a view of poetry as a kind of music of words. What is important in poetry is neither the expression of the inner self of the poet, as some romantic poets had thought, nor the imitation of something in the external world, as Aristotle had said. Poetry, like music, is an autonomous art. Music makes patterns of sequences of tones. Poetry makes patterns of sequences of words. The notes in a piece of music tell us nothing about the external world, and the meaning of a word in poetry is also part of its substance, no more related to the outside world than its sound. Hopkins, in a famous letter to Bridges, affirms the similarity of music, painting, and poetry. Pattern is the one thing needful in all three: ". . . as air, melody, is what strikes me most of all in music and design in painting, so design, pattern or what I am in the habit of calling 'inscape' is what I above all aim at in poetry." [5]

It might seem, from the sentences which follow in the letter just quoted, that Hopkins means by "inscape" uniqueness of pattern, what

[5] Claude Colleer Abbott, ed., *The Letters of Gerard Manley Hopkins to Robert Bridges* (London: Oxford University Press, 1955), p. 66; hereafter cited as "L, I."

Duns Scotus calls the *haecceitas* of a thing, its ultimate principle of individuality: "Now," says Hopkins, "it is the virtue of design, pattern, or inscape to be distinctive and it is the vice of distinctiveness to become queer. This vice I cannot have escaped" (L, I, 66). Poetry would seem to be a matter of making a pattern of words which is so highly pointed that it is unlike any other pattern of words. A poem should have the same unspeakable stress of pitch that a man's selftaste has.

This is not really the case, nor does inscape here mean anything like Scotus' *haecceitas*. The inscape of a poem, far from being a unique, unrepeatable pattern, is the design which different parts of the poem share, and which detaches itself from the chiming of these parts. Hopkins' theory of poetry is much like his theory of music.

In his experiments in musical composition Hopkins was most interested in melody and rhythm (see J, 457-497). The kinds of music which most fascinated him were those, like canon and fugue, in which a basic pattern is stated and then developed in overlapping variations. In a late letter to Bridges, he made explicit the central idea of his theory of music: ". . . the air becomes a generic form which is specified newly in each verse" (L, I, 305). The inscape of a piece of music is that generic form, present in all specifications of itself, but usually visible only through our perception of their similarity or rhyming.

The inscape of poetry is analogous. Poetry is not distinguished from other uses of words by its intensity or complexity of meaning. The meaning is there only as a necessary support for the pattern. The design of a piece of verse would be just as visible, perhaps more visible, to someone who did not know the language in which it was written. Such a person would be better able to recognize the precise sound-shape of the words. The inscape is this shape of sound: "Poetry is speech framed for contemplation of the mind by the way of hearing or speech framed to be heard for its own sake and interest even over and above its interest of meaning. Some matter and meaning is essential to it but only as an element necessary to support and employ the shape which is contemplated for its own sake. . . . Poetry is in fact speech only employed to carry the inscape of speech for the inscape's sake—and therefore the inscape must be dwelt on" (J, 289). The inscape is a pattern of sound, and therefore "verse is . . . inscape of spoken sound, not spoken words, or speech employed to carry the inscape of spoken sound . . ." (J, 289). As in music the inscape is the generic form which recurs in varied forms throughout the composition, so the inscape of verse is a pattern of sound which may be repeated, and usually must be repeated in different specifications in order to detach it from its particular manifestations. The basic method of

poetry as of music is repetition, the repetition of different forms of the
same inscape. This inscape must echo and reverberate through the poem
in order to become visible. The term "inscape," at least as Hopkins uses
it in his theory of poetry and music, means just the opposite of the Scotist *haecceitas*. It means that which a number of particulars have in common rather than that which one particular shares with no other: "Now if
this [the dwelling on the inscape for its own sake] can be done without
repeating it, *once* of the inscape will be enough for art and beauty and
poetry but then at least the inscape must be understood as so standing by
itself that it could be copied and repeated. If not/repetition, *oftening,
over-and-overing, aftering* of the inscape must take place in order to
detach it to the mind and in this light poetry is speech which afters
and oftens its inscape, speech couched in a repeating figure and verse is
spoken sound having a repeating figure" (J, 289).

Hopkins begins in his early diaries with a fascination for the relations
of word-sounds, and is led step by step to develop an intransigent theory
of poetry. The letters to his fellow poets, Bridges, Patmore, and Dixon,
are full of professional discussions of the craft of poetry. He seems to be
more interested in technical questions of rhythm, meter, and form than
in questions of content. The striking peculiarities of his verse are ways
of attaining the utmost refinement of inscape. There must be nothing
flaccid or lax, no blurring or smudging of the pattern, but each part of
the poem must be wound up to an intense stress or pitch of distinctiveness. Comprehensibility, grammar, and clear logical form may be sacrificed to the attainment of strongly marked pattern. Sprung rhythm,
internal rhyme, consonant chiming, alliteration, "vowelling"—all the
special characteristics of Hopkins' verse, all his "stress . . . on the naked
thew and sinew of the English language" (L, I, 267, 268), are there to
achieve the highest possible degree of what he called "brilliancy, starriness, quain, margaretting" (J, 290). These techniques of patterning work
together to produce the extraordinarily sinewy and burly texture of
Hopkins' poetry, its heavy substance and strongly marked inner structure, as of bones, veins, and tendons binding together a body and making
it one. His description of "Harry Ploughman" might be taken as a
description (and example) of the texture of his own poetry:

>   Hard as hurdle arms, with a broth of goldish flue
>   Breathed round; the rack of ribs; the scooped flank; lank
>   Rope-over thigh; knee-nave; and barrelled shank—
>   Head and foot, shoulder and shank—
>   By a grey eye's heed steered well, one crew, fall to;
>   Stand at stress. (P, 108)

If Hopkins' poetry had substance without sinew it might be a loose heap of words turned things. The inner structure, the stress between word and word, makes the poem stand "as a beechbole firm" (P, 108). Each word or group of words is a stress of individualized sound. The poem is made up of the stresses between these stresses. It is "one crew" of parts all working together in harmonious unison. "Starriness" and "margaretting" are not attained through sharpness or crispness of pattern. They are attained only through the *repetition* of a crisp pattern which makes its inscape visible, as stars shine together against the dark field of the night sky, or as flowers bloom together in a meadow.

Hopkins' theory of poetry as the inscape of speech for the inscape's sake has organized and conquered the whole realm of words through an extension of the principle of rhyme. Different modes of echoing mean that all words taken together form an elaborate system of interrelated reverberations. Poetry is the exploration and exploitation of these possible "figures of sound" (J, 289). But in defining poetry in this way Hopkins has cut it off from the poet and from nature. He has reduced one kingdom to order only at the cost of isolating it as radically as a man's self-taste isolates him from the rest of creation. The figures of sound in poetry have an order and harmony of their own, but these are without relation to the poet. The poet is a skilled craftsman, coldly manipulating materials which remain external to him. His own personal distinctiveness remains untouched, unexpressed, uncommunicated.

Perhaps the principle of rhyme can be applied in other areas beside that of the sounds of words. It would be some satisfaction to find more order in the apparent chaos of the world, even if that order were to have no relation to the solitude of the self.

Alongside Hopkins' interest in the sounds of words there is an equally strong interest in the way words are a means of possessing nature. Hopkins knows that detached observation of nature is not a possession of it. There must be a strong grappling action on the part of the mind to go out and meet the powerful energy with which things are what they are. There must be what he calls a "stem of stress between us and things to bear us out and carry the mind over" (J, 127). This stem of stress is words.

If Hopkins makes the assumption that words of similar sound are derived from a common root, he also assumes that this root word is often onomatopoeic. Though he knows that the onomatopoeic theory of the origin of language is somewhat discredited, he is led by his feeling for words to reaffirm it. "In fact," he says, "I think the onomatopoetic theory has not had a fair chance" (J, 5). If words are arbitrary labels for things, they give no substantial possession of the things they name, but are only signs pointing in the direction of their meaning. An onomato-poeic word imitates in its substance and inscape the substance and in-scape of the thing it names. Hopkins does not particularly like words which are a superficial echo of the sound of a thing. The words which most attract him are those which are a kinesthetic imitation of their meaning, and give a deep bodily, muscular, or visceral possession of the world. For him language originates in a kind of inner pantomime, in fundamental movements of the body and the mind by which we take possession of the world through imitating it in ourselves. Words are the dynamic internalization of the world.

Browning, too, likes words which, as they are pronounced, give a kinesthetic possession of the thing named. But Browning is most inter-ested in the rough, solid weight of matter which all things share; conse-quently his onomatopoeic words are thick with harsh consonants express-ing the universal density of material substance. Hopkins, on the other hand, has a strong sense of the variations in texture, substance, and struc-ture of the things of the world. He likes the way a word, by the unique-ness of its inscape, is a perfect match for one certain quality in the world and one only (though this quality may of course be repeated in different phenomena). Interspersed among the lists of words of similar sounds in Hopkins' early diaries are places where he experiments with the way a single word opens up a precise area of the world, and gives him a way to seize it: "Altogether *peak* is a good word. For sunlight through shutter, locks of hair, rays in brass knobs etc. Meadows peaked with flowers" (J, 47).

The inscape of words for the inscape's sake, words as a means of grasp-ing the things of the world—these two apparently incompatible orienta-tions toward language exist side by side. Though there does not seem to be any way in which they can be harmonized, nature still seems worth studying and naming. What characterizes Hopkins' sense of nature and of the way nature may be grasped in words?

At first it seems that there are no pervasive principles of organization. What pervades are principles of isolation.

The descriptions of nature in the journals are written from the point of view of scientific detachment. Even when it is a question of describing a subjective reaction to a scene this is given as objectively as the rest of the data: "I felt an instress and charm of Wales" (J, 258); "I felt a certain awe and instress . . ." (J, 249). Hopkins distinguishes his self-taste from the flavor of anything he sees, and this self-possession makes

it possible for him to see things clearly. He remains himself; the cloud
or waterfall remains itself, seen at a distance. Hopkins does not want to
melt into the totality, to expand into vagueness, or to lose the sharp
taste of himself in a possession of the "all." He will describe what is there
to be seen, as completely and accurately as possible, and finds little
difference in value between one phenomenon and another. He takes as
much interest in analyzing the precise way in which steam rises from a
cup of cocoa, as in describing the grandest sunset (J, 203, 204).

If the spectator remains spatially detached from what he sees, there is
a temporal separation too. The journal entries were written up, sometimes more than a year after the experience, from notes taken at the
time. There is always a more or less prolonged interval between the
actual experience and its final crystallization in language.

A distance also exists between one item in the scene and another.
The diaries and journals are made up of detached entries, each existing
by itself and separated by a gap from those around it. There is no
attempt to connect them together in some over-all pattern of meaning.
The basic principle of the journals is the assumption that each cloud or
tree or waterfall is unique, and must therefore be described in an individualized pattern of words.

Everywhere evident in the journals is an amazing linguistic virtuosity.
Hopkins invents with effortless ease new combinations of words for each
nuance of the appearances, of nature. A respect for the idiosyncrasy of
each thing is the law of this virtuosity. Hopkins views every item in
nature as unique in pattern, texture, and inner structure, and it would
seem that no more can be said about his journals than this. His celebrated terms, "inscape" and "instress," seem, when they apply to natural
things at least, to refer, respectively, to the individual pattern of a
thing and to the inner energy which upholds that pattern. The journals
are the record of a long series of isolated encounters with unique inscapes. Each encounter already implies the insight into nature expressed
in the octave of "As kingfishers catch fire," the idea that each thing in
nature has its own distinctive note or tone, which it manifests in being
itself, "doing" itself, "going" itself (P, 95). Nothing is like anything else,
except in being "arch-especial" (P, 84).

If this is Hopkins' nature and his relation to nature, disorder and
isolation predominate. But certain motifs recur . . . ; there *are* principles of organization. Though for Hopkins no two clouds or trees repeat
each other, certain qualities are characteristic of his apprehension of
nature, and tend to be present in whatever he is describing. . . .

. . . What all thing[s]
are all different, eac[h]
rather, things are [
"throughout one v[
All things have i[
fact that all th[
being unlike. [
gous to the re[
be found ev[
Beauty" (P[
to express[

100

them echo and chime, and therefore th[
dappled things."
Nature in "Pied Beauty" lives [
pattern of couple-color is only m[
chestnuts have fallen, and are [
a fresh firecoal, perfect imag[
itself by its very act of be[
ploted and pieced—what [
next; and each trade, [
activity of making and [
Though nature h[
Like the lark's so[
losing its first fre[
two couple-colo[
counter to on[
stands by i[
known in [
it is a co[
appear[
not u[
may[
be[

> Fresh-fi[
> Landscape p[
> And áll trádes,

> All things counter, original, sp[are, strange]
> Whatever is fickle, freckled (who [
> With swift, slow; sweet, sour; adazzle, [
> He fathers-forth whose beauty is past change:
> Praise him.

Piedness, like beauty and like rhyme, is a relation between t[wo]
which are similar without being identical. This relation organizes "Pied
Beauty" at every level. Each individual thing, the poem says, is pied or
dappled. Though it is all one thing, it is different from one place to
another. A dappled or brinded cow is all the same cow, but in one place
it is one color, in another another. This difference may exist in time or
in space. A thing may be pied by having rose-moles, or by changing
from swift to slow, from adazzle to dim.

Hopkins does not speak of individuals in "Pied Beauty." Each thing
is given in the plural: skies, trout, chestnut-falls, finches' wings, fields,
and trades. Only in the line: "All things counter, original, spare, strange"
does Hopkins make explicit the notion that there is a "pied" relation
among members of the same species. No two brinded cows are exactly
alike, though they are all cows. So the rhymelike relation of pied beauty
holds between all cows, skies, trout, and so on. But only groups of dappled things have visibly the relation of likeness in difference which makes

he poet says: "Glory be to God for

in movement and change. The sky's
omentary; the trout are swimming; the
like that evanescent and glowing thing,
e of a dynamic energy which is spending
ng itself. The finches fly; the landscape is
is fallow one year is "plough" or "fold" the
ith its special gear and tackle and trim, is an
changing the world.
re lives in dynamic change it never repeats itself.
g it "goes on . . . through all time, without ever
nness, being a thing both new and old" (L, I, 164). No
red skies, trout, or finches' wings are alike. They are
e another, original, "spare," in the sense that a spare part
elf, and strange, in the sense that they cannot be wholly
terms of past experience. Though the poet can recognize that
v, a trout, or a sky, to some degree it evades his categories and
strange, a strangeness which makes him recognize that he does
nderstand how it is what it is. "Who knows how?" he asks, which
mean both: "How can I tell you all the ways in which things can
fickle or freckled?" and also: "It is impossible to understand how this
comes about." This failure to understand the thing fully, though it
registers on the senses, opens up the gap between sensation (or "simple
apprehension") and perception (or "understanding") which is so important to Hopkins as a Scotist (see S, 174). When a thing appears strange,
man becomes aware that to place it in a concept does not do justice to
its uniqueness and originality. He comes to see the coarseness of such
words as "cow," which must do duty for all cows, though each cow, as
can be seen in the case of brinded cows, is in some sense original and
strange. To name a thing rightly the poet must go beyond nouns, for
the noun will tell how a thing is like other things of the same species,
but not how it is different from them. Beauty lies in the copresence of
the two, unlikeness with likeness, sameness with difference.

Words for the qualities of things, adjectives, are in one way more
anonymous than nouns, since they can be applied indifferently to all
things which share the quality in question. The Thomistic account of
the way we know God in nature moves, as does "Pied Beauty," from
perception of specific objects through perception of qualities which many
species share to recognition of the God who fathers all. In another way

qualities are closer to the true strangeness of sense-experience, for they exist at a level beneath that of concepts and a little closer to the immediacy of sensation. They are also more likely to suggest in their very sound the experience they name. "Freckled," "sweet," "sour," "brinded," "adazzle," "dim"—each of these seems to have been picked at least partly for the way its sound echoes its sense. Every quality-word names a special attribute of the sensible world, an attribute which may recur, but each time with its special "counterness" to other qualities. All words are general, but adjectives have a radically different form of generality from nouns.

What is the relation between qualities and pied beauty? Adjectives measure degrees of similarity or difference within a certain category of experience. Qualities are a matter of more or less. Even colors are more or less intense, and other qualities are even more unequivocally a matter of degree. Something sweet is more or less sweet than other things, and sweetness exists only by comparison with its opposite, sourness, just as swiftness suggests slowness; brightness, dimness. Since sweetness and sourness can be measured by the same means (taste) they are in some sense the same. They are another case of sameness and difference. Adjectives are words by which we name the way all things are "counter, original, spare, strange," and so Hopkins is quite right to say "Glory be to God" for "Whatever is fickle, freckled, (who knows how?)/With swift, slow; sweet, sour; adazzle, dim."

His identification here of objective qualities (swift, slow) with qualities which much more depend on our senses for their existence (sweet, sour; adazzle, dim) shows his desire to bring spectator and scene together. The freckledness of a thing, its fickle disparity from itself in space or in time, is its way of having being, but this is immediately possessed through our sense-knowledge of the thing. Adjectives name qualities in things which are both subjective and objective at the same time.

Hopkins wants us to think that all words have this intimate participation in the nature of what they name. Reality has simultaneously the dynamic activity and instress of verbs, the solidity and substantiality of nouns, and the sensible vividness of adjectives. Signs of this are his fondness for participles, and his use of one part of speech in place of another. He likes to build up groups of words which form a single linguistic unit combining adjective (often as participle), verb, and noun. Sometimes nouns are turned into adjectives. The whole compound forms one word possessing the powers of all the major parts of speech. In "Pied Beauty" we have "landscape plotted and pieced" and "fresh-firecoal chestnut-falls." The phrases are dappled or pied and express in their structure the fact that the world is made up of groups of dissimilar things which are nevertheless similar and rhyme.

The rhymelike relation of beauty in the poem is more than that within individuals which are pied, or even among individuals of the same species which are the same and yet different. There is also a relation of piedness between different species, expressed here, as in the journals, by metaphor. The chestnut-falls are like fresh-firecoals, the skies are like a brinded cow, the moles on a trout are like roses, but likeness is not identity. We understand the chestnut-falls by means of the firecoals, but only by realizing that they are different as well as alike. Behind them both there is some general quality or qualities which they participate in, but each differently, just as all cows, however unique their pattern of color, participate in the species "cow."

All things are like one another in one way or another. All things rhyme. In this poem the things mentioned are, or can be, some shade of red or brown: skies, brinded cows, rose-moles on trout, firecoals, chestnuts, finches' wings, landscape, and even the gear and tackle of a trade such as shoemaking. The list of dappled things for which Hopkins says "Glory be to God" forms a "chord of colour" (J, 260). And all the things in the list share the quality of being pied; they are thus in yet another way rhymes of one another. Any two of the pied species taken together form a larger piedness enclosing the smaller one.

It is not an accident that two of the examples (sky and landscape) are universal in scope, for clearly the whole world, taken as a unit, is a case of pied beauty. The poem includes the four universal elements: earth, water, air, and fire. The fields, trout, skies, and firecoals are synecdoches, and the poem is cosmic in scope. Every piece of nature is in itself pied, and at the same time it is part of a larger and more inclusive piedness. The relation of sameness and difference, of the one and the many, of general and specific, pervades the whole universe.

The structure of the universe is echoed and imitated by the sound and structure of the poem. The relation of sound between the pairs of quality-words ("swift, slow"; "sweet, sour"; "adazzle, dim") is one of piedness. The pairs of words are opposite in meaning, and yet similar in sound, and this similarity in sound leads us to seek a relation of meaning. The poem's structure of sound, like its structure of meaning, and like the universe it imitates in little, is a complex network of relations of likeness in difference—pied beauty within pied beauty, and larger cases of pied beauty embracing smaller. There is an elaborate pattern of alliteration, assonance, and rhyme which creates a canon of sound repeating in another form the meaning of the poem. The relation between the two stanzas is pied. There is some carry-over in rhymes from stanza to stanza, but some of the rhymes are unique to their stanzas. The first three lines of the second stanza are like either half of the first stanza, but the last two lines are different. The poem is what Hopkins called a "curtal-sonnet" (P, 10). It is like an ordinary sonnet, but different, and so the relation of this sonnet to the usual sonnet is another case of pied beauty. The poem's structure of rhythm and sound seems to be all for the purpose of making the poem a model in little of the universe it names.

What of the first line of the poem and the last two? The poem describes the universe as a total harmony of pied beauty, but only as a way of praising God, its creator. What is the relation here between God and nature?

At first it appears that the first line of the poem and the last say much the same thing: a pious thanks to God for having provided this wonderful world of linked multiplicity: "Glory be to God for dappled things," and "Praise him." But at the end of the poem the statement relating the pied universe to God has a new meaning, for the poem has shown that the most inclusive case of the relation of sameness and difference is the relation of God to the universe. The creator and the creation rhyme.

God's beauty is "past change." He is single and eternal, not at all fickle or freckled, but this God of undifferentiated oneness has fathered forth the pied universe. Its seeds have lain in him, ready to flow forth and spring into material existence. God and the universe have the relation of pied beauty. The eternity, changelessness, and unity of God are set against the temporality, spatiality, self-division, and changefulness of the world, but one is the source of the other, and "like father, like son." The creation must somehow be made in the image of its progenitor.

Perhaps the ultimate case of piedness is God himself. If God is in one sense certainly "past change," beyond it altogether, and not pied beauty but the beauty of the One, in another sense God's perfection lies in the fact that he is the origin of difference, the meeting place of opposites. He may be past change not in the sense of transcending it, but in the sense of being beyond it toward the future as the goal of earthly changing beauty. All things flow from God and flow back to God. God is the most wonderful example of piedness, for in him the most radically different things, diversity and unity, are reconciled and made one.

If this is the case, we can see why Hopkins says "Glory be to God for dappled things" and "Praise him." The poem works from the first line

back around to an apparent repetition of it through an exploration of
the nature of pied beauty in the middle lines. The last line is really
repetition with a difference—it rhymes in meaning with the first line.
At the end of the poem the reader knows that he should not simply say
"Glory be to God for dappled things," blandly and neutrally. By understanding the dappled or pied nature of the universe he best understands
the nature of God, though God's beauty is past change, and this knowledge makes it possible to praise God. The whole poem leads up to the
two words which make up the final half line. These two monosyllables,
in the sprung rhythm of the poem, take up as much time as seven
syllables elsewhere in the poem. They are like two great concluding
chords in a fugue: *Praise him.*

Why is it that God is best known through dappled things? The answer
is double, epistemological and ontological at once. Man's only knowledge
is through sensation. A single pure homogeneous sensation would be invisible, inaudible, without taste or feeling. The sensation would be there
but man would not be aware of it. Man knows through comparison.
Even the uniqueness of his self-taste can only be known by seeking similar tastes in the world. The need to set two different sensations against
one another in order to know either one of them is the chief mark of
man's epistemological limitation, and one reason he cannot know God
directly. Piedness is necessary to knowledge of the world, and God cannot be known directly as the pure One.

There is more to the matter than this. In one sense the dappledness
of things is a sign of their deficiency from the wholeness of God, for
things which are fickle and freckled are differentiated in space and change
in time, waver and are not consistent with themselves. In another sense
pied things are the best earthly image of God's perfection. Something
unpied is only one limited thing, one quality, one action, and that thing,
quality, or action is a far cry from the infinite perfection of God in his
fullness. But pied beauty is precisely a *concordia discors,* a unifying of
diversity, and thereby a finite image of the infinite God. Hopkins may
well say "Glory be to God for dappled things," for it is through fickle,
freckled things, things which combine in themselves "swift, slow; sweet,
sour; adazzle, dim," that limited mortals can best know God, and, by
knowing, rightly "praise him."

Hopkins' long exploration of nature in his journals and poems begins
with a respect for the integrity of concrete particulars. It culminates in
the notion that "the world is charged with the grandeur of God" (P, 70).
His vision of nature as pied beauty is balanced in tension between a
strong sense of the uniqueness of each thing and a feeling of the omni-

presence of God in all things. Inscapes, canons of feeling, metaphors, God as father of all—the principle of rhyme has been extended further and further until the whole universe, in itself and in its relation to its maker, is revealed as "like notes of a scale and a harmonic series" (S, 200). Poetry, to borrow further Hopkins' phrases for the angelic concord, is "like the playing on these notes, like the tune, the music" (S, 200). There are innumerable possible poems, but each of them is another exploration of the music of creation, another tune played on the scale and harmonic series of things.

How can the two theories of poetry in Hopkins be reconciled? A poetry which imitates the objective chiming of nature has nothing to do with a poetry which is the autonomous inscape of the sound of words. Neither of these two forms of poetry seems to have anything to do with the poet's distinctive self-taste. It was the painful isolation of that self-taste which drove the poet to his exploration of the way things rhyme. He can write word music of absolute beauty or poems of the most exquisite perfection imitating nature; he will still be as isolated as ever.

The case is even worse than this. There is in Hopkins a *third* theory of poetry, incompatible with the other two, and developed with the same fullness and cogency.

In a letter to Bridges, Hopkins affirms his belief that there is in the bee a specific shaping power which drives it to build naturally in hexagonal figures. This shaping power is like the instinct which makes birds of the same species sing the same song (L, I, 281). If the bee, the cuckoo, and the thrush express their inscapes in an outward form, so do all other natural things. The sharply patterned outward form which manifests inscape Hopkins calls the "sake," "that in the thing by virtue of which especially it has [its] being abroad, and that is something distinctive, marked . . ." (L, I, 83). All created things possess inscape. But this inscape manifests itself in what things *do,* as the bee makes honeycomb, as thrush and cuckoo sing their specific songs. Each mortal thing "deals out that being indoors each one dwells," and this is its way of being (P, 95).

The poet is a mortal thing too, and his way of existing is like that of any other created being. The bee builds honeycomb. The stone rings. The poet poets. In writing poetry the poet expresses the innate pattern of his inscape. Poetry, like other arts, is creative not in the sense that it makes something out of nothing, but in the sense that it imposes upon the raw material of its art, words, a distinctive and highly pitched pattern. This pattern is a copy or echo of the pattern of selfhood in the poet. The poet, like other creative men, sheds multiple replicas of himself, as a dandelion sows seeds on the wind: "But MEN OF GENIUS ARE SAID TO CREATE, a painting, a poem, a tale, a tune, a policy; not indeed the colours and the canvas, not the words or notes, but the design, the character, the air, the plan. How then?—from themselves, from their own minds" (S, 238).

Hopkins' discussions of music, poetry, and painting in his letters and journals presuppose the notion that a unifying inscape is necessary to make a work of art "beautiful to individuation" (L, I, 210). The source of this unifying inscape is the artist himself. The artist and his work are different versions of the same inscape. They rhyme. Like a man who leaves his fingerprints on everything he touches, the poet makes his poems, whether he wishes to do so or not, in such a way that they match the pattern of his individuality. The poet is like a stamp or mold which shapes everything according to its design.

In this third theory of poetry Hopkins commits himself to the notion that all authentic art is original and distinctive. "The effect of studying masterpieces," he wrote in a famous letter, "is to make me admire and do otherwise. So it must be on every original artist to some degree, on me to a marked degree. Perhaps then more reading would only *refine my singularity*" (L, I, 291). A true artist is not one example of a species, but "each poet is like a species in nature (*not* an *individuum genericum* or *specificum*) and can never recur" (L, III, 370). The individualized spirit in the artist is the cause of the individualized pattern or inscape which is the one thing necessary in art. In the sonnet to Henry Purcell, Hopkins praises Purcell's music because it is the direct expression of the composer's "arch-especial . . . spirit." Purcell's music is "none of your d——d subjective rot" (L, I, 84) because it expresses something deeper than subjective feelings. Just as a seabird opening his wings unintentionally reveals the "quaint moonmarks" on his under-plumage which stamp his species, "so Purcell, seemingly intent only on the thought or feeling he is to express or call out, incidentally lets you remark the individualizing marks of his own genius" (L, I, 83). Hopkins likes inscape in art not for its own sake but because it is a revelation of the distinctive quality of the poet's soul. In Purcell's music it is "the forgèd feature" he likes best, and this distinctiveness of design is "the rehearsal/Of own, of abrúpt sélf" (P, 85). In another poem on music and architecture Hopkins says again that the harmony of art is an expression of the harmony of the artist's mind:

> Who shaped these walls has shewn
> The music of his mind,
> Made known, though thick through stone,
> What beauty beat behind. (P, 163)

This third view of poetry seems at last to have freed the self from isolation. The poet can make copies of his own self-taste which are comprehensible to others, and we can, through art, come to understand the "own, abrupt self" of a genius like Purcell. Those who are not artists may still remain imprisoned in themselves, but art is the liberating power which allows some men to go outside themselves, and even to find something which does not rebuff them with blank unlikeness. The artist has the pleasure of seeing himself mirrored everywhere in his own work. Like God, he has the power to emanate from himself in waves of creative instress which sweep through unformed matter and shape it in his own image. Whereas God possesses the molds of all possible created things, the poet oscillates at but one frequency, and can shape things in but one pattern. Each poem is the casting forth of a new "sake," a new expression of the inscape of the poet.

How can poetry do three things at once? There seems to be a contradiction at the heart of Hopkins' theory and practice of poetry. One kind of poetry permits an escape from the prison of selfhood, but this mode of poetry seems to have no relation to the other kinds. How could poetry express at once the inscapes of nature, the inscapes of words, and the inscape of the poet? Each of these realms has been organized in itself by an extension of the principle of rhyme, but there seems to be no rhyming between the three realms. Hopkins' exploration of language has led him to discover a division and disintegration of his world, for he finds that words can be used in three radically different and incompatible ways.

Hopkins' thinking so far has seemed like the gradual putting together from dispersed fragments of a great edifice, a bridge spanning the universe and binding its multiplicity into oneness. At the last moment the project has collapsed, and left three great towers standing in isolation from one another. Where is the power which will complete the construction of a unified world?

The first hint of a principle of unification is given in Hopkins' undergraduate notes on Parmenides. The brief essay on words, which comes earlier in the same notebook (J, 125, 126), is an expression of Hopkins' insight into the three-faced nature of words. Each word expresses a sub-

jective state, is a thing in itself, and names something in the objective
world: "A word then has three terms belonging to it, ὅροι, or moments
—its prepossession of feeling; its definition, abstraction, vocal expression
or other utterance; and its application, 'extension,' the concrete things
coming under it" (J, 125). The essay can offer no way of reconciling
these three aspects of a word. It vibrates back and forth between the
concepts of language which would be suggested by each one. The notes
on Parmenides suggest the beginnings of an escape from this dilemma.

There is one thing, Parmenides assumes, which self, words, and nature
all share: they have being, they exist, they *are*. If this is the case the
fact that a thing, word, or thought *is* may be more important than what
it is. Authentic thinking and authentic language are possible only if
thought and words participate in the nature of what is thought or
named. This participation may be in the fact that thoughts, words, and
things all have being. "Being" here must be thought of as univocal, not
equivocal; the word must mean the same thing when applied to each of
the three realms. Hopkins quite rightly picks out the concept of the
univocity of being as central in Parmenides. His notes are more than a
partial translation and commentary. They contain at crucial points statements of Hopkins' own thought, statements whose importance is suggested by the fact that they are among his earliest uses of the terms
"inscape" and "instress." Hopkins has an intuitive comprehension of
Parmenides' vision of things, and he sees in that vision an escape from
the conflict involved in his own triple view of words. His comments on
Fragment Two of Parmenides' poem are an affirmation of his own sense
of the univocity of being. Being, for Hopkins as for Parmenides, holds
nature together, and makes language and our knowledge of nature possible. The instress and inscape of individual things and the drama of
our intercourse with things are diverse manifestations of the universal
power of being, and Hopkins, like Parmenides, has felt its permeating
power. "But indeed," he says, "I have often felt when I have been in this
mood and felt the depth of an instress or how fast the inscape holds a
thing that nothing is so pregnant and straightforward to the truth as
simple *yes* and *is*" (J, 127).

This passage is of great importance in Hopkins, for it marks the first
step toward a final unification of his world. Being brings everything together, and is "throughout one with itself" (J, 130). Being must not be
considered an abstraction, a passive condition of existing. Being is a vital
force, a creative energy. It is spoken of repeatedly in Hopkins' notes on
Parmenides as "the flush and foredrawn" (J, 127), as an energy which
collects things together and gathers them into one. Being is instress, that

which foredraws things and holds each thing fast in itself. Since this gathering power is the same everywhere, the most important characteristic of any individual thing is that which it shares with all other things—namely, the fact that it is. The best way of recognizing this is not by a description of the distinctive individuality of a thing but by a "simple *yes* and *is*." These are the fundamental words, the words on which the very possibility of language depends. Unless we can say: "Yes, there is something rather than nothing," or: "It is," we can say nothing at all, for all words are merely different ways of saying "yes" and "is." As the instress of being lies behind all the particularities of inscape, so the verb "to be" lies behind all words and makes them possible. The instress which foredraws all nature is the same as the "is" which gathers all language together, for language is a manifestation of thought, and thought, like external instress, is a foredrawing act. As Parmenides said: "Τὸ γαρ αὐτὸ νοεῖν ἔστιν τε καὶ εἶναι: The same thing exists for thinking and for being." [6] The mind's act of thinking is one manifestation of the stress of being. The inscapes of nature are another. Language is the stem of stress which carries the mind over into things and things over into the mind. The same energy of being manifests itself in thinking, in language, and in things. Therefore all language is an expression of this ubiquitous being, and being and thought are the same: "To be and to know or Being and thought are the same. The truth in thought is Being, stress, and each word is one way of acknowledging Being and each sentence by its copula *is* (or its equivalent) the utterance and assertion of it" (J, 129).

The stress of being in the mind in answer to the stress of being in nature is necessary not only for universal statements but also for particular judgments. Unless there were being within and without, joined by the stem of stress of language, we could not even say, "This blood is red," much less, "Blood is red," for all speech is another way of expressing the "it is" which is the fundamental foredrawing act of the mind. What the mind knows is always and in every act of knowing the instress of being. All particularities are merely "husks and scapes" (J, 130) of this: ". . . the mind's grasp—νοεῖν, the foredrawing act—that this is blood or that blood is red is to be looked for in Being, the foredrawn, alone, not in the thing we named blood or in the blood we worded as being red. . . . Everything else is but a name . . . or disguise for it—coming to be or perishing, Yes and No . . . , change of place, change of colour" (J, 129).

[6] G. S. Kirk and J. E. Raven, *The Presocratic Philosophers* (Cambridge, England: The University Press, 1957), p. 269.

Nature, language, and thought are seen by Parmenides as the same in being, and this concept of being suggests to Hopkins a way in which he can unify the realms which seemed destined to remain disparate. Nor is selfhood left out of this universal gathering. An individual inscape in nature is a mode in which the instress of being appears; the selfhood of a man is another scape or husk of being. Every created thing, man included, is an approach toward being, limited and baffled by its degree of nonbeing. The distinction between external objects and subjective selves is unimportant. All things, including man, are modes of the one being: "For the phenomenal world (and the distinction between men or subjects and the things without them is unimportant in Parmenides: the contrast is between the one and the many) is the brink, limbus, lapping, run-and-mingle/of two principles which meet in the scape of everything —probably Being, under its modification or siding of particular oneness or [of?] Being, and Not-being, under its siding of the Many" (J, 130).

In the Parmenidean fragments Hopkins as early as 1868 finds a way to unify self, words, and world. This does not mean that he is a Victorian Presocratic, depending for the very keystone of his thought on Parmenides, although it is true that his reading of Parmenides is a turning point in his thinking, and prepares him for the decisive encounter some years later with Scotus and St. Ignatius.

The central principle of Catholicism, as Hopkins sees, is the doctrine of the Incarnation. For him a basic difference between Catholicism and Protestantism is their divergent interpretations of the Sacrament of Communion. Protestantism has moved from the doctrine of transubstantiation toward the idea that the communion service is a commemoration of the Last Supper. The bread and wine are signs or symbols pointing toward something which remains absent. The Zwinglian interpretation of the Eucharist prepares the way for the situation in poetry and in life which is characteristic of nineteenth-century man, and is experienced by Hopkins before his conversion. The thinning of the meaning of the communion service spreads out to diminish the divine meaning of the whole world. The heavens no longer declare the glory of God. The deity retires to an infinite distance, and the universe becomes drained of spiritual presence and meaning. The creation becomes "a lighted empty hall," and poetry becomes the manipulation of symbols which no longer participate in the reality they name.

Hopkins' conversion is a rejection of three hundred and fifty years of the spiritual history of the West, three hundred and fifty years which seem to be taking man inexorably toward the nihilism of Nietzsche's

"Gott ist tot." Like the Catholic revival in Victorian England of which it is part, Hopkins' conversion can be seen as an attempt to avoid falling into the abyss of the absence of God. Hopkins, like other Catholic converts, is willing to sacrifice everything—family, academic career, even his poetic genius—in order to escape the poetic and personal destiny which paralyzes such men as Matthew Arnold, and leaves them hovering between two worlds, waiting in vain for the spark from heaven to fall.

In letters written at the time of his conversion and afterwards Hopkins emphasizes the doctrine of the Real Presence as the core of Catholicism. "The great aid to belief and object of belief," he writes in a letter, "is the doctrine of the Real Presence in the Blessed Sacrament of the Altar. Religion without that is sombre, dangerous, illogical, with that it it . . . *loveable*" (L, III, 17). The doctrine of the Real Presence is, as Hopkins says in the letter written to his father announcing his conversion, the only thing which keeps him from losing his faith in God: "This belief once got is the life of the soul and when I doubted it I shd. become an atheist the next day" (L, III, 92). Belief in the Incarnation and its repetition in the Eucharist offer the only escape from a world which has been rendered universally "sordid" by the disappearance of God (L, III, 226). Christ, in condescending to take upon himself not only the pains of manhood, but also its meannesses, transfigured these degrading characteristics of human life and made them radiant with spiritual significance. Belief in the Incarnation makes it possible to face the full triviality of human life, but at the same time it redeems this triviality and makes it part of the imitation of Christ: "I think that the trivialness of life is, and personally to each one, ought to be seen to be, done away with by the Incarnation . . ." (L, III, 19).

The doctrines of the Incarnation and the Real Presence are more than proof that there was and is some connection between the divine and human worlds. Ultimately, with the help of Scotus and other theologians, Hopkins broadens his theory of the Incarnation until he comes to see all things as created in Christ. This doctrine of Christ is a Catholic version of the Parmenidean theory of being, and it is the means by which Hopkins can at last unify nature, words, and selfhood.

To say that all things are created in Christ means seeing the second person of the Trinity as the model on which all things are made, non-human things as well as men. "We are his design," said St. Paul; "God has created us in Christ Jesus" (Eph., 2:10). To see things as created in Christ means seeing Christ as the Word, the Being from whom all words derive: "God's utterance of himself in himself is God the Word, outside himself is this world. This world then is word, expression, news of

God. Therefore its end, its purpose, its purport, its meaning, is God and its life or work to name and praise him" (S, 129). Christ is the perfection of human nature, but he is also the perfection of birds, trees, stones, flowers, clouds, and waterfalls. He is, to give the Scotist term for this concept, the *natura communis,* the common nature who contains in himself all natures. He is the creative Word, the means by which God created all things. As Christopher Devlin puts it: "GMH thinks of Christ's created nature as the original pattern of creation, to a place in which all subsequent created being must attain in order to be complete" (S, 341). Each created thing is a version of Christ, and derives its being from the way it expresses Christ's nature in a unique way. All things rhyme in Christ.

This vision of Christ as the common nature is the culmination of Hopkins' gradual integration of the world. Christ is the model for all inscapes, and can vibrate simultaneously at all frequencies. He is the ultimate guarantee for the validity of metaphor. It is proper to say that one thing is like another only because all things are like Christ. The long exploration of nature in Hopkins' journals leads to certain key entries in which he comes to recognize that everything expresses the beauty of Christ:

> I do not think I have ever seen anything more beautiful than the bluebell I have been looking at. I know the beauty of our Lord by it. (J, 199)

> As we drove home the stars came out thick: I leant back to look at them and my heart opening more than usual praised our Lord to and in whom all that beauty comes home. (J, 254)

Such passages reveal what is distinctively Scotist about Hopkins' vision of nature, and demonstrate the significance of that journal entry where he says: "just then when I took in any inscape of the sky or sea I thought of Scotus" (J, 221). Scotus, like Parmenides, and unlike St. Thomas, affirms the doctrine of the univocity of being.[7] Scotus refers to Parmenides, and defends, against Aristotle's attempted refutation, Parmenides' proposition that all being is one. (See S, 284, and Duns Scotus, *Oxoniense,* I, iii, 2 and viii, 3.) If Parmenides is the Greek philosopher who comes closest to Hopkins' intuition of nature, Scotus is the theologian who seems to him "of realty the rarest-veinèd unraveller" (P, 84). Like

[7] See Cyril L. Shircel, *The Univocity of the Concept of Being in the Philosophy of John Duns Scotus* (Washington: The Catholic University of America Press, 1942), Allan Bernard Wolter, *The Transcendentals and Their Function in the Metaphysics of Duns Scotus* (Washington: The Catholic University of America Press, 1946), pp. 31-57, and Étienne Gilson, *Jean Duns Scot* (Paris, 1952). For the doctrine of analogy in Aquinas, see George P. Klubertanz, *St. Thomas Aquinas on Analogy* (Chicago: Loyola University Press, 1960).

Parmenides, Scotus believes that the term "being" means the same thing when we ascribe it to God and when we ascribe it to any creature.

The difference between Scotus and Aquinas on this point is a complex technical matter, and authorities tend to stress their ultimate agreement, or the verbal nature of their disagreement.[8] Even so, it would perhaps not be falsifying too much to say that Scotus and Aquinas represent opposing tendencies of thought, and that these tendencies, if carried to their extremes, would lead to two radically different concepts of nature and of poetry.

The concept of the analogy of being leads to an hierarchical view of nature. Each thing, in this view, possesses only a material and created equivalent of the immaterial and uncreated attributes of God. Things are *analogous* to the nature of God, and each thing in nature stands not for the whole nature of God, but for a particular attribute of the deity. The book of nature is a set of hieroglyphs or symbols, each one of which tells us something specific about God, the lion his strength, the honey his sweetness, the sun his brightness. In short, the concept of the analogy of being leads to something like the view of nature on which medieval and Renaissance poetry, with its horde of specific symbols, is based.

The idea of the univocity of being leads to a different view of nature, and therefore to a different kind of poetry. In this view natural things, instead of having a derived being, participate directly in the being of the creator. They are in the same way that he is. Each created thing, in its own special way, is the total image of its creator. It expresses not some aspect of God, but his beauty as a whole. Such a view of nature leads to a poetry in which things are not specific symbols, but all mean one thing and the same: the beauty of Christ, in whom they are created.

Hopkins sometimes speaks as if he believes in the analogy of being, as when he says of created things: "They glorify God. . . . The birds sing to him, the thunder speaks of his terror, the lion is like his strength, the sea is like his greatness, the honey like his sweetness; they are something like him, they make him known, they tell of him, they give him glory . . ." (S, 238). In spite of such passages, and in spite of places in Hopkins' poetry where he uses the specific symbolism of the Middle Ages and Renaissance, the main tendency of his vision is toward seeing inscapes as versions of the whole nature of Christ. Natural things are all, and all equally, charged with the grandeur of God, and this overwhelming fact is more important than anything specific about the nature of God which may be learned from the special qualities of created things:

[8] See, for example, Gilson, *Jean Duns Scot*, pp. 101-103.

"All things therefore are charged with love, are charged with God and if we know how to touch them give off sparks and take fire, yield drops and flow, ring and tell of him" (S, 195). God's beauty is like an ubiquitous fluid or electric energy molding everything in the image of the Son.

This idea is the basic presupposition of Hopkins' nature poems. In "The Starlight Night," the night sky, with its treasure of stars, is like bright people or cities hovering in the air, like "dim woods" with "diamond delves," like "grey lawns cold where gold, where quickgold lies," like "wind-beat whitebeam," like "airy abeles set on a flare," like a flock of doves flying in a barnyard, like May blossoms on orchard trees, and like "March-bloom . . . on mealed-with-yellow sallows" (P, 70, 71). The poem, like so many of Hopkins' nature poems, is made up of a list of natural phenomena set in apposition to one another. The poem says: "Look at this, and this, and then this!" The things listed are all metaphors of the night sky and of one another. They are parallel because they all equally contain Christ. "The Starlight Night" ends with the affirmation that the night sky and the things with which it has been compared are like barns which house the precious grain, Christ. Christ is the treasure within all things.

The octave of "As kingfishers catch fire" is sustained by the same presupposition. The fact that all things cry, "Whát I dó is me: for that I came" is more than evidence that things express their inscapes by "doing" themselves. The echo here of the words of Jesus[9] tells us that in doing what they came for, in speaking themselves, nonhuman creatures are revealing their likeness to Christ and speaking his name. Like just men, kingfishers and dragonflies are of the truth, hear Christ's voice, and speak it again.

In the same way the basis of "The May Magnificat" is a comparison of the Blessed Virgin and nature. As Mary carried Christ within her and magnified him, all nature in May is quick with Christ, the universal instress which reveals itself in a thousand different inscapes: "This ecstasy all through mothering earth/Tells Mary her mirth till Christ's birth" (P, 82).

"Hurrahing in Harvest" is the most ecstatic expression of Hopkins' vision of the ubiquity of Christ in nature. The poem "was the outcome of half an hour of extreme enthusiasm" (L, I, 56). It was enthusiasm in the etymological sense, for the seeing of Christ everywhere in the earth

---

[9] See John, 18:37: "Pilate therefore said to him: Art thou a king then? Jesus answered: Thou sayest that I am a king. For this was I born, and for this came I into the world; that I should give testimony to the truth. Everyone that is of the truth, heareth my voice."

and sky of this autumn scene was a supernatural harvest for the spectator. "Gleaning" Christ from the multitudinous spectacle, threshing
him out from the husks which hid him, Hopkins took him as it were in
the communion of love, and was himself lifted up into an inscape of
Christ: "I walk, I lift up, I lift up heart, eyes,/Down all that glory in the
heavens to glean our Saviour" (P, 74).

The doctrine of the common nature takes Hopkins one all-important
step beyond the recognition that all things rhyme. The latter led to a
sense that all nature is integrated, but is foreign to man. Hopkins' doctrine of Christ allows him to integrate man into the great chorus of
created things. Man too is a scape of Christ, and reflects Christ's image
back to Christ at the same time as he affirms his own selfhood. A man,
like other created things, says "Christ" at the same time as he speaks his
own name. All men are rhymes of Christ:

> . . . the just man justices;
> Kéeps gráce: thát keeps all his goings graces;
> Acts in God's eye what in God's eye he is—
> Christ—(P, 95)

In imitating Christ man is also imitating natural things, and expressing his kinship with them. To know nature is also to know oneself, for
the natural world is a mirror in which a man may see hints and reflections of his own selfhood. Hopkins' epistemology presupposes a new version of the Presocratic "theory of sensation by like and like" (J, 130). I
am a "scape" of the common nature, Christ. Each natural thing is also
a scape of Christ. Therefore I contain in myself and recapitulate in little
all the variety of the creation, kingfishers, dragonflies, stones, trees,
flowers—everything. To know them is to know myself, for they are rhymes
for me, and for my model, Christ.

Hopkins has at last completed the edifice which seemed destined to
remain in fragments. Everything has been brought under the aegis of
rhyme. In doing this he has brought into harmony his three theories of
poetry. Poetry can be at once self-expression, the inscape of words, and
the imitation of nature. To imitate natural things is to express the self,
for are not all natural things created in the image of man, since man too
is in the image of Christ? To express the self is to imitate nature, for
the best means of self-expression is those exterior things which so
naturally and delightfully mirror the self. To express the inscape of the
self in terms of the inscapes of nature is also to express the inscapes of
words. Christ is himself the Word, the origin of all language. He is what
"Heaven and earth are word of, worded by" (P, 65). The inscapes of

nature flow from Christ the Word, and the inscapes of language flow from the same source. There is a natural harmony between the sounds of words and their meanings, and a poet seeking to express the harmonies of one will naturally express the harmonies of the other. Far from being the place where we are forced to confront the unbridgeable gulfs between world, words, and self, poetry is the medium through which man may best express the harmonious chiming of all three in Christ.

The Dialectic of Sense-Perception

by Geoffrey H. Hartman

I

The windhover takes its name from its ability to hover steady over one spot in the face of the wind. The subject of the poem is, in the octave, the poet's admiration for a balance achieved in the face of violent motion by countermotion; in the sestet, the sacrifice of both admiration and admired ideal to the transcendent example of Christ. The poem's argument thus turns on Hopkins' interpretation of Christ and Christian action, and will be discussed in detail later on.

The immediate difficulty of "The Windhover" lies less in the complexity of its ideas than in its aesthetic surface. Hopkins tends to use rather simple ideas without theological complication, as if his purpose were confined to the medieval *manifestatio*—an illustration, not argumentation, of sacred doctrine. But his poems do not seem to progress by thought to which word and image are subordinate, rather by word and image distilling thought. Where another poet might use statement, elaboration, suggestion, or grammatical emphasis, Hopkins will use word on word, image on image, as if possessed with a poetic kind of *horror vacui*. Consciousness of the word is so strong in "The Windhover" that the poem's very continuity seems to derive from an on-the-wing multiplication of the sound of one word in the next, like a series of accelerating explosions: "morning" to "morning's" to "minion"; "king" takes the *in,* "daylight" picks up the *d* of *dom* and "dauphin" the *in,* as well as an echo of the *au* from "caught"; a sort of climax is reached in the triple adjective before the main noun with its repeated *d* and *aw.* In the next lines the *r* is multigraphed and combined with the dominant nasal glides of "striding," "rung," "rein," falling away into the *in* and *im* before the movement is broken to a new direction with the wheeling of the bird in the fifth line, where a fresh beat of the wing is felt

"The Dialectic of Sense-Perception" by Geoffrey H. Hartman. From *The Unmediated Vision.* Copyright 1954 by Yale University Press. Revised and retitled by the author. Reprinted by permission of the publisher.

("then off, off forth on swing"). Moreover, the clash of words is hardened, not softened, by every kind of alliterative and assonantal device, and the poem from the first line on is marked by an excitedness of individual perception ("caught" is an intensive verb, hinting the swift, empathic, mastering glance of the observer) that omits the smoothing article and relative pronoun.

Every means is used to gain an asyndetic style with a minimum of grammatical subordination. Hopkins is a master of extreme suspension (hyperbaton) but not for the sake of subordinating one word or thought to another. The two main objects of the first three verses, falcon and air, are strongly suspended by apposition and adjective- noun- verb- qualifiers, but only to crowd each line with an asyndetic rush-of-breath movement, maximizing the density of the verse. Just as windhover, air and dawn are seen not as three separate elements, but as one whirl of action, so noun, verb and modifier are similarly viewed as one massed element with minimized grammatical distinctions. Hopkins favors the verbal noun (of which he constructs new examples: "the hurl," "the achieve") because it brings out the freshness of a verbal root at the expense of a purely linguistic form having no direct source in sense perception. What, we can imagine Hopkins asking, corresponds in my sense-seizure of this bird to noun, verb, adjective and the rest? Grammatical distinctions have no intrinsic value, and become subordinate to word-painting. Thus such images as bow-bend (line 6) make evident the indifference of linguistic form. "Bow" is an Anglo-Saxon equivalent of "bend," and adds no element of meaning to "bend" that might not have been rendered by "bend" alone; both words refer equally well to a curve or to the flexing of the knee necessary in skating or taking a curve. Yet these meanings, common to either word, might not have been conveyed by either in isolation with the exact physical stress. Hopkins, aware of the atrophied or simplified sense-root of words, combines them to suggest their original identity in a physical percept.

The physical nature of sight, sound, and movement are vividly rendered in "The Windhover." Hopkins is much aware of spatial position and angles of sight ("I caught . . ."). Rarely do we find such awareness of air as a medium, actively affecting vision, distributing light, lighted in return, inseparable from the object it surrounds. The notebooks are full of fine observations wherein sight is conceived as a physically near, self-conscious gathering in and going out: "Cups of the eyes, Gathering back the lightly hinged eyelids. Bows of the eyelids." Hopkins has written a poem to compare the Blessed Virgin to the air we breathe ("Wild air, world-mothering air . . ."). But air is also a field of sound. The "whorled ear" corresponds to the "cup" of the eye. Sound and sight are combined in "The Windhover" by such words as "rolling," "rung," "the hurl," where an act and its echo appear as simultaneous. Air is a true theater of action, dense with event. The density of space and the physical nature of sound and sight are found in all of Hopkins' poetry. We may add this passage from the poem "Spring" where the thrush (itself a sight-sound image) "through the echoing timber does so rinse and wring/the ear, it strikes like lightnings to hear him sing. . . ."

The rhythm of the poem moves against a like density. In the first eight lines of "The Windhover" only two connectives are found, both more ecstatic than conjunctive. The poet employs a system of hard fillings which, on the level of meter, forces weak words into a position of emphasis and, on the level of syntax, jams a group of grammatically assorted words before the suspended noun ("Of the rolling level underneath him steady air"). A counterpoint rhythm evolves that respects the abrupt and singular nature of each word, while emphasizing the one-breath swing of every line, hovering at the repeated end-rhyme, moving forward in a series of glissando movements, but never receding from the forward surge.

While rhythm is not necessarily imitative of a physical movement, with Hopkins it is. The hurl and gliding of his verse render the "hurl and gliding" of "The Windhover." We do find a similar rhythm in some other poems (e.g., "Look at the stars! look, look up at the skies! . . . Down in dim woods the diamond delves! the elves'-eyes!") and this makes us suspect that the thrust and glide of his verse is descriptive of more than the particular motion of the windhover, that the windhover's motion is only a type of a more fundamental rhythm. But the rhythm, in any case, has a physical basis, and many comments could be added to show that Hopkins conceived his words and technique in terms of physical imitation. Of his use of the rather ugly "back" in "The Leaden and the Golden Echo" he writes, *"Back* is not pretty, but it gives that feeling of physical constraint which I want."

There is, even in the best of Hopkins, an unwillingness to release his mind from the physical contact of words, which are conceived not only as the means but also and very strongly as the materials of expression, and used with the undiluted stroke of some modern painters who wish to let color or *touche* speak for itself. Rhythm, sound, and sight involve for Hopkins a sense of the body, the total and individual body, and his poems and notes are full of pride and despair at the inseparably sensuous character of his vision ("my taste was me;/Bones built in me, flesh filled, blood brimmed the curse"). The drama of Hopkins is played out between his senses and the thing observed, and perception becomes act in the full sense of the word. But though perception is sensuous and distinctively individual, neither the act of sight nor the true medium are found to change the nature of the thing perceived. In the poem comparing the Blessed Virgin to the air we breathe, Hopkins addresses the reader. How the air is azured, he cries; lift your hand skyward and the rich blue sky will lap round and between the fingers:

> Yet such a sapphire-shot,
> Charged, steepèd sky will not
> Stain light. Yea, mark you this:
> It does no prejudice.
> The glass-blue days are those
> When every colour glows,
> Each shape and shadow shows.

So in his poem on spring the blue is described as all in a rush with richness; air diversifies, reveals, intensifies the intrinsic character of leaf, blossom and timber. There is no blending or blurring between object and object, object and air, object and observer, such as is often found in impressionist painters who are just as sensitive to the "act" of sight as Hopkins; nor is echo (as for example in Shelley) the disembodiment of sound, its spiritual form, but each reverberation in Hopkins is a singular, incisive beat which "strikes like lightnings."

Hopkins' poetry is first an expression of sense experience and wants at first to be taken as such. *The act of sight has become a moral responsibility,* and whereas Milton or Wordsworth might talk about a chastity of the mind, Hopkins would talk about a chastity of the sense. A poet who can write "The Windhover" or "Harry Ploughman" shares the great religious subject of the century of Marvel and Milton—the dialogue between the resolved soul and created pleasure—but in a special way. He works in the belief that "Man's spirit will be flesh-bound when found at best" and claims for his theme the dialogue between the created senses and created beauty. We will not understand "The Windhover" unless we first understand this dialogue. Hopkins once avowed that "God's Grandeur" was written to accommodate its fine first images, which would not mean that the poet does not think, or thinks by spurts, but that he renders his thoughts in terms of natural perception. Moral and religious meaning do not belatedly disclose themselves to reason, judgment or rationalization, they are given in the very act of perception, and when Hopkins catches sight of the windhover, he sees it first in its individual and brute beauty.

II

"The Windhover" bears a religious dedication: *To Christ our Lord,* and yet contains no explicit element of traditional religious symbolism except, possibly, the falcon. Its imagery is one of natural perception and its one simile, comparing the motion of the bird to a skate heel's turn on a bow-bend, expresses only ease and balance, physical grace. Hopkins, at times, even tries what has rarely been done before him in a sonnet: to introduce technical terms and observations. Thus "rung" may be a word adopted from falconry to suggest the spiral ascent of the windhover.[1] But more significant is the mention of "blue-bleak embers," for Hopkins has noticed the bluish tinge of coals when in full heat but not yet burst or died; and instead of using "blue" absolutely in order to indicate Mary's color and the color of the sky, like the more conventional religious poet, he will use it only in context of a technical observation on the physical world, and may see the presence, or here the absence, of Mary in a piece of coal. The religious dedication is quite genuine, even required. As in other poems that start with some kind of invocation ("Glory be to God for dappled things"), end with a benediction ("Praise Him"), but in between offer a series of fiercely sensuous and quite untraditional symbols, it indicates that dedication to God is also possible by means of natural perceptions which are, as it were, the first fruits of the senses.

Although religious and natural perception fall together in Hopkins, this is not without its difficulty. The poems after "The Windhover" echo with a plaint on the "skeined stained veined variety" of life. Our present purpose is to find by what means and with what success Hopkins reconciles the sensuous and the religious imperatives, how he passes from a vivid and immediate sensing to religious insight without rejecting or modifying the former. It should first be said, however, that Hopkins is in no way a mystic, except perhaps in one of his late sonnets, "Carrion Comfort," where the combat with God is conceived as a personal one. Even here the concern is merely that of all his poems in its extremity:

[1] The suggestion of R. V. Schoder, "What does the Windhover mean?" in *Immortal Diamond: Studies in Gerard Manley Hopkins,* ed. Norman Weyand (New York: Sheed and Ward, 1949), chap. 9. There is, however, no reason to think that "rung" refers only to the falcon's spiral ascent. We point out, with respect to "buckle," that Hopkins uses words to indicate physical actions or their effect, and the word may be used to suggest more than one thing: (1) the stress exerted on a bell, and its ringing out, (2) the stress on the rein of a horse to control and direct it, creating perhaps a whiplike snaking in the rein parallel to that in the "wimpling wing," (3) the spiral of flight. Hopkins might have said that all three actions have the same "inscape" or "instress."

in my actions, in my perceptions, is it God I feel and credit, or myself?
"O which one? is it each one?"

The mystic, seeing the windhover, might be snatched away by it,
divinely raped like Ganymede by Zeus the Eagle. Hopkins describes the
particular bird, his individual pattern in the air. This, if it cannot suggest the mystic, might make of Hopkins a divine analogist, who sees or
seeks in the windhover resemblance to godly action, and such a view is
implicit or explicit in most studies on the poet. But Hopkins sets no
store by a system of correspondences, perhaps because he acknowledges
just one correspondent, Christ—"the Master,/*Ipse*, the only one, Christ,
King, Head"—and so the image of the windhover must give way in the
poem's second part to the figure of Christ. Yet this Christ, as in the first
part, is not symbolized through the traditional symbols or the original
story of the New Testament. He is found rather in clay and coal. The
real and increased question before us is how Christ can be considered
not only the component of natural perception but also the component
of a material or physical world.

What catches the eye of the poet is the windhover's mastery of the
wind, the control of a proud rider over his tumultuous horse, the strong
stress and balance. The simile on the skate heel's smooth turn is also
based on a feeling for stress, and whatever image we choose in Hopkins,
perhaps "When weeds, in wheels, shoot long and lovely and lush" or
"With the gnarls of the nails in thee, niche of the lance," or "For rose-
moles all in stipple upon trout that swim," the odds are that there will
be found in it a sensitivity if not to actual stress then to touch, muscular
action, and pressure. *The sense of pressure or stress is the sixth and radical sense in the experience of Hopkins.* It is evident to the tongue on
reading his poetry. Even words like "rung" (upon the rein) and "rolling,"
which seem to take their effect from a simultaneity of sight and sound,
stem from this deeper sense. There is also a construction in Hopkins which
does not often seem to have been remarked, about which one is not
absolutely sure, but which may be exemplified in our poem by "plough
down sillion." It gives a figure of thought rather than of speech, and is an
attempt to describe muscular action: the strip of land is there to have a
plow pushed through, a thing is conceived in terms of the physical action
prompted by it.[2] So thing and perceiver, thing and actor, tend in the

---

[2] Father Schoder, on the other hand, thinks "shine" refers to the plough. This may
be so, but the view neglects the kinaesthetic element in Hopkins' imagery. Elsewhere
"down" clearly refers to, or mimics, a strong, almost muscular movement:

> I walk, I lift up, I lift up heart eyes,
> Down all that glory in the heavens to glean our Saviour
>   ("Hurrahing in Harvest")

sight of Hopkins to be joined to each other as if by electrical charge; they are connected like windhover and wind in terms of stress given and received.

Action under stress or by stress is not only a particular condition in Hopkins' universe, but the one condition showing forth the *resilience* of things, their inexhaustible individuality. Whether we consider the relation of eye to object, of creature to creature, or of any of these to the medium—air, water, earth—in which they live, we find that Hopkins has rendered this relation in terms of resilience. There is, for example, the pressure of eye against object and answering pressure of object against eye, each intensifying the "deep-down-thing" freshness of the other. The water in which the trout moves, the movement itself, does not disturb but increases the poet's sensuous apprehension. The blue sapphire-light of the sky which the leaves and blooms of the pear tree are said to brush does not with its strong monotone draw out other shapes and colors but adds to their resistant individuality. The fact is further pointed up in the poem "Spring" by describing the pear tree as "glassy." Even when, as in a snowfall, it seems least possible to remark the individual forms of things, Hopkins still manages to do so:

> It tufted and toed the firs and yews and went to load them till they were taxed beyond their spring. The limes, elms, and Turkey-oaks it crisped beautifully as with young leaf. Looking at the elms from underneath you saw every wave in every twig . . . and to the hangers and flying sprays it restored, to the eye, the inscapes they had lost.[3]

His concern is evidently with the spring of the trees, their resilience; and we meet the word "inscape" which together with "instress" is the poet's technical term describing the individual form of resilience as the quality or effect of a particular thing. The above is also noteworthy in point of style, for by the double indirect object ("to the hangers," "to the eye") Hopkins indicates the compulsion exercised by object on eye.

The act of hard perception, then, where the naked eye becomes an instrument of analysis, does not decrease a thing's individuality, but affirms it.[4] The stronger the pressure of sight or sense, the greater the sensuous yield, but also the resilience, of what is observed. Parallel to God's grandeur, it "gathers to a greatness, like the ooze of oil/Crushed" ("God's Grandeur"). Nowhere is the resilience or "springiness" of the world so directly expressed as in this sonnet, and we realize that there the

[3] *The Journals and Papers of Gerard Manley Hopkins,* ed. Humphry House and Graham Storey (London: Oxford University Press, 1959), p. 196.
[4] Cf. *Journals and Papers,* p. 204: "What you look hard at seems to look hard at you."

eternal and unchanged regeneration of the act of sensing and of the world is taken by Hopkins as a mark of the divine. Yet Hopkins' sonnet, however original, is not *sui generis*. It expresses a deep and common religious experience also described in Herbert's "The Flower":

> How fresh, O Lord, how sweet and clean
> Are Thy returns!

But whereas Herbert is witty, homely, almost *ad hominem,* not bothering in the least about oil, foil, and the like to express his delight, citing just a common, unspecified flower, Hopkins cannot speak except with the whole body, with the awareness and justification of all his senses. Hopkins is engaged on a theodicy, and has taken for his province the stubborn senses and the neglected physical world.

But this idea of the world's resilience, however strong in Hopkins and however made clear to the imagination, is an old idea, active in Heraclitus and other pre-Socratic philosophers, incorporate in Aristotle's principle of the eternity of matter, and set forth by the poet himself in the first part of "That Nature is a Heraclitean Fire"—"Squandering ooze to squeezed dough, crust, dust." But to be more in his celebration of oil, clay, and coal than an extreme, modern, industrial pagan, Hopkins must surpass Greek philosophy. And this he does by interpreting the resilience of the world to mind or body, to thought or use, as the source of that individuation of which the culminating point is found in Christ.

For Hopkins leaves aside all speculation on whether the physical universe has or has not a soul and what kind of soul. He is concerned in it with only one thing, its "pitch of self," and he knows that each thing's pitch of self is distinctive and incomparable with any other, and that man's pitch or individuality is the highest. The religious poet before Hopkins often based himself on *Romans* 8:19, (*Etenim res creatae exerto capite observantes expectant revelationem Filiorum Dei*) in order to be permitted to think of the purpose of nature in the divine economy. One of Vaughan's most tragic poems is written under this heading:

> Can they their heads lift, and expect
> and groan too? Why th'elect
> Can do no more.

and Hopkins himself has a poem written on the same theme which addresses the Ribbelsdale landscape simply as "Earth, sweet Earth. . . . That canst but only be, but dost that long." [5] The landscape, then, like

---

[5] Two texts of this poem quote "Nam expectatio. . . ." (*Poems of Gerard Manley Hopkins,* third edition [London: Oxford University Press, 1948], p. 240).

the modern poem, does not *mean,* but simply *is.* Its patience of being, its steady *expectatio,* is its meaning. Hopkins has broken with the common belief that nature is the language of God; or, rather, this language is not to be understood in conceptual terms but accepted in its concrete immediacy and resilience to sight. Hopkins does not ask what is nature for, How can man use nature for his spiritual or material welfare: when he catches sight of the windhover, final and mediate cause are out of mind, he is concerned with a description of the bird's individual beauty or mode of action, knowing that whether it has a soul or not, a purpose or not, it has resilience and a "pitch of self," which, if felt and acknowledged, will affirm in man his own greater resilience and "pitch of self": "that taste of myself, of *I* and *me* above and in all things, which is more distinctive than the taste of ale or alum, more distinctive than the smell of walnutleaf or camphor."

We see then that man is more highly pitched than anything else. He is as Hopkins elsewhere says, the "clearest-selved spark" of nature. These two metaphors of pitch and flame are fundamental to Hopkins, first because pitch and flame are the two evident types of resilience,[6] and because in them the action of a thing and its nature are identified. This is clear in "As kingfishers catch fire":

> As kingfishers catch fire, dragonflies draw flame;
> As tumbled over rim in roundy wells
> Stones ring; like each tucked string tells,
>   each hung bell's
> Bow swung finds tongue to fling out broad its name;
> Each mortal thing does one thing and the same:
> Deals out that being indoors each one dwells;
> Selves—goes itself; *myself* it speaks and spells;
> Crying *What I do is me: for that I came.*

"Tucked," "hung," "swung" are not simple, sensory adjectives, but (like, perhaps, "plough down" in "The Windhover") indicate a physical act inseparable from the nature of the thing they qualify: the grammatical sign betrays their status: they are not qualities but proleptic forces: they should be joined to the noun, as they sometimes are, by dashes: the

---

[6] W. A. M. Peters, in *Gerard Manley Hopkins* (London: Oxford University Press, 1948), p. 19, makes an interesting suggestion in noting that Hopkins tends to associate the sound of bells and fire, and that we should read, or at least hear

> AND the fire that breaks from thee then, a billion
> Times *tolled* lovelier, more dangerous. . . .

"The words 'fire' and 'tolled,' " he says, "show how the instresses of the bird in action, of fire, and of tolling bells, are joined in one poetic experience."

craftsman who constructed this bell though he (no doubt) conceived it
instantaneously, created on the first day resilience, on the second day its
infinite thingness or self out of resilience, and on the third day its capacity for self-revelation.

But supposing this bell to be of the same make as man, since no distinction exists in this poem between inanimate and animate nature, there
being mentioned only "Each mortal thing," then the craftsman must have
been faced with this problem: everything has durance, thingness, revelation through resilience; as bird is manifest in flame, so bell in pitch, so
earth in being plowed; but what is the manifest of man? The poem
continues:

> I say more: the just man justices;
> Keeps grace: that keeps all his goings graces;
> Acts in God's eye what in God's eye he is—
> Christ—for Christ plays in ten thousand places,
> Lovely in limbs, and lovely in eyes not his
> To the Father through the features of men's faces.

Christ is for Hopkins the manifest of man, as ringing is of the bell,
fire of kingfishers, hurl and gliding of the windhover. We perceive the
identity established in the poems of Hopkins, an identity of all things,
all mortal things, in resilience, infinite individuality, God. But this identity, close to the central principle of Aristotelian philosophy, and expressed in the first part of "That Nature is a Heraclitean Fire," is then
transcended by a further identity, exclusive to man, in resilience, highest
pitch of self, Christ, hence—resurrection! To "That Nature is a Heraclitean Fire" is added "and of the comfort of the Resurrection":

> Manshape, that shone
> Sheer off, disseveral, a star, death blots black out; nor mark
> Is any of him at all so stark
> But vastness blurs and time beats level. Enough! the Resurrection,
> A heart's-clarion!

In this way Hopkins goes from the perception that crushed oil gathers
again to "a greatness," to the affirmation of Christ. For if all nature have
resurgence, should not man? And how can the resurgence of man be
conceived except through Christ's example? Yet Hopkins prefers to take
his instances of resilience from the world of coal and clay, from the
earth as earth, because resurgence is there more evidently inexhaustible
than in the animal creation, and when he sees the windhover he catches
sight of him not in isolation but in battle with an element, as if the
windhover had not like man quite freed himself, selved, from the earth.

This may not satisfy the philosophic mind pointing out that resilience far from being the source of individuation is dependent on the indifferent and undifferentiated character of the earth, and that man's individuality is at the expense of resilience and resurgence. Christ, as he appears in Hopkins, is dangerously near to physical man, while man is still dangerously near to physical beauty, so that Hopkins' work becomes an ode on the eternal nativity of Christ in the world of the senses. In that ode, "The Windhover" is one of the finest stanzas.

III

The poet in the octave marks the "pitch" of the battling windhover, his individual brute beauty, and this is seen deeply in terms of resilience. The poet is in a stage of mere attention, not of analogy; and the hidden heart does not stir for the windhover itself as much as for a bird in general, its balance under extreme stress. Now, a poet is known by his invocations. If Hopkins had felt the windhover to be an immediate symbol for Christ he would have addressed it as spontaneously as he apostrophizes God in "The Wreck of the Deutschland" or "The Loss of the Eurydice"; but when his invocation "O my chevalier" comes in the sestet, the riders have changed, and it is no longer the windhover astride the wind, but Christ's example mastering the poet, which is referred to.

The sestet results from a sudden intrusion of the thought of Christ. For the ideal marked and admired in the windhover by the poet was of elegant balance in the center of stress, and this stress is sought by, not imposed on the falcon who seems to know that a storm center is necessary to display the "achieve" and the "mastery." Yet Christ while also of his own will seeking the center of stress did this not for the sake of elegant balance, but to suffer without mastery the "unshapeable shock night." "Buckle," therefore, addressing the windhover or its accouterments of sensuous magnificence, would be in the nature of an optative and mean more than "buckle on meeting this heart which, thinking of the ascetic Christ, must refuse its admiration"; it suggests, "Let yourself like Christ militant for sacrifice submit to a storm center greater than the power of beauty, valor, or act, and let this example grapple with, become a buckler for, dent my heart." [7]

[7] In a discussion of what the word is, generically speaking, Hopkins concludes that it is properly neither the thing referred to nor the response called up in the reader but "the expression, *uttering* of the idea in the mind. That idea itself has its two terms, the image (of sight or sound or *scapes* of the other senses), which is in fact physical and a refined energy accenting the nerves, a word to oneself, an inchoate word, and secondly the conception." *Journals and Papers*, p. 125. This precept dis-

Thus the flame breaking from windhover or the Christ-assaulted heart indicates self-sacrifice in the maximum of stress. But why should the AND be in capitals and the resulting flame be described as a billion times lovelier (aesthetically seductive) and more dangerous (morally seductive) than the windhover's previous image? The AND expresses the poet's surprise that the splendor of self-sacrifice should surpass the splendor of equilibrium: the image of the flaming windhover or of the crucified Christ becomes a greater spiritual temptation than could ever have been exerted by the former image of elegant equilibrium. Then Hopkins, in the final tercet, adds "No wonder of it," for he finds that even the humblest things bear the mark and splendor of sacrifice imprinted on them like a physical law, even the lowliest thing galls itself and flames, so that the poet feels ("ah, my dear") fear? regret? resignation? perceiving Christ's Passion as a universal and haunting phenomenon. He has not escaped brute beauty: the very means which caused him to reject the windhover have revealed to him a different beauty, less elegant indeed, but just as brutally evident, lovely and dangerous.

The poet, then, sees the sacrifice of Christ imprinted like a physical law in even the lowliest corner of nature. He thought Christ superinduced on the windhover to be unique, but finds the call to sacrificial action also in coal. This law, which holds for all nature, is simple and contains three things: maximum stress, the disintegration that follows maximum stress, the flame that follows or is the visible sign of disintegration. In such processes Hopkins comes to see an imitation of Christ's Passion, Crucifixion, and Resurrection; and this fact haunts him, that what should be written large in matter has not become organic to man.

If we regard the images of the sestet, we find them all kinaesthetic in nature, determined by the sense of stress or muscle. Even syntax helps toward this: the grammatical status of "Buckle" cannot be fixed with absolute precision, Hopkins often using words to describe more than qualities, things, relations: "Buckle" mimics a muscular movement, a physical act. "Buckle" is not meant to suggest simply the actual object or the act of buckling, but the process whereby when two stresses clash one has to give way, to buckle or be buckled, and this would catch the senses

---

penses with certain exclusive hypotheses concerning the "meaning" of "buckle." There is, in Hopkins, an audacious attempt to conceive words generically, as beings in their own right and not merely as carriers of an idea. In some later poems there is a method of rhythmic stuttering, as it were, that would make the word a point, the strongest non-referential intention of speech (see, e.g., "I cast for comfort I can no more get," *Poems*, p. 111). The final tendency is toward purely vocative speech, what Hopkins might call the inscape of speech. And "buckle," therefore, is in the nature of a pure speech movement, an "explosive."

by a displacement of, for example, light flashing from an uneven breast-plate—"AND the fire that breaks from thee then." For whereas a lesser poet than Hopkins might have used "fire" in a purely figurative sense, in Hopkins the figurative sense is always derived from physical phenomena. The same thing can be shown of the other images in the poem which are also conceived as emitting light: the coal obviously, but also the "shine" of "plough down sillion": it is neither the shining plow nor the new earth but the kinaesthetic effect of plow-breaking-through-earth. Thus our three images are seen to express contacts and disintegrations that have caused a surprising outward burst of splendor greater than the original splendor of equilibrium.

Stress, disintegration, and flame are caught as one process and almost rendered as such in Hopkins' poetry. But we may go somewhat further to determine how Christ enters this purely physical observation. Here is a skyscape recorded by the poet:

> . . . below the sun it was like clear oil but just as full of colour, shaken over with slanted flashing "travellers," all in flight, stepping one behind the other, their edges tossed with bright ravelling, as if white napkins were thrown up in the sun but not quite at the same moment so that they were all in a scale down the air falling one after the other to the ground.[8]

Though in tenor entirely descriptive, the passage reflects a kind of instinctive epistemology on Hopkins' part: the brilliance of the particular depends on individuation, but individuation also, because group intensity is lacking, tends to destroy brilliance; therefore the moment of greatest brilliance in the particular is in its just-emergence from the group, when a measure of off-balance catches the sun—in the moment of disintegration.

Another passage should be given in support, this time in description of a thunderstorm:

> I noticed two kinds of flash but I am not sure that sometimes there were not the two together from different points of the same cloud or starting from the same point different ways—one a straight stroke, broad like a stroke with chalk and liquid, as if the blade of an oar just stripped open a ribbon scar in smooth water and it caught the light; the other narrow and wire-like, like the splitting of a rock and danced down-along in a thousand jags.[9]

The two flashes are compared to the splitting of a rock, and the ribbon scar caused by the stroke of an oar on smooth water. Both images,

[8] *Journals and Papers*, p. 207.
[9] *Journals and Papers*, p. 212.

kinaesthetic, repeat that the greatest brilliance of the particular is in the moment of disintegration or off-balance from the group to which it belongs, and both remind us of the images in "The Windhover." If we now recall that Christ for Hopkins is the highest pitch of self, the summit of human individuation, we also perceive the identity inevitably made between the highest pitch of self, Christ, and the greatest brilliance of the particular, disintegration. Thus the antinomy of self and self-sacrifice would be resolved: the oil has to be crushed before it may gather to greatness. This identity shows the temptation undergone by Hopkins to equate Passion and Salvation. It is not absent from "The Windhover."

In this poem the balance of the bird in the storm wind is rejected for the buckle that flames up when struck or made uneven, the furrowing act of the plow that catches light like the furrow made by the stroke of an oar on smooth water, for the dull embers that suddenly flare forth in falling apart like volcanic rock or jagged lightning or like the grandeur of God which "will flame out, like shining from shook foil" or like the body of the crucified Christ who galled himself and gashed gold-vermilion. The brilliance, brutality, stress and necessity of individuation are connected and apperceptively fused with the sacrifice of Christ and turned by him into a figure for resurrection. The windhover, chevalier in perfect mastery of his winged horse, fitted out with all the accouterments of an elegant-brute-beauty, suddenly falls, buckles, flames, and Christ appears, chevalier of true-brute-beauty, and valor and act.

III

Two Mannerists: James and Hopkins

by Giorgio Melchiori

Henry James' art had a recognizable influence not only on the contemporary novel, but—perhaps less directly—on contemporary poetry as well. This fact has been acknowledged more than once,[1] but it does not seem to have occurred to the critics that there might be an affinity between James and some of the poets living in his own age. I believe that a parallel examination of the most striking characteristics of James and Hopkins will be rewarding and revealing in this respect.

Indeed, except that they were born within a year of each other (respectively in 1843 and 1844) it is hard at first sight to detect any connection between James and Hopkins. It is obvious besides that they completely ignored each other's existence. James' mature novels were written well after Hopkins' death, and Hopkins' poems were only published three years after James' death. And one could easily contrast the Catholic priest relating in his poems his own ecstatic experiences, with the international worldling exploring in his novels the morbid sensitivity of a refined society. But the fact is that each of them has struck readers of later generations by some features so peculiar to himself as to be considered almost personal idiosyncrasies. In view of the utterly different spheres in which they moved it is the more surprising to realize that these very peculiarities, distinguishing each of them from his contemporaries,

"Two Mannerists: James and Hopkins" by Giorgio Melchiori. From *The Tightrope Walkers* (New York: Macmillan and Co., 1956), pp. 13-33. Copyright © 1956 by Giorgio Melchiori. Reprinted by permission of the author and Routledge & Kegan Paul, Ltd., London. Slightly abridged.

[1] E.g. M. D. Zabel, "The Poetics of Henry James," in *Poetry*, XLV (1935), pp. 270-76; and several references in F. O. Matthiessen, *The Achievement of T. S. Eliot* (New York, 1935).

are common to both. Here is what can be considered as a typical passage
from James:

> And how much, as it was, for all her bridling brightness—which was
> merely general and noticed nothing—*would* they work together? . . . Yet,
> none the less, when, at the end of five minutes, in the cab, Jim Pocock
> had said nothing either—hadn't said, that is, what Strether wanted, though
> he had said much else—it all suddenly bounced back to their being either
> stupid or wilful. It was more probably on the whole the former; so that
> that would be the drawback of the bridling brightness. Yes, they would
> bridle and be bright; they would make the best of what was before them,
> but their observation would fail; it would be beyond them; they simply
> wouldn't understand.[2]

There is no mistaking the author of this passage: the Jamesian syntax
is obvious in each line—the sentences are broken and proceed hesitat-
ingly, feeling their way for the exact word. In this process, grammar is
mercilessly twisted, following the involutions of thought; the language
too is characteristic and unlike that of the other nineteenth-century
novelists: it is on the whole sustained, but it alternates words of the
literary usage and colloquialisms; finally, there is a certain concreteness
in the imagery (though this is not so apparent in this particular passage):
a verb like *bounced back* is vividly descriptive, while *bridling brightness*
gives point and flavour to the whole passage.

James is looking for a complexity of effects (expressed in as complex a
form) which no other prose writer of his time was pursuing. Even
Meredith's prose for all its intellectual subtlety is plainer and less
strained. Instead the same type of syntactic elaboration is to be found in
the following:

> A bugler boy from barrack (it is over the hill there)—boy bugler, born,
> he tells me, of Irish mother to an English sire (he shares their best gifts
> surely, fall how things will), this very day came down to us after a boon he
> on my late being there begged of me, overflowing boon in my bestowing;
> came, I say, this day to it—to a First Communion.

But this is not prose; it is a transcription, without line divisions, of
eight lines of a poem by Hopkins.[3] Here too we find the crowding of
secondary clauses in a complex sentence, the breaks and hesitations in
the flow of speech, the colloquialisms alternating with the literary words.
It is very unlike the work of the poets of the last century, the overflowing

[2] *The Ambassadors* (London, 1948), p. 219.
[3] *The Bugler's First Communion*, in *Poems of Gerard Manley Hopkins*, second edition (London: Oxford University Press), pp. 42-3.

sonority of Swinburne, the musical ease of Tennyson, or even the diffused monologizing of Browning. It fits with Hopkins' definition of poetical language, which should be "current language heightened, to any degree heightened and unlike itself, but not an obsolete one." [4] This is obvious in all Hopkins' poems: from the current language he gets not only single words and expressions, but also constructions, and those repetitions and interrupting clauses which are characteristic of the spoken language. This can be seen, in the passage already quoted, in the parenthetical sentences, the expressions *he tells me, surely, fall how things will,* and *I say.* And the same interjectional clauses are found in his most complex and elaborate poems, as for instance *The Wreck of the Deutschland.*[5]

> And after it almost unmade, what with dread,
> Thy doing.   (stanza 1)

There are the hesitations, the broken syntax common in normal speech, as in the passage quoted "came, I say, this day to it—to a First Communion," or again in the *Deutschland:*

> But how shall I . . . make me room there:
> Reach me a . . . Fancy, come faster—
> Strike you the sight of it?   (stanza 28)

And in this same poem we can see other examples of colloquial construction: the exclamation in mid-sentence:

> Finger of a tender of, O of a feathery delicacy.
>   (stanza 31)

or the stammering repetition due to the violence of feeling:

> . . . where, where was a, where was a place?
>   (stanza 3)

Finally there are passages of a deliberately chronicle style:

> On Saturday sailed from Bremen,
> American-outward-bound . . . .   (stanza 12)

There is no doubt that these linguistic and syntactic features, that both unite and contrast with the high poetical elaboration are peculiar to

---

[4] Passage from a letter quoted in W. H. Gardner, *Gerard Manley Hopkins, A Study of Poetic Idiosyncrasy in Relation to Poetic Tradition* (London, 1948), I, p. 115.

[5] *Poems,* ed. quoted, pp. 11-21. Compare with the line of Hopkins' quoted below, "Finger of a tender of, O of a feathery delicacy," the following from a note of Henry James (*Letters,* ed. P. Lubbock [London, 1920], I, p. xxi): "Thus just these first little wavings of the oh so tremulously passionate little old wand (now!) make for me, I feel, a sort of promise of richness and beauty and variety."

Hopkins, and are among those that most distinguish his style. As for his
other characteristics, his striking compound words, alliteration, assonance,
internal rhymes, etc., the difference between himself and his contemporaries is one of degree and intensity rather than original invention;[6]
and it was in this preoccupation with the "current language" that his
"sprung rhythm" also originated, which is, according to his definition,
"the rhythm of common speech and of written prose, when rhythm is
perceived in them." [7]

The same preoccupation with the "heightening" of current language
and expression seems responsible for the peculiarities of James' style, especially in his later (or "major") phase. It is significant that James, when
revising *The Portrait of a Lady,* as Matthiessen tells us,[8] adopted more
colloquial forms—as e.g. *can't, she'd* for *cannot, she would*—and substituted concrete and organic images for abstract descriptions. He reached
in this way a sense of greater solidity, but at the same time he complicated the construction of his prose to such an extent as to become the
easy target of satire (the early parody by Max Beerbohm is a masterpiece
in its kind).

Hopkins' later poems show an identical tendency. His two well-known
sonnets, *Tom's Garland* and *Harry Ploughman,* which are considered
among his most involved, show a deliberate use of colloquial expressions,
to the point of abbreviating *his* to *'s;* and even in subject matter he wants
to be as down to earth as possible. But the syntax is utterly broken and
the rhythm is extremely loose, so that the structure of the sonnets becomes extremely complicated:

> Tom Heart-at-ease, Tom Navvy: he is all for his meal
> Sure, 's bed now. Low be it: lustily he his low lot (feel
> That ne'er need hunger, Tom; Tom seldom sick,
> Seldomer heartsore, that treads through, prickproof, thick
> Thousands of thorns, thoughts) swings though.[9]

Like James' prose, these Hopkinsian poems seem unrecitable, but it
should be remembered that Hopkins wrote of *Tom's Garland:*[10] "de-
claimed, the strange constructions would be dramatic and effective," and
of *Harry Ploughman* he said that it was "altogether for recital, not for

[6] The use of parallel devices by Hopkins' contemporaries has been studied and amply
exemplified in W. H. Gardner's two volumes, mentioned above.

[7] "Author's Preface" to the *Poems of Gerard Manley Hopkins,* ed. cit., p. 5.

[8] F. O. Matthiessen, *Henry James, The Major Phase* (London, 1946). The last chapter
contains a thorough study of the changes made in the revision.

[9] *Poems of Gerard Manley Hopkins,* p. 63.

[10] This and the next quotation are from letters reproduced in the notes to *Poems,*
pp. 114-16.

perusal." In the same way James, in the preface to *The Golden Bowl,*
where his style has reached a maximum of complexity, writes that:

> the highest test of any literary form conceived in the light of "poetry"—
> to apply that term in its largest literary sense—hangs back unpardonably
> from its office when it fails to lend itself to *vivâ-voce* treatment.[11]

Both writers then were anxious to produce work which could stand
the test of declamation, but were looking at the same time for more
complex and penetrating speech forms, such as could render the subtlety,
the fineness of their feelings and of their mental processes. This ambition,
which distinguishes them among their contemporaries, is at the root of
their endless and deliberate stylistic search. It was a search for the utmost
precision of expression and immediate communication of feeling and
sensation. This effort towards an ever-increasing directness is reflected too
in their use of imagery; they tend to avoid abstract descriptions and to
use instead concrete images, at times rather precious ones. So Hopkins
works out a comparison between a lark and a winch:

> Left hand, off land, I hear the lark ascend,
> His rash-fresh re-winded new-skeinèd score
> In crisps of curl off wild winch whirl, and pour
> And pelt music, till none's to spill nor spend. . . .[12]

or describes the action of human muscles in metaphors taken from nature
and from military service:

> . . . Each limb's barrowy brawn, his thew . . .
> Though as a beechbole firm, finds his, as at a roll-call, rank
> And features, in flesh, what deed he each must do—
> His sinew-service where do.[13]

James for his part could speak at length of life as a tin mould, either
fluted and embossed, with ornamental excrescences, or else smooth and
dreadfully plain, into which, a helpless jelly, one's consciousness is
poured—so that one "takes" the form, as the great cook says. . . .[14]
or he could change the description of a face of a woman from the earlier
abstract terms ("It had an air of intelligent calm—a considering, pondering look that was superior, somehow, to diffidence or anxiety") into a
concrete metaphor taken from business life:

[11] H. James, *The Art of the Novel* (critical prefaces, edited with introduction by R. P.
Blackmur [New York: Charles Scribner's Sons, 1947]), p. 346.
[12] *The Sea and the Skylark, Poems of Gerard Manley Hopkins,* p. 28.
[13] *Harry Ploughman, Poems,* p. 64.
[14] *The Ambassadors,* ed. cit., p. 129.

It was as calm as a room kept dusted and aired for candid earnest occa-
sions, the meeting of unanimous committees and the discussion of flourish-
ing business.[15]

All these, in James and Hopkins, are images (similes, comparisons,
metaphors) bordering on the conceit, unafraid or unaware of the ridiculous which might have sprung from this union of apparently unrelated
terms: a lark and a winch, a limb and a military exercise, the form of life
and the mould for a jelly, a face and a room. They are at the same time
demonstrations of a supreme preciosity, showing how a genuine intellectual power can sustain and make acceptable also extreme exercises in
artistry.

We may wonder why two writers unknown to each other should have
shared the same peculiarities. But some of them are essentially the
products of an exalted artistry, more conscious and more passionately
felt than that of most of their contemporaries; and we must remember
that these two authors lived through the so-called "aesthetic period,"
dominated by the doctrine of "art for art's sake," when problems of form
had assumed an extraordinary importance. Perhaps then the link between the two may be found in a dominant figure of the period: Walter
Pater.

Hopkins was, during his formative years, at Oxford, a pupil of Pater,
and was certainly influenced by the aesthetic theories that his teacher
(only five years older than himself) was then developing. Hopkins' Platonic dialogue *On the Origin of Beauty,* written at this time and, it appears, for Pater, contains theoretical statements that the poet never rejected, and that are the fruit of Pater's teaching.[16] The dialogue insists
particularly on the beauty and importance of symmetry and asymmetry
both in nature and art, acknowledging the validity of both kinds of
pattern, symmetrical and asymmetrical, as the basis of beauty. Transfer-
ring the exemplification onto the musical plane, Hopkins says that there
are two kinds of beauty, diatonic and chromatic. The first is characterized
by parallelism in all its forms, while the second includes, when applied to
poetry, "emphasis, expression (in the sense it has in music), tone, intensity, climax and so on." Now, this distinction is very important. Hopkins is in this way contrasting the fundamental features of two kinds of
artistic expression—the one based on symmetry (parallelism), balance of
parts, which had dominated the middle part of his century; the other
instead essentially asymmetrical and following a sort of undulating line of

[15] The revision of *The Reverberator,* quoted by Matthiessen, *Henry James: The
Major Phase,* cit., p. 61.
[16] See W. H. Gardner, *op. cit.,* pp. 6 ff.

development, representing graphically the variations and hesitations of feelings and emotions. What Hopkins calls "chromatic beauty," then, is that of an art expressing with the utmost intensity and closeness the intellectual reactions to sensations and emotions. The musical terms used by Hopkins in this connection are the more striking when we think that his essay is dated 12 May 1865, and that on the 10th of June of the same year Wagner's *Tristan und Isolde,* the apotheosis of the chromatic scale, had its first performance in Munich. Hopkins' definition of chromatism fits perfectly with the general character of Wagner's opera, in which those features listed by the Welsh poet have an extraordinary prominence. It seems that, with the help of Pater, Hopkins (who was then twenty-two years old) realized that the accepted Victorian standards of formal balance, emotional restraint, and material solidity, were not the only ones by which a work of art could be created or judged. He put on the same plane the other kind of "beauty," irregular, unrestrained and at the same time subtler and more elaborate. And though at first he objectively considered the two aspects of beauty as equal, it is apparent from his poems that he adopted the second, the "chromatic," asymmetric beauty. In other words, Hopkins lived at a time when one style was being succeeded by another contrasting one, and adopted the second.

As for James' debt to Pater, it is a fully acknowledged fact. Stuart Pratt Sherman has amply dealt with the aesthetic ideals shared by Pater and James,[17] throwing light on their passionate love of and search for beauty. This is as well one of the fundamental motives of Hopkins' poetry:

> How to kéep—is there àny any, is there none such,
>   nowhere known some, bow or brooch or braid or
>   brace, làce, latch or catch or key to keep
> Back beauty, keep it, beauty, beauty, beauty, . . . from
>   vanishing away? [18]

And this same anxious quest for beauty (beauty intended as something to be caught in a moment and fixed and kept for endless contemplation) is the mainspring of James' art and the reason for his involved style. The object of his search is so precious that he moves with an extreme caution, feeling his way all the time, trying the different angles of approach. The process is described at length in James' own preface to *The Wings of the Dove.* After fixing the centre of the composition, "pre-

[17] In an essay reproduced in *The Question of Henry James,* ed. F. W. Dupee (New York, 1947), pp. 86-106, "The Aesthetic Idealism of Henry James," (written 1917).

[18] *The Leaden Echo and the Golden Echo,* in *Poems of Gerard Manley Hopkins,* p. 54.

paratively and, as it were, yearningly—given the whole ground—one began, in the event, with the outer ring, approaching the centre thus by
narrowing circumvallations. . . ."

James is fully conscious of his supersubtleties and archrefinements; he
adopts a form deliberately extravagant, and while trying to communicate
deeply human feelings and to penetrate human consciousness, the beauty
of expression he pursues becomes identified with preciosity of form. The
style of James (and, for that matter, of Hopkins) shows then the characteristics recurring in certain periods in the history of art and poetry—
in the periods when the ideals of serenity and formal balance are broken
by a spirit of uncertainty and search; the search makes for refinement
both in themes and in expression, for a subtler and subtler penetration
of meanings and attention to details rather than to the structure as a
whole. So that there is a loss of balance and at times of proportion: details are worked out with a goldsmith's care, and this makes for an
enormous gain in insight and precision—but the total effect is frequently
lost sight of, or is reached through accumulation rather than through a
harmonious disposition of the structural parts. Uncertainty too contributes to the lack of total balance or, with reference to graphic representations, lack of symmetry; it induces a preference and a taste for
undulating, twining, whorling lines.

These formal features—as I was saying—have characterized the styles
of certain artistic periods—the styles that art historians have called (in
their chronological succession) Hellenism, Flamboyant Gothic, Mannerism, Rococo. It is what Peter calls, in his *Marius the Epicurean,* Euphuism, widening the terms of reference of a word defining the first phase of
Mannerism in the English literature of the Elizabethan age. Euphuism,
according to Pater, is based on the passionate love of form, and more
specifically of words. It is "determined at any cost to attain beauty in
writing." [19] But beyond what may seem merely external peculiarities,
common to the "Euphuists of successive ages," like their archaism on the
one hand, and their neologies on the other, beyond "the theory of Euphuism, as manifested in every age in which the literary conscience has been
awakened to forgotten duties towards language, towards the instrument
of expression," [20] there may be deeper motives justifying the departure
from the "simpleness" and "broadness" of "the old writers of Greece,"
the classical art. Cannot this same sense of the "forgotten duties towards
language" be found in Hopkins' ceaseless experiments with words and
constructions, in his interest in rhythm and structure, in his extraordi-

[19] *Marius the Epicurean* (1885), fourth edition (London, 1898), I, p. 98.
[20] *Marius the Epicurean,* ed. cit., I, p. 97.

nary mixture of neologisms, archaisms and colloquial idioms, his assertion of what Pater calls "the rights of the *proletariate* of speech"?[21] On the other side, could not this description of the faults and achievements of Flavian (the "Roman Euphuist" in Pater's book) fit as well Henry James' work? Pater writes:

> From the natural defects, from the pettiness, of his euphuism, his assiduous cultivation of manner, he was saved by the consciousness that he had a matter to present, very real, at least to him. That preoccupation of the *dilettante* with what might seem mere details of form, after all, did but serve the purpose of bringing to the surface, sincerely and in their integrity, certain strong personal intuitions, a certain vision or apprehension of things as really being, with important results, thus, rather than thus,— intuitions which the artistic or literary faculty was called upon to follow, with the exactness of wax or clay, clothing the model within. . . . And it was this uncompromising demand for a matter in all art, derived immediately from lively personal intuitions, this constant appeal to individual judgement, which saved his euphuism, even at its weakest, from lapsing into mere artifice.[22]

Indeed, Hopkins and James are both euphuistic writers in this, in Pater's, sense. This means that they adopted a certain attitude to the form of their writing in clear contrast with the rules of the period immediately previous to theirs, or, in other words, shifted the stress from one set of stylistic characters to another. From the clear line of development followed in the narrative of Dickens or Thackeray, or in the poetry of Tennyson or Matthew Arnold, they pass to more tortuous and tormented forms; to the effects of straightforwardness and harmony they prefer those of nicety in details and preciosity in construction. They represent a different phase of sensibility from that which dominated the middle period of the nineteenth century. They actually usher in a new (or a different) style which will characterize the next half-century. I am using the word style in the sense in which art historians use it—as the complex of formal features and intellectual characteristics common to a certain artistic period. The style of which Hopkins and James are the first major representatives is, as we have seen, of the type that Pater called Euphuism. It is a great merit of Pater to have tried to free the word from that derogatory connotation it had assumed—in fact even now, in the last edition of Roget's *Thesaurus*,[23] we find *euphuism,* to-

[21] *Ibid.*, I, p. 95.
[22] *Ibid.*, I, pp. 102-3.
[23] Longmans edition, 1936, 579.

gether with *mannerism* (historically the style of which Euphuism is just one stage), appearing under the heading *Inelegance*. . . .

. . . [But] the stature of single authors has only an indirect relation to the styles of their respective periods. They will of course adopt them since they speak the language of their age, and they will inevitably modify them, carrying them a stage further through the exceptional powers of their creative personalities. James and Hopkins, as we saw, were both keenly interested in stylistic principles, but their work, as that of all true artists, was not exclusively preoccupied with them. The problems of style and technique were interesting for them only in so much as through them they could construct perfect instruments for the expression of their inner world of meanings. That this world existed and was of paramount importance for them, is obvious. It expresses itself in the powerful visual images of Hopkins—in a poem like *The Windhover* an intellectual image is expressed in extremely vivid visual terms, confirming that predominance of the sense of sight in the nineteenth century which made Emerson remark (as Matthiessen reminds us) "the age is ocular." [24] For his own part James stated in the preface to *The Ambassadors* "Art deals with what we see." [25] But, as is the case with Hopkins, James' descriptions of places, like those of persons, are from the inside; they not only endow a room or a landscape with personality (a thing Dickens did in a masterly way), but add a wealth of psychological nuances and convey all the subtle interreactions of place, occupant and observer.

. . . Kate Croy, wating for an interview with her father in the sitting-room of a London boarding house, "takes in" her surroundings:

> She had looked at the sallow prints on the wall and at the lonely magazine, a year old, that combined, with a small lamp in coloured glass and a knitted white centre-piece wanting in freshness, to enhance the effect of the purplish cloth on the principal table: she had above all, from time to time, taken a brief stand on the small balcony to which the pair of long windows gave access. The vulgar little street, in this view, offered scant relief from the vulgar little room; its main office was to suggest to her that the narrow black house-fronts, adjusted to a standard that would have been low even for backs, constituted quite the publicity implied in such privacies. One felt them in the room exactly as one felt the room—the hundred like it, or worse—in the street. Each time she turned in again, each time, in her impatience, she gave him up, it was to sound to a deeper depth, while she tasted the faint, flat emanation of things, the failure of fortune and of honour. . . . To feel the street, to feel the room, to feel the table-cloth and the centre-piece and the lamp, gave her a small, salutary

[24] Matthiessen, *Henry James*, cit., p. 32.
[25] *The Art of the Novel*, cit., p. 312, quoted also by Matthiessen.

sense, at least, of neither shirking nor lying. This whole vision was the worst thing yet. . . .[26]

Many similar passages could be quoted from James' books: for instance the description of Madame de Vionnet's house in *The Ambassadors* (book VI, chap. I). Here, as well as there, there is a place, an observer and an inhabitant reacting on or against each other. But attention should be called to the last words of the passage quoted, "this whole vision," where vision is used both in the sense of "scene" and of "sudden revelation." James is conscious of having succeeded in interpreting and representing —through the picture he has drawn of the room, the list of a few articles of furniture—the essential characteristics, the deep nature itself, of a place: this is his vision. He has, in Hopkins' word, *inscaped* that room. And to *inscape* (the word is a coinage of his own) was one of the supreme aims of Hopkins himself. The most satisfactory definition of the word *inscape,* amply used by Hopkins especially in his notes and letters, is that given by W. A. M. Peters: "inscape is the unified complex of those sensible qualities of an object . . . that strike us as inseparably belonging to and most typical of it." [27] This obviously is the equivalent of James' *vision,* and Hopkins follows this principle consistently in all his work. The sonnet *Hurrahing in Harvest* may be taken as an example. Here are the last six lines:

And the azurous hung hills are his world-wielding shoulder
Majestic—as a stallion stalwart, very-violet-sweet!—
These things, these things were here and but the beholder
Wanting; which two when they once meet,
The heart rears wings bold and bolder
And hurls for him, O half hurls earth for him off under his feet.[28]

The third and fourth lines mark the achievement of the inscape—the communication between things and the beholder, the vision, which in Hopkins produces a feeling of exaltation which he called *instress.* But for Hopkins inscape in itself is not already poetry. Poetry is inscaping of speech, meaning that after receiving the inscape of an object (and putting it into ordinary speech) poetry must inscape this same speech, must make a new unified complex of the sensible qualities of the words used, so that they strike us as inseparable from and most typical of the speech. Poetry is, then, the inscape of objects squared. This is what Hopkins tried to say in some lecture notes of his:

[26] *The Wings of the Dove.*
[27] W. A. M. Peters, *G. M. Hopkins: A Critical Essay towards the Understanding of His Poetry* (London, 1948), p. 1.
[28] *Poems of Gerard Manley Hopkins,* ed. cit., p. 31.

Poetry is speech framed for contemplation of the mind by the way of hearing or speech framed to be heard for its own sake and interest even over and above its interest of meaning. Some matter and meaning is essential to it, but only as an element necessary to support and employ the shape which is contemplated for its own sake. (Poetry is in fact speech only employed to carry the inscape of speech for the inscape's sake—and therefore the inscape must be dwelt on. Now if this can be done without repeating it, *once* of the inscape will be enough for art and beauty and poetry but then at least the inscape must be understood as so standing by itself that it could be copied and repeated. If not repetition, *oftening, over-and-overing, aftering* of the inscape must take place in order to detach it to the mind and in this light poetry is speech which afters and oftens its inscape, speech couched in a repeating figure and verse is spoken sound having a repeating figure.)[29]

It appears very clearly from this passage that Hopkins was passionately concerned with the verbal level and the formal level of poetry. It is, as we saw before, a typical "euphuistic" attitude. In this passage one finds the reason for what was called Hopkins' mannerism, his use of repetition and alliteration, of a new rhythm and a new syntax, in a word, of his bewildering artistry.

But let us take now the last passage of James' quoted, from *The Wings of the Dove*. Here are the same characteristics, the alliteration, the repetition, the rhythms, the extra syllables, the breaks:

Each time she turned in again, each time, in her impatience, she gave him up, it was to sound to a deeper depth, while she tasted the faint, flat emanation of things, the failure of fortune and of honour.

We saw that this keen interest in form, style, technique, common to both, was partly due to the influence of the aesthetic movement, but the fact to be emphasised is that James and Hopkins are not akin only for these surface-features: they both used the stylistic and technical achievements which they had developed as instruments to reach and explore deeper levels of consciousness. They actually went so far in this search, and transformed their instruments of expression to such an extent, that James found only very few immediate followers, while Hopkins was ignored by all. They shared the fate of all pathfinders: only many years after their disappearance their work was rediscovered and appreciated, and actually became a powerful influence on younger writers. Through their links with the aestheticism at the end of the last century James

[29] *The Note-Books and Papers of Gerard Manley Hopkins*, ed. H. House (London, 1937), p. 249.

and Hopkins are firmly rooted in their own time; but by their constant work of deeper and deeper penetration they brought to full maturity already existing tendencies in taste and art. This maturity of a new art became generally apparent and accepted only in the 'twenties of this century, so that the two writers can be considered as transition figures between the age of Biedermeier, of Victorianism, and the *mannerist* age between the two wars. But their work belongs obviously to the second.

One final remark before closing this essay. Hopkins, as we saw, with his sprung rhythm and his use of *current language heightened,* broke the existing formal poetic pattern by including in it technical elements directly derived from prose usage. Conversely James used imagery in a way characteristic of poetry, and introduced, as I had occasion to remark before, alliterative and repetitive patterns taken from the poetic technique. They contributed then to that approach between the techniques of prose and poetry which is more apparent now, when novels assume frequently a lyrical tone while poems have definitely broken the metrical pattern and rejected the "poetical" language.

Hopkins and Whitman

by F. O. Matthiessen

Much the most searching examination of the general problem presented by Whitman's form was made by a man who, born twenty-five years after the author of *Leaves of Grass,* became the period's most thoroughgoing student of language and rhythm. Gerard Manley Hopkins devised his "sprung rhythm" "because it is the nearest to the rhythm of prose, that is the native and natural rhythm of speech, the least forced, the most rhetorical and emphatic of all possible rhythms, combining, as it seems to me, opposite and, one would have thought, incompatible excellences, markedness of rhythm—that is rhythm's self—and naturalness of expression." He felt compelled to his innovation by the vogue of such emptiness as Swinburne's "perpetual functioning of genius without truth, feeling, or any adequate matter to be at function on," by this poet's increasing failure in his later work to recognize that "words only are only words." At the other pole was Wordsworth; but he, notwithstanding his "spiritual insight into nature," was, in Hopkins' view, a transparent instance of the chief fault in English poetry after Milton, its weakness in rhetoric. By rhetoric Hopkins meant something far more exact than Whitman did, even though they are on common ground in the younger poet's declaration, "My verse is less to be read than heard . . . it is oratorical, that is the rhythm is so." Rhetoric had seemed valuable to Whitman, as to Emerson, only at those moments when it flamed into eloquence and lost the necessity for any restraining rules. To Hopkins it meant "all the common and teachable element in literature, what grammar is to speech, what thorough bass is to music, what theatrical experience gives to playwrights."

Yet Bridges believed that he detected Whitman's influence, as he read the draft of "The Leaden Echo and the Golden Echo" which Hopkins had sent him in 1882. Hopkins' answer is one of the most clarifying documents in the history of the development of modern poetry. He doubted the influence, since all he had ever read of Whitman were three poems, "Come Up from the Fields Father," "To the Man-of-War Bird," "Spirit that Form'd this Scene," and a few quotations in a review. He knew that this did not preclude the possibility of a strong impression on his style, since "they say the French trace their whole modern school of landscape to a single piece of Constable's exhibited at the Salon early this century." And he confessed what he "should not otherwise have said, that I always knew in my heart Walt Whitman's mind to be more like my own than any other man's living. As he is a very great scoundrel this is not a pleasant confession. And this also makes me the more desirous to read him and the more determined that I will not." He must have been referring to Whitman's homosexuality and his own avoidance of this latent strain in himself. For when he later sent Bridges his sonnet, "Harry Ploughman," where this feeling rises closest to the surface in his pleasure in the liquid movement of the workman's body, he hoped that there was not "anything like it in Walt Whitman, as perhaps there may be, and I should be sorry for that."

But despite the compelling and dangerous attraction that his Jesuit training taught him to cast out, he believed Bridges to be quite mistaken in supposing imitation in his poems. He granted that both Whitman and himself wrote "in irregular rhythms," but there the likeness ended. For Whitman intended no other than a free rhythmic prose, a "rugged," or as he called it in "Spirit that Form'd this Scene," a "savage" art and rhythm, which would fit its neglect of conventional technique to the vast Platte Cañon of Colorado, where this poem had been written in 1881. It was always Hopkins' contention against Bridges' incredulity that his "sprung rhythm" was "the most natural of things," since "it is the rhythm of common speech and of written prose, when rhythm is perceived in them." It was indisputable, too, that Whitman's native instinct had rediscovered something similar to what Hopkins believed he had found by learning Anglo-Saxon: that before the language had bent itself to classical influence, and had still depended in its poetry wholly on speech stresses and on a variable number of unstressed syllables between, it was "a vastly superior thing to what we have now." Still there was all the difference in the world between Whitman's occasional unconscious approximations and Hopkins' deliberately planned and highly wrought effects, for "in a matter like this a thing does not exist, is not *done* unless it is wittingly and willingly done; to recognize the form you are employing and to mean it is everything."

However—and here is one of the flashes that can illuminate a whole period of cultural development: "Extremes meet, and (I must for truth's sake say what sounds pride) this savagery of his art, this rhythm in its last ruggedness and decomposition into common prose, comes near the last elaboration of mine . . . The above remarks are not meant to run down Whitman. His 'savage' style has advantages, and he has chosen it; he says so. But you cannot eat your cake and keep it: he eats his off-hand, I keep mine."

Both these extremes had been called into being by the inordinate expansiveness of the age. It had distended the language that men used away from the formal denotations of the eighteenth century, and had admitted such a range of connotations to meet new demands that the exact sense of any single one of them was hard to pin down. Whitman, as we have seen, luxuriated in such unlimited possibilities for suggestion, just as he spoke of "the middle range of the nineteenth century" as "a strange, unloosen'd, wondrous time." But Hopkins' way was a hitherto unparalleled concentration. In his dissatisfaction with the vague poeticisms of Tennyson and Morris, he held that the true "poetical language of an age should be the current language heightened." Although Whitman would have agreed that the only sound basis for poetry was ordinary speech, Hopkins carried the practice of his theory, in this respect as in all others, to far more rigorous lengths. Appalled by the flux of contemporary art, he argued with Bridges on the merit of "terseness": "it is like a mate which may be given, one way only, in three moves; otherwise, various ways, in many."

When Hopkins said that he wanted to bring some of the resources of music into his poems, he did not mean Whitman's indefiniteness of association, for Hopkins spoke as a trained musician, an accomplished composer of fugues, who aimed to utilize in his language the most telling correspondence between sound and sense, and to give his compositions in verse an ordering comparable to the intricacies of counterpoint. In his comprehension of the significance of technical expertness in every art, he showed how different a thing tradition could be for a nineteenth-century European than for a typical American. With a no less complete rejection of contemporary practice than Whitman's, he did not therefore throw over other men's work altogether but dredged his way back to earlier values, which he assumed as his birthright, to Milton's rhetoric and the harmonies of Purcell. When Bridges taxed him with obscurity, he kept insisting that he was clearing the ground for a new popular style. The first essential was a return to strictness in the use of words, and it is manifest to us today that his compact method of joining them together compels them "to be understood as he meant them to be, or understood not at all." [1] In his intense precision of design, or "inscape" as he named it, he is in revolutionary opposition both to Whitman's happy diffuseness and to Bridges' conventional decorum. He is likewise opposed to the belief of the late-century French poets that the symbol suggests far more than it can state, or—as Eliot has defined it for his own practice—to the belief that the symbol can be at once "consciously concrete" and "unconsciously general."

However, inasmuch as Hopkins' most matured poems are so subtle and recondite as to require repeated reading, and even then some of them might still be imperfectly comprehensible without his own prose arguments, it is obvious that as the author of a popular style he fell even farther short than Whitman. Yet they both were insistent on the centrality of man. You would expect as one of Whitman's key declarations: "In the centre of all, and object of all, stands the Human Being, towards whose heroic and spiritual evolution poems and everything directly or indirectly tend, Old World or New." It might appear much less likely that an isolated Jesuit priest would declare, in a sonnet called "To what serves Mortal Beauty?"

> To man, that needs would worship block or barren stone,
> Our law says: Love what are love's worthiest, were all known:
> World's loveliest—men's selves.

Hopkins was like Whitman in his ingenuous delight in the variegated surfaces of daily existence, in "all trades, their gear and tackle and trim." Moreover, writing during the days of the French Commune, he said, "I must tell you I am always thinking of the Communist future. . . . I am afraid some great revolution is not far off. Horrible to say, in a manner I am a Communist." For he could see that their ideal was just. "I do not mean the means of getting to it are. But it is a dreadful thing for the greatest and most necessary part of a very rich nation to live a hard life without dignity, knowledge, comforts, delight, or hopes in the midst of plenty—which plenty they make. They profess that they do not care what they wreck and burn, the old civilization and order must be destroyed. This is a dreadful look out but what has the old civilization done for them?"

This would chime in exactly with what Whitman thought about Europe. But he had great confidence that the United States, "the born offspring of Revolt," was different from any other country. He believed that here alone "all forms of practical labor are recognized as honorable,"

---

[1] Robert Graves and Laura Riding, *A Survey of Modernist Poetry* (London: Heinemann, 1928), p. 90.

and consequently he could hope that the average bulk of mankind, "a magnificent mass of material, never before equal'd on earth," would continue to go forward in natural progress. However, after the Civil War, he began to know more fully that there was "nothing more treacherous" than the attitude "of nearly all the eminent persons" here towards the advance of democracy. He drafted a scheme for "Songs of Insurrection" to warn against "the more and more insidious grip of capital."

He tackled the problem most sharply in notes for another undelivered lecture, on "The Tramp and Strike Questions" (1879). The panic of 1873, with its aftermath of hard times, which reached their crisis four years later in the great railroad strike, the first occasion when federal troops fired on American workers, had compelled Whitman to think of our conditions in some of the same terms as Hopkins. He now realized that the critical issue was the struggle for adequate distribution of wealth, since "beneath the whole political world, what most presses and perplexes to-day, sending vastest results affecting the future, is not the abstract question of democracy, but of social and economic organization, the treatment of working-people by employers, and all that goes along with it— not only the wages-payment part, but a certain spirit and principle, to vivify anew these relations." At the time when most respectable citizens were deploring the violence of the strikers, Whitman asserted that "the great American revolution of 1776 was simply a great strike, successful for its immediate object," but whether a lasting success still remained to be tested. For "if the United States, like the countries of the Old World, are also to grow vast crops of poor, desperate, dissatisfied, nomadic, miserably-waged populations, such as we see looming upon us of late years— steadily, even if slowly, eating into them like a cancer of lungs or stomach —then our republican experiment, notwithstanding all its surface-successes, is at heart an unhealthy failure."

That these two so different poets had the same misgivings concerning the state of society shows how central such issues were. The conditions they foresaw and the question of how to deal with them remain the cardinal problems for the writer today. And their solutions, Whitman's drift towards socialism and Hopkins' conversion to Catholicism, are still the two extremes that are embraced, by Malraux and Eliot, by Auden and Hemingway (who, so far as I know, has not discussed in print the grounds for his faith). In his letter about the crisis dramatized for him by the Commune, Hopkins continued that as civilization

. . . at present stands in England it is itself in great measure founded on wrecking. But they [the people] got none of the spoils, they came in for

nothing but harm from it then and thereafter. England has grown hugely
wealthy but this wealth has not reached the working classes; I expect it has
made their condition worse. Besides this iniquitous order the old civilization
embodies another order mostly old and what is new in direct entail from
the old, the old religion, learning, law, art, etc. and all the history that is
preserved in standing monuments. But as the working classes have not been
educated they know next to nothing of all this and cannot be expected to
care if they destroy it. The more I look the more black and deservedly black
the future looks, so I will write no more.

But Hopkins' comprehension of the desperate conditions of mankind
not only made the substance of his poem "Tom's Garland: upon the Un-
employed"; it also served to heighten the tension that you feel almost
everywhere in his work. His rejection of much that Whitman had included, his closing the doors against the open road, did not mean ease.
His subject, which grew ever more obsessive, was struggle, the unending
necessity to fight against inner division. His moments of triumph came
when he could portray the fusion of man's energies at their full exertion,
a harmony between discipline and spontaneity. He delighted in the
movement of the windhover, in its unexampled splendor as it mounted
above the earth:

> I caught this morning morning's minion, kingdom of daylight's
>   dauphin, dapple-dawn-drawn Falcon, in his riding
> Of the rolling level underneath him steady air, and striding
> High there, how he rung upon the rein of a wimpling wing
> In his ecstasy!

The difference from the movement of Whitman's man-of-war bird is
overwhelming. However similar Whitman's exuberance in the wings
matching the gale (similar enough for Hopkins to have possibly received
the hint for his theme from it),[2] his eagle's muscles are flaccid by contrast:

> Days, even weeks untired and onward, through spaces, realms gyrating,
> At dusk that look'st on Senegal, at morn America,
> That sport'st amid the lightning-flash and thunder-cloud,
> In them, in thy experiences, had'st thou my soul,
> What joys! what joys were thine!

It is no adequate comparison of powers thus to put the opening of
what Hopkins called "the best thing I ever wrote" beside the conclusion

[2] The likelihood becomes greater in view of the proximity between the publication
of Whitman's poem in the London *Atheneum* in 1876, where Hopkins said that he
read it, and the composition of "The Windhover" in the following spring.

of one of Whitman's merely average productions.[3] Still Hopkins might
have justly contended that any group of Whitman's lines would show the
same logical consequences of extreme protestantism, of his downright
statement that formal verse was as outmoded as sacraments and dogma.
Whitman also declared that he had an instinctive "aversion to the church
notion of an atonement," because of "its essential vulgarity, its wanton
treachery" to what he believed to be the "high and imperative" recognition that man was made to be free. To the Catholic this would furnish
the most compelling evidence why Whitman's rhythms had naturally
fallen into the final looseness of decomposition. Whitman said that he
could not read Tolstoy's *Confession,* since he had never been worried by
the question of whether he should be saved or lost. Yet in his desire to
keep all doors open, he was willing to grant that the "introspective, sin-
seeking" element in the Russian "may better represent the present day
than I do." However, his complacence did not leave his view of freedom
so undeveloped that he thought any road as good as another or that the
individual's impulse constituted the only law. When he surveyed the
instances of usurping individualistic lawlessness in the era of the robber
barons, he had reached his main position in *Democratic Vistas* (1871):
that the crucial task for the American future was some reconciliation of
the contradictory needs for full personal development and for "one's
obligations to the State and Nation," to "the paramount aggregate." Although this conception of the One and the many would not have satisfied Hopkins, when Whitman went on to say that "most people entirely
misunderstand Freedom," which we can attain only "by a knowledge of,
and implicit obedience to, Law," he at least approached Engels' disciplined comprehension of freedom as "the recognition of necessity."

It is wholly obvious to us now that Bridges was wrong in his notion
that Hopkins' work was a case of "unexampled liberty." His reaction
against flabbiness had driven him rather to an excessive control, which
finally amounted to constriction. The "terrible pathos" that became his
habitual tone sprang never from doubt, but from the bitterest anguish,
from the absence of movement in a life driven in on itself, from the unflinching scrutiny of his weakness before the perfection of God. But what
is expressed has hardly any of the resolution of tragedy, since all action
has been reduced to suffering. In his unsurpassable courage to endure, his
world finally became as narrow as the cell in a monastery.

[3] A much more energetically imaginative poem on a similar subject is Whitman's
"The Dalliance of the Eagles."

Sprung Rhythm and English Tradition

by Walter J. Ong

. . . Within a rhythmic tradition such as that which was carried from Old English into Elizabethan times, it was natural for his [Hopkins'] contemporaries to single out Spenser as "the new poet." For into the tradition Edmund Spenser hardly fits. Something might be done to introduce him in part into the tradition on the score of "Februarie" and "Maye" in *The Shepheardes Calender,* although this is uncertain, but all the important rhythmic achievements of this poet tend to divert English verse into pure running-rhythm channels with no sense-stress tributaries.

We are so close to the Spenserian tradition even yet that it is difficult to realize the extent of the revolution Spenser effected. His full influence in establishing the eighteenth- and nineteenth-century feeling for a "continuous literary decorum," which so easily associated itself with the quiet throbbing of the smooth alternating-stress verse he perfected, is only beginning to be recognized as comparable to that of his greater disciple Milton, for whom he had everywhere paved the way. Saintsbury was not only making a supposition common in his day, but he was calling attention to a fact when he said that Spenser was the Joshua who brought English prosody into its promised measure and rhyme.[1] Saintsbury's supposition would find little support now: that Spenser's achievement was inevitably progress is at best a gratuitous assumption. But the importance Saintsbury assigns to Spenser is not exaggerated. To appreciate the revolutionary effect of Spenser's verse, we need only look to the diffidence of Elizabethan prosodists toward the "feet" which become the stock in trade of prosody in the late Spenserian tradition we have known. And to see the extent of his influence long after his death, we can recall that all the

"Sprung Rhythm and English Tradition" (editor's title) by Walter J. Ong. From "Hopkins' Sprung Rhythm and the Life of English Poetry," in *Immortal Diamond,* ed. by Norman Weyand, S.J. (New York: Sheed & Ward, Inc., 1949), copyright 1949 by Sheed & Ward, Inc., pp. 159-68, 170-72. Reprinted by permission of the publishers, New York and London.

[1] George Saintsbury, *A History of English Prosody* (London: Macmillan and Co., 1906-1910), I, 351.

poets disapproved of by the eighteenth century, and by the nineteenth
following its lead, have uniformly been those who are outside the Spenserian tradition. Generally speaking, to the eighteenth and nineteenth
centuries rhythmic crudity was equivalent to non-Spenserian verse movement. It is significant that eighteenth-century prosody outlaws alliteration.[2]

It is a simple fact that the smooth Spenserian rhythms cannot stand
much sense interpretation or declaim. But no need for declaim was felt
by the Augustans. The demand was for a standard currency, a guaranteed
emotional tender insured against inflation. Since it provided this, the
Spenserian tradition cannot be said to have achieved nothing: it does one
of the things which poetry can do. And yet the reduction of all poetry
to this sort of thing was bound to be disastrous. This reduction forms
one facet of the "dissociation of sensibility" which T. S. Eliot has described [3] and which took place when Spenser's influence was in the
ascendency. Here, indeed, the language was developed (along a simple
enough line), but the feeling became more and more vulgarized as it became more and more standard, less responsive to its object, for no matter
what their object, all vehicles had to follow the same road, not because it
reached the destination, but because it was smooth. Of course, this road
runs out in album verse and poetry as a "polite accomplishment." Moreover, this is the road which leads verse off the English stage: as verse in
general loses ability to declaim, the age of prose drama is ushered in.

It is difficult not to believe that the taste for smoothness which remained an accepted touchstone of good English poetry from Dryden's
day, when Mr. Waller had only lately improved our numbers, till some
time around the turn of the present century, is intimately associated with
the whole intellectual milieu of this period. In this bright and shining
world of a successful Newtonian physics, a Cartesian mathematical solvent
for all reality, and a naïve materialism, there is something which inevitably gave body to a "continuous literary decorum." Like the decimal
measurement systems, Spenserian smoothness represented great achievement to the enlightened mind.

The effects of Spenser's canonization persist on all sides in Hopkins'
age. They appear in the fact, already mentioned above, that Hopkins,
reading the English poetry ordinarily read in his day, never came across
the greater bulk of the poetry which would have interested him most, as
the natural antecedent of his own. They are manifest in Saintsbury, who,

[2] *Ibid.*, III, 541.
[3] "The Metaphysical Poets," *Selected Essays, 1917-1932* (New York: Harcourt, Brace
and Co., 1932), p. 247.

which no one had bothered to construct metric containers. But there were other odd places, for wherever departure was made from the usual running rhythm, the sense-stress pattern had a chance to assert itself. The various attempts to reproduce Latin or Greek quantitative meter in English seem to fall back in reality on a sense-stress rhythm. George Canning pays unconscious tribute to the methods of sense-stress verse when his lampooning attack on Southey's experiments in quantitative meter slips into alliteration and a movement not unlike Old English four-stress verse:

> *N*eedy *Kn*ife-grinder! *wh*ither are you going?
> *R*ough is the *r*oad, your *wh*eel is *ou*t of order—
> *Bl*eak *bl*ows the *bl*ast; your *h*at has got a *h*ole in't,
>   So *h*ave your *b*reeches.[12]

The same tendency to support with characteristic sense-stress devices the irregularity of pattern which these "classical meters" attempt is found in Tennyson's *Ode to Milton* done in "alcaics":

> O *m*ighty *m*outh'd inventor of harmonies,
> O *s*killed to *s*ing of *T*ime or *E*ternity.[13]

The same thing had been observable in the "classical meter" of the Renaissance, as in Richard Stanyhurst's *A Prayer to the Trinity*:

> *B*lessed I *i*udge *h*im that in *h*ert is *h*ealed,
> Cursed I know *h*im, that in *h*elth is *h*armed.[14]

But here one notes a more marked tendency to reproduce the Old English four-stress line so noticeable elsewhere in the poetry of Stanyhurst's contemporaries.

In turning from the verse of the simple alternating stress, the nineteenth-century writers were all in one way or another falling back on the sense-stress patterning which is so much the bone and sinew of English rhythm. Evidence of the revival of the pattern is often in individual instances equivocal, but the evidence in the whole body of English verse toward the end of the nineteenth century as against the middle of the eighteenth is unmistakable. Moreover, there are such signs as the alliteration to be found here and there. This is probably for the most part

---

[12] "Sapphics: The Friend of Humanity and the Knife-Grinder," *Poetry of the Anti-Jacobin,* with notes by Charles Edmonds (London: G. Willis, 1854), p. 20. Italics mine.
[13] *The Poetic and Dramatic Works of Alfred, Lord Tennyson* (Boston: Houghton Mifflin Co., 1898), p. 267. Italics mine.
[14] "A Prayer to the Trinity," *Translation of the First Four Books of the Aeneis of P. Virgilius Maro: With Other Poetical Devices Thereto Annexed* [1582], ed. by Edward Arber ("The English Scholar's Library of Old and Modern Works," No. 10 [London: 1880]), p. 133.

entirely unconscious, it is not uniform throughout the poems, and yet it comes in quite too persistently to be accidental. It is the old functional alliteration asserting itself again, as it had asserted itself in Old English and was to assert itself in Hopkins' sprung rhythm. It is the alliteration which poets fall back on as a natural help to heighten stress for sustaining a rhythm not built on a regularly pulsing beat. . . .

Hopkins, then, had found the tradition of a sense-stress rhythm, which we may also call the declamatory rhythm or the interpretive rhythm of English—a rhythm inherited from Old English as one of the bases of verse until the "reform" and "smoothing" of English numbers, principally under the influence of Edmund Spenser and his followers. Basically, this sense-stress rhythm is a rhythm which grows not from the tendency of English to stress every second or third syllable (whether sense demands this stress or not), but from the tendency of each sense stress, especially in emotional utterance, to constitute itself a kind of rhythmic unit, either alone or together with a varying number of slack syllables which may precede and/or follow it. These rhythmic units can be of more or less equal weight while retaining great variety of movement—falling, rocking, or rising—and various lengths.

Perpetuated largely in the playwrights and in the line of wit poets, who preserved the tone of direct address in their verse and with this the preeminence of sense stress associated with stage delivery, this sense-stress rhythmic tradition persisted quite noticeably as a secondary or "counterpointed" rhythm until Pope, and was, indeed, never quite eliminated even at the height of the Spenserian influence during the eighteenth and nineteenth centuries. During these lean years, sense-stress rhythm survived after a fashion in out-of-the-way places such as songs and popular saws and nursery rhymes (more genuinely, it seems, in the songs than in the saws or rhymes—but this would take long to show). Hopkins notes it in these places. It also persisted in a way in various metrical experiments. Always different from and always somewhat like the "running" or "common" rhythm of English, this sense-stress rhythm is ready at all times to assert itself in English verse, especially when syllabic count is neglected. In Hopkins' day it was reviving to some extent in places other than his own verse.

The rhythm had existed all the time in prose, in the rhythms of speech where the restraint of reformed numbers was not felt. Hopkins himself finally came to understand this. Even before he did, he realized the hold of the rhythm on the language ("I do not claim to have invented *sprung rhythms* but *sprung rhythm*," he tells Bridges), but the reading menu which his age prescribed kept Hopkins from ever knowing how much the forces back of sprung rhythm had normally made themselves felt in English verse.

This limitation of his knowledge did not stop accomplishment, for Hopkins' rhythmic achievement was primarily the work not of theory but of an extremely keen ear aided by a singularly open and objective mind, and it was made possible by the unusually true and consistent sensibility reflected in Hopkins' understanding that "a perfect style must be of its age."

Hopkins' achievement in reviving sense-stress rhythms is largely traceable to this understanding. On the strength of it, he turned in his poetry to language which is the normal tender for emotion, a currency heavy with the Anglo-Saxon small change of the English tongue. Hopkins' preference for the short word is apparent in every line of his verse.

General neglect of the longer Latin derivatives is indeed not essential to sense-stress rhythm. "Free verse" has never been remarkable for Anglo-Saxon preferences, and its rhythm is no less sense-stress because the stresses consequently occur at a greater distance from one another than is usual in Hopkins, who is able to say of his own sprung rhythm verse that it uses more than three successive slacks only "for particular rhythmic effects." Moreover, an Anglo-Saxon vocabulary is, conversely, quite consonant with the smooth rhythms of Gray's *Elegy,* which in many stanzas can be convicted of no more Latinity than Hopkins' "That Nature Is a Heraclitean Fire."

And yet, beyond the shadow of a doubt, Hopkins' diction does make the characteristic movements of his verse more unmistakable. By and large, the number of sense stresses in English decreases as words become longer, since each word, no matter how long, ordinarily is ready to receive no more than one sense stress. Filled with short words, and thus adaptable to a high proportion of sense stresses, Hopkins' verse moves so as to underline heavily the principles on which it is based. Stresses are packed close together to form a kind of condenser which gives each stress a higher charge than other diction might do. This is eminently stress verse. And it is stress verse all the more because of Hopkins' revivification of the alliteration and other sound echoes which make the verse of high stress live. Hopkins succeeded in reaching to the very "inscape" of his medium. His achievement is its "clearest-selved spark."

Poetry and the Language of Communion

by Sigurd Burkhardt

By way of showing how poets respond to the threat of disintegration, to the awareness that traditional harmonies and cohesions are no longer to be relied on, I should like to consider three poems, all on the same subject but far apart in time and in form. The first is Robert Herrick's *To Daffodils:*

1. Fair Daffodils, we weep to see
    You haste away so soon:
As yet the early-rising Sun
    Has not attain'd his Noon.
        Stay, stay
    Until the hasting day
        Has run
    But to the Even-song;
And, having prayed together, we
    Will go with you along.

2. We have short time to stay, as you,
    We have as short a spring;
As quick a growth to meet Decay,
    As you or anything.
        We die,
    As your hours do, and dry
        Away,
    Like to the Summer's rain;
Or as the pearls of Morning's dew
    Ne'er to be found again.

This apostrophe to flowers is perhaps a song rather than a poem; it may be a violence to strip it of its musical envelopment. Still I think we are

"Poetry and the Language of Communion" (editor's title) by Sigurd Burkhardt. Originally published as "Poetry, Language, and the Condition of Man" (partly written in collaboration with Roy Harvey Pearce) in *The Centennial Review*, 4 (Winter, 1960). Revised by the author and reprinted by permission of *The Centennial Review*, Michigan State University.

safe in noting two things about it as significant: that daffodils are being addressed, and that the stanzaic pattern is forbiddingly complex. The subject itself—the analogy between human and floral life—is a topos as old as the Bible; the basic rhetorical figure—the apostrophe—is equally old. But the tone is singular: a pleading, at times almost hectic, to the flowers to acknowledge the relationship which alone can make the direct address meaningful. The point in history at which an address to inanimate things ceased to be taken literally and became figurative lies in the dim past; but the point at which such an apostrophe is felt to be a positive incongruity, an artifice no longer reconcilable with the speaker's sense of reality, is very much more recent and varies from person to person, perhaps from mood to mood. Herrick, I think, reaches that point in this poem. To trace out rhyme schemes is no longer fashionable critical practice, but here we need one, because the poem is a rhymer's tour de force; it stretches almost to the breaking point our capacity for hearing the tonal correspondencies. As the speaker has difficulty in believing that human and inanimate nature are still sufficiently of a piece to talk to each other, so we have difficulty in hearing that the lines of the poem fully answer each other. German has an expressive term for lines which, in generally rhymed stanzas, remain without the fulfillment of an answering line; it calls them "orphans." There are two near-orphans in Herrick's stanza: the first and the ninth lines. Is it altogether an accident that it is the word "we" at the end of line 9 which stands in this position of almost complete bereavement (and pronounced syntactical isolation), harking back to an answering echo that has become almost too faint to hear? And again, is it an accident that in line 6 of the second stanza the flow of the verse, until then easy though varied, becomes disturbed and clogged through the juxtaposition of the words "your hours"? "Hours" itself is wilful; from the logic of the analogy we should expect a simple "you." But if we consider "hours" as a pun on the first-person-plural possessive, we see that the disturbance arises from the too close joining of the two pronouns— "we" and "you"—to join which would have seemed the very point of the poem.

We might say, then, that the poem is a splendid farewell to itself, or to its mode. This particular kind of grace, of madrigal lightness and intricacy, does not, I believe, recur in English poetry. The faith in the universal harmony of all creation, which ought to be the real substratum for such modes of speech, is only a charming fiction. And though there is hardly a limit to the fictions the poet may permit himself, fictions about his medium are forbidden him upon pain of poetic death. What

makes this poem live—as the anthologies show it does—is not the fiction
but rather the poet's awareness of it *as* a fiction. Because an apostrophe
is a figure of *speech* in the most literal sense, and because the poet is
the most conscious and responsible of speakers, he knows himself com-
mitted to something untenable, something beautiful but already beyond
recall; the "Stay, stay" calls out not only to the daffodils in the first line,
but also to those in the title—that is, to the poem as a whole.

   Two and a half centuries separate Hopkins' elegy from Herrick's,
and they tell.

Spring and Fall

TO A YOUNG CHILD

> Márgarét, are you gríeving
> Over Goldengrove unleaving?
> Léaves, líke the things of man, you
> With your fresh thoughts care for, can you?
> Áh! ás the heart grows older
> It will come to such sights colder
> By and by, nor spare a sigh
> Though worlds of wanwood leafmeal lie;
> And yet you wíll weep and know why.
> Now no matter, child, the name:
> Sórrow's spríngs áre the same.
> Nor mouth had, no nor mind, expressed
> What heart heard of, ghost guessed:
> It ís the blight man was born for,
> It is Margaret you mourn for.

Now it is not the "we" of common humanity that speaks to flowers, but
the poet who speaks to a child. The child responds to the falling of
leaves somewhat as Herrick, speaking for all of us, does to the withering
of the daffodils; but the poet initiates her into the harsher verities of
human life and growth. He does not call Margaret's grief pointless, on
the contrary: he says that she is, by intuitive wisdom, grieving over the
ineluctable future time when she will no longer grieve. Thus the poem
translates into an adult sensibility the kind of correspondence which
formed the already precarious base of Herrick's poem. To put it somewhat baroquely, Hopkins goes about his work with a compassionate
severity, destroying the fairy-tale Goldengrove in which the child still
finds the objective correlative of her sorrow, and leaving in its place
worlds of wanwood, but on the other hand giving that sorrow a new
dignity by showing it its true object: man's—Margaret's—self.

In this separation, words and images assume a particularity which they do not have in the earlier poem. Perhaps my interpretation of Herrick's "your hours" seemed a little strained; but if it occurred in this poem, my calling attention to it would, I daresay, seem quite natural, because it would be entirely of a piece with "heart heard, ghost guessed," with wanwood and leafmeal, etc. What I take to be the first sign of disintegration in Herrick has become the dominant formal feature in Hopkins; the words do not easily blend into the total utterance, but insistently call attention to themselves as entities, as particulars, which the meter, moreover, compels us to linger over and take in fully.

This means that Hopkins has drawn the linguistic consequences of his knowledge. The relative ease with which we read Herrick's poem derives from the sense of correspondence which still structures it: where Nature is in tune with man's feelings, language need not carry a very heavy burden; the greater, encompassing harmony is pre-established, as it were. Call this harmony into question, as Hopkins does, and the burden on language immediately becomes greater. It has to exert itself to hold things together; we can see the alliterative tendons straining.

But something has been gained by the loss; as man has been turned in upon himself, so has language. In being forced to structure itself more rigorously from within, it has gained a new resilience. I will risk the assertion that the rhyme of the final couplet would have been impossible before Hopkins, except where the intention was comic; it has so work-a-day a cadence that it seems, or did seem, unavailable to serious lyric poetry. Here however, it does its work with dignity and even poignancy. Why? Mostly, I think, because the poem as a whole has prepared us to accept words as particulars, with an inherent worth. Perhaps it is a blight which has turned Goldengrove into wanwood and splendid phrases like "pearls of morning's dew" into "It is Margaret you mourn for." (Margaret, by the way, is Greek for "pearl.") But it is the human lot and the human phrase, as moving in their way as any beautiful but false compare.

That this conquest of a new linguistic province for poetry has not been a matter of course, we see from the strange second couplet. Why this painfully contorted sentence, which seems to yield nothing but a strained and inharmonious rhyme? My guess is that the principle of contortion is not a "poetic" one, in the common acceptance of that much abused term, but a purely linguistic—and thus a truly poetic—one. The sentence creates no effect that would speak immediately to our feelings (unless we have learned to *feel* language, as the poet does); what it does is to crowd together, at the beginning, all its nominal ele-

ments and to relegate the verbal elements to the end. Is not the point
of this to show the linguistic impossibility of that pristine innocence and
sense of harmony in which all things stand side by side, inviolate, substantial and yet intimately related?—a harmony so unbroken that there
is no subject lording it over an object and no verb to intervene between
the two, relating only what itself has separated? In a sense, the child's
inarticulate, ineffable intuition of coherence is true; but the poet knows,
more keenly than anyone else, that what cannot be said cannot, humanly
speaking, be true. And yet it seems that what *can* be said must be false.
It is at this point that the final and "vulgar" phrasing comes to the
poet's rescue. In "the blight man was born for" and "Margaret you
mourn for"—already anticipated in the "care for" of line four—the
form of statement which before was all but unintelligible becomes available; in a curious way subject and object have become one, and no
verb separates the substantives. There has been a price to pay: the
truth of language is man's truth; its limitations are man's blight; the
pathetic fallacy is, humanly speaking, just that—a fallacy. But at least
the truth of man's fellowship and common fate can be wrested from
language, and that, as the poem proves, is no mean triumph.

The Course of a Particular.

Wallace Stevens

Today the leaves cry, hanging on branches swept by wind,
Yet the nothingness of winter becomes a little less.
It is still full of icy shades and shapen snow.

The leaves cry . . . One holds off and merely hears the cry.
It is a busy cry, concerning someone else.
And though one says that one is part of everything,

There is a conflict, there is a resistance involved;
And being part is an exertion that declines:
One feels the life of that which gives life as it is.

The leaves cry. It is not a cry of divine attention,
Nor the smoke-drift of puffed-out heroes, nor human cry.
It is the cry of leaves that do not transcend themselves,

In the absence of fantasia, without meaning more
Than they are in the final finding of the ear, in the thing
Itself, until, at last, the cry concerns no one at all.

If we were asked to supply a title for Stevens' poem, it is a safe guess
that we would not hit on the one chosen by the poet. Herrick's title adds

nothing to our understanding which we would not know after reading the first two words of the poem; Hopkins' we might guess and do at least not puzzle over. But I doubt that we could read Stevens' poem correctly without the pointer supplied in the title; even with it it is difficult enough. This means, surely, that a confidence has become still more shaky: the confidence, let us say, of the apostrophe, of the direct address; the trust that the poet will be understood, because his voice is the common voice of man. Where Herrick says "we" and speaks to Nature and where Hopkins says "you" and speaks to a child, Stevens says not even "I" but "one"; and if he speaks to anyone, it is with a mediacy and from an isolation so great that he is bound to be diffident about being understood at all. Hence the starkly abstract title, a warning that what follows will speak for itself with an uncompromising absoluteness.

The "particular" that runs its course through the poem is the cry of the leaves—or perhaps, more cautiously, "the leaves cry." The course itself is a merciless stripping, a structured and mounting negation, until we have the thing "itself," untranscending, uncommunicative, cut off from all connection with gods, heroes, man, and even, so it seems, with that impersonal "one," who has no attributes left except the rapidly failing ability to hear and the ebbing will to be part. At first the leaves cry in a setting, temporal and spatial; but, bleak as the setting is, it is too much, is got rid of. The phrase itself must speak, or rather cry . . . what, or to whom? The "one" hearer lacks the energy and resists the temptation to hear more than is said—and nothing *is* said. The meaning of the cry would have to be contributed by the "one" and to do so would not only be an exertion, but a violation of the truth of the thing, the cry, itself. And so, finally, the particular stands naked, separate, intransitive, closed off by a full stop. It has become absolutely itself.

In this minimal integrity, the particular has to counterbalance a heavy bulk of statement—statement which, except in the first stanza, is weighed down with bureaucratic jargon. Compared with "concerning someone else," "there is a resistance involved," or "in the absence of," Hopkins' "It is Margaret you mourn for" seems the essence of purity. And so does the particular—"the leaves cry"—itself. We get the feeling that to say more than this barest of sentences is already too much, too risky, involving us, on the one hand, in fantasias of togetherness and on the other in a mode of speech so drained of all concreteness and felt reality that it seems to issue from a Hartford, Conn., office building. Anything that might smack of artifice, of vividness, is stringently avoided; even images

are too much, it seems, because the human mind is so constituted that
it takes images as metaphors and finds a specious consolation in the
sense that things have, after all, a meaning, are related, cohere. It is
this consolation Stevens deprives us of; he will not supply us with any
props for our illusions. This is the language you speak, he seems to say,
and consequently this is the way you are; it would be a lie to pretend
that things are meaningful.

I distrust the practice of assigning philosophical labels to poetry, but
Stevens' stripping of language to the bare bones of statement is too
obviously analogous to the existentialist's stripping man of all his attributes to be ignored. "The leaves cry" is the linguistic counterpart to
the existentialist "I am"; we have here the same desperate search for the
irreducible, the same will to take nothing for granted. We have observed
the interiorisation of "form" from Herrick to Hopkins; with Stevens it
has become pure structure. Rhyme, meter, richness of image and sound
—all the devices which, being external and immediately perceptible em-
blems of order and splendor (however fleeting), affirm an ordered and
in some sense splendid world outside of the poet's created act, a world
within which he can act because he shares it with his audience—all these
are no longer available. Traditionally, poetry has been in some way
celebratory; however precarious the poet felt the possibility of communion to be, he celebrated the sense that it was still and once more
possible. With Stevens—and much modern poetry—all the energy seems
to be spent on the mere assertion that communion must be *made* possible. The act of creation has become absolute—and for this reason
stark. By a curious but necessary paradox, the unlimited freedom of
the absolute creator turns into the grimmest kind of necessity; it is
this paradox which Stevens' particular, in the counterplay of form and
content, embodies. "The leaves cry" is, as an assertion, creatively sovereign; real leaves do not *cry*. But as a *form* of statement it is terrifyingly
compelled; if less were said, it would no longer be a statement at all.

In "Carrion Comfort" Hopkins cries:

> Not, I'll not, carrion comfort, Despair, not feast on thee;
> Not untwist—slack they may be—these last strands of man. . . .

This is anything but confident or even elegiac, but it is still grand.
Though God—the sonnet ends: "I wretch lay wrestling with (my God!)
my God."—has become inscrutable to the point where prayer and blas-
phemy are almost one, He is still there. The demands on Stevens are
starker. Whatever is said and heard "is not the cry of divine attention";

"these last strands of man" are, for him, not those that tie man to God but more likely those that tie subject and verb into minimal utterance. Elsewhere Stevens calls the poem "the cry of its occasion"; but the cry is not allowed to deteriorate into a "Howl." Like Hopkins, Stevens will not feed on despair, for "Said words of the world are the life of the world." The emphasis is on the "said," the human speech act which invests words with life-giving meaning.

"Leaves, like the things of man . . ."—that is the simile which, over and over again, demands to be tested. What we call, loosely and meta-phorically, the "meaning of our lives," the poet tests literally against the meaning of our discourse. A theory of meaning—whether implicit or explicit—is in fact a whole philosophy, because it stipulates the all-important third party who must be the guarantor of communion. Who or what guarantees that the meaning I attach to my words is the same as the meaning my listener derives from them? Is it a divinely established harmony, a firmly and beautifully woven texture of creation, in which all creatures have discourse with one another? Is it the more tenuous— I would say Post-Reformation—order, which still allows men the com-munity of their individual wrestling with God? Or is it the group-made, haphazardly enslaving system of mere social habit, the probability-calcu-lus kind of communion, the order of slogan and jargon and conditioned response? For the poet, the shift from Divine Providence to actuarial tables is a linguistic one. And as our certainties loosen and dissolve, his business is to discover and recreate the integers of speech—to tighten, at whatever cost in grace and ease, "these last strands of man."

Instress of Inscape

by Austin Warren

The early Hopkins follows Keats and the "medieval school" (as he called the Pre-Raphaelites). The latest Hopkins, who wrote the sonnets of desolation, was a poet of tense, economic austerity. Their nearest parallel I can summon would be Donne's "holy sonnets": "Batter my heart" and "If poisonous minerals." For the mode of "Andromeda" and the later sonnets (1885-89), Hopkins himself projected "a more Miltonic plainness and severity": He was thinking of Milton's sonnets and the choruses of *Samson*. In 1887 he invoked another name: "My style tends always more towards Dryden."

The middle period, which opens with the "Wreck of the Deutschland" (1875) and closes with "Tom's Garland" and "Harry Ploughman," both written in 1885, is the period of experiment. But it is also the most Hopkinsian—the most specially his own.

Middle Hopkins startles us by its dense rich world, its crowded Ark, its plenitude and its tangibility, its particularity of thing and word. There is detailed precision of image ("rose moles all in stipple upon trout that swim"). The poet is enamored of the unique, the "abrupt self."

The exploration of Middle Hopkins—its style, the view of life and art implicit in its style—may well start from the institutions and movements from which the poet learned, in which he participated. The motifs are the Ritualist Movement, Pre-Raphaelitism, Aestheticism, linguistic renovation, England, the Catholic church. In Hopkins' celebration of the sensuous, the concrete, the particular—his "instress of the inscapes" —all of these converge.

As a Catholic, Hopkins was an incarnationist and a sacramentalist: the sacraments are the extensions of the Incarnation. As a Catholic he believed that man is a compound of matter and form and that his body, resurrected, will express and implement his soul through all eternity. "Man's spirit will be flesh-bound when found at best. But unencumbered. . . ." Like all Catholic philosophers, he believed in an outer world independent of man's knowing mind—he was, in the present sense of the word, a "realist."

Hopkins was an Englishman, of a proud and patriotic sort. This is not always remembered, partly because he became the priest of a church viewed by other Englishmen as Continental, or Italian, or international. But there is an English way of being Catholic. Hopkins was not an "old Catholic" of the sturdy, unemotional variety nourished on Challoner's *Garden of the Soul;* no convert could be that. But, like his admired Newman, and unlike Manning and Faber (also converts), he was "Gallican," not ultramontane; British, not Italian, in his devotional life and rhetoric. He remembers when England was Catholic, when the pilgrims frequented the shrine of Our Lady of Walsingham.

> Deeply surely I need to deplore it,
> Wondering why my master bore it,
> The riving off that race
> So at home, time was, to his truth and grace
> That a starlight-wender of ours would say
> The marvellous Milk was Walsingham Way
> And one—but let be, let be:
> More, more than was will yet be.

The four real shapers of Hopkins' mind were all Britons; we might go farther and say that all were British empiricists—all concerned with defending the ordinary man's belief in the reality and knowability of things and persons.

Two of them were encountered at Oxford. Pater, who remained his friend, was one of his tutors. Against the abstractions of the academic world, Pater boldly defended the concrete—in the visual arts and music, in perception. "Every moment some form grows perfect in hand or face, some tone on the hills or the sea is choicer than the rest . . ." Though Hopkins could not conceivably have written so representatively, abstractly ("hills . . . sea . . . choicer") the famous Conclusion to *The Renaissance* pleads for a stressing of the inscapes. Hopkins followed some lectures by Pater on Greek philosophy; perhaps he heard, in an earlier version, Pater's lectures on Plato and Platonism, in which, with monstrous effrontery, the Doctrine of Ideas was praised as giving contextual interest to the concrete.

With Ruskin, whose *Modern Painters* he read early and admiringly, Hopkins revolted against the neoclassical grandeur of generality praised by Johnson and expounded by Reynolds. The influence of Ruskin—art medievalist, devout student of clouds, mountains, trees—is pervasive in Hopkins' sketches (five of which are reproduced in the *Note-Books*) and in his journalizing, his meticulously technical descriptions of church architecture (often neo-Gothic) and scenery.

Hopkins follows the general line of Ruskin in more than art. He does not find the humanly satisfactory and well-furnished world such an effect of its Creator as the watch of the watchmaker. Nor does he, after the fashion of some mystics and Alexandrians, dissolve Nature into a system of symbols translating the real world of the Spirit. Like Ruskin, he was able to recover the medieval and Franciscan joy in God's creation. And, like Ruskin, he protested against an England which is "seared with trade . . . and wears man's smudge." His political economy, as well as it can be construed, was Ruskinian—what may be called tory socialist or distributist.

It was to Newman, his great predecessor, that Hopkins wrote upon deciding to become a Roman Catholic. And Newman's closest approach to a philosophical work, his *Grammar of Assent* (1870), interested Hopkins enough so that in 1883 he planned to publish (had Newman agreed) a commentary on it. There were marked temperamental and intellectual differences between the men. Newman, much the more complex and psychologically subtle, could feel his way into other men's minds as Hopkins could not. Hopkins was the closer dialectician and scholar. He did not share Newman's distrust of metaphysics (including the scholastic), his tendency to fideism; but he was, like Newman—in words the latter used of Hurrell Froude—"an Englishman to the backbone in his severe adherence to the real and the concrete."

The great medieval thinker who most swayed Hopkins' spirit to peace, Duns Scotus, was also a Briton, had been an Oxford professor. He was "of reality the rarest-veinéd unraveler": he was able to analyze, disengage from the complex in which they appear, the thinnest, most delicate strands ("vein" may be either anatomical or geological). Perhaps "rarest-veinéd unraveler" is a kind of kenning for the philosopher's epithet, the Subtle Doctor. Scotus, the Franciscan critic of the Dominican Aquinas, was centrally dear to Hopkins as undertaking the philosophical validation of the individual. In the individual's relation to his species, Aquinas taught that the "matter" individuates, while the "form" is generic: that is, that the individuals of a species reproductively multiply their common originative pattern. Scotus insisted that each individual has a distinctive "form" as well: a *haecceitas,* or thisness, as well as a generic *quidditas,* or whatness.

After having discovered this medieval Franciscan, Hopkins, upon "any inscape of sky or sea," thought of Scotus. The word, of Hopkins' coinage, occurs already in his Oxford notebooks. Modeled presumably on "landscape," "inscape" stands for any kind of formed or focused view, any pattern discerned in the natural world. A central word in his vocabulary and central motif in his mental life, it traverses some range of meaning: from sense-perceived pattern to inner form. The prefix seems to imply a contrary, an outerscape: that is, an "inscape" is not mechanically or inertly present but requires personal action, attention, a seeing and a seeing into.

The earliest "Notes for Poetry" cite: "Feathery rows of young corn. Ruddy, furred and branchy tops of the elms backed by rolling clouds." "A beautiful instance of inscape *sided* on the *slide,* that is successive sidings on one inscape, is seen in the behavior of the flag flower." In 1873, two years before the "Deutschland," he "saw a shoal of salmon in the river and many hares on the open hills. Under a stone hedge was a dying ram: there ran slowly from his nostrils a thick flesh-coloured ooze, scarlet in places, coiling and roping its way down so thick that it looked like fat."

He made notes on ancient musical instruments and on gems and their colors: "beryl—watery green; carnelian—strong flesh red, Indian red. . . ." His love of precise visual observation never lapsed, nor did his taste for reserach. Like Gray, he had a meticulous antiquarianism, suited to botany or archeology, to notes and queries, details, studies in place names, amateur etymologies.

Perhaps his most brilliant prose celebrates the Self and its wonders: "That taste of myself, of I and me above and in all things, which is more distinctive than the taste of ale or alum." Other selves were mysterious. As a shy man, he found it easier to reach natural "inscapes." He wrote no psychological portraits matching for sharpness and delicacy his notations of ash trees. The men in his poems are seen as from a distance—sympathetically but generically.

But he gloried in the range and repertory of mankind. Chesterton was concerned that, lying down with the lamb, the lion should "still retain his royal ferocity"; and Hopkins, also, wanted monks to be mild and soldiers to be pugnacious. He imagined Christ incarnate again as a soldier. He didn't want other men to be like himself; he was drawn to his antitypes—to soldiers; miners; Felix Randall, the blacksmith, and Harry, the ploughman; to manual laborers. Moreover, each of these men he wished to be functioning not only characteristically but intensely, violently, dangerously—on their mettle, like the Windhover, like Harry

Ploughman, like the sailor of the "Eurydice" who, "strung by duty, is strained to beauty."

In poetry he desired both to record inscapes and to use words as objects. His was a double particularity.

Poetry, he wrote shortly before composing the "Deutschland," is "speech framed to be heard for its own sake and interest even over and above its interest of meaning. Some [subject] matter and meaning is essential to it but only as an element necessary to support and employ the shape which is contemplated for its own sake. Poetry is in fact speech for the inscape's sake—and therefore the inscape must be dwelt on."

In 1862 he was already collecting words. The earliest entries in the *Note-Books* are gritty, harshly tangy words, "running the letter,": "grind, gride, grid, grit, groat, grate" and "crock, crank, kranke, crick, cranky." He collected dialectical equivalents: "whisket" for "basket," "grindle-stone" for "grindstone." He notes linguistic habits: that an observed laborer, when he began to speak "quickly and descriptively,—dropped or slurred the article." He attends to, and tries to define, the sundry modes of Latin pronunciation. He inquires concerning the character of the Maltese language; wants to learn Welsh—not primarily in order to convert the local Wesleyans back to their ancestral faith.

In his early poetry Hopkins followed Keats and the "medieval school." Even in his middle style there remain vestiges of the earlier decorative diction, frequent use of "beauty," "lovely," "dear," "sweet" ("that sweet's sweeter ending"). But as early as 1866, "The Habit of Perfection," though dominantly "medieval," anticipates the later mode:

> This ruck and reel which you remark
> Coils, keeps, and teases simple sight.

"The Wreck of the Deutschland" (1875) inaugurates Hopkins' middle period (his first proper mastery). The diction is quite as extraordinary as the rhythm. Characteristic are homely dialectal words, sounding like survivors from Old English, and compound epithets suggestive of the same archetype. From the concluding stanzas of the "Deutschland" come these lines:

> Mid-numbered He in three of the thunder-throne!
> Not a dooms-day dazzle in his coming nor dark as he came. . . .

and

> Dame, at our door
> Drowned, and among our shoals,
> Remember us in the roads, the heaven-haven of the
> Reward. . . .

From "The Bugler's First Communion":

> Forth Christ from cupboard fetched, how fain I of feet
>   To his youngster take his treat!
> Low-latched in leaf-light housel his too huge godhead.

That Hopkins was influenced by Old English poetry is an easy assumption. In his excellent *New Poets from Old: A Study in Literary Genetics,* Henry Wells observes that all the technical features representative of that poetry appear conspicuously in Hopkins; judges him far nearer to Cynewulf than to Chaucer; and finds a plausible parallel to a passage in *Beowulf.* But, by his own statement, Hopkins did not learn Anglo-Saxon until 1882 and seems never to have read either *Beowulf* or Cynewulf. In any case, he was already a student of Welsh poetry and an attentive reader of linguistic monographs. Like Pound and Eliot, he belongs among the poets who can be incited to poetry by scholars' prose.

In 1873-74, while teaching a course in rhetoric at Manresa House, Hopkins wrote the observations collected in the *Note-Books.* In his notes he used the 1859 *Lectures on the English Language* by the American scholar, George P. Marsh, a book calculated to incite a poet. Marsh has a real interest in the future (as well as the past) of the language and a real interest in the literary (as well as the pragmatic) use of words. The whole direction of his book suggests that literary experiment can find much to its purpose in literary history and that new poetry can be engendered by old. Ending his lecture on "Accentuation and Double Rhymes," he urges: "We must enlarge our stock [of rhyming words] by the revival of obsolete words and inflections from native sources," or introduce substitutes for rhyme; in the following chapter he excitingly discusses alliteration (with illustrations from *Piers Plowman*), consonance, e.g., "bad, led"; "find, band" (with illustrations from Icelandic poetry and invented English examples), and assonance (with illustrations from the Spanish). Hopkins' quotations from *Piers* are Marsh's; only in 1882 did he study *Piers,* and then without admiration, regarding its verse as a "degraded and doggerel" form of Anglo-Saxon sprung rhythm.

To both Bridges and Dixon, curious concerning the new poetic method of the "Deutschland," Hopkins says nothing of Old English or of *Piers Plowman* but speaks of nursery rhymes, the choruses of Milton's *Samson,* and his readings in Welsh poetry (which he began studying in 1875). "The chiming of the consonants I get in part from the Welsh, which is very rich in sound and imagery." Traits common to Old English and Middle Hopkins (scant use of articles, prepositions, and pronouns; constant use of compound words) are shared by both with Welsh poetry.

There is a third lineage for the diction of Hopkins. Through Barnes and Furnivall, at least, he derives from an imprecisely defined group of Victorian historians and philologists, who challenged the dominance of the Latin and Romance—the "civilized," learned, abstract—elements in our language. One of these linguistic protestants was the Oxford historian, E. A. Freeman, who chronicled the Norman Conquest and himself resisted it. As early as 1846 he was praising the Teutonic part of our language as affording "expressions mostly of greater strength than their Romance synonyms for all purposes of general literature"; and he used the phrase "pure English" for a diction purged of these synonyms. Another Anglicizer was F. J. Furnivall, a founder, in 1864, of the Early English Text Society, and a constant editor of texts, who began his intellectual career under the influence of Ruskin and Maurice and declared that his interest in early literature was not linguistic but social. Another founder of the E.E.T.S., R. C. Trench, gave a chapter of his *English, Past and Present* (1855) to a consideration of "English as it might have been" without a Norman Conquest. Though our present cerebral and technical words derive from the classical languages, he argues that the Anglo-Saxon might have developed—chiefly by compounding, as German has done—such a vocabulary. Even "impenetrability" could have been matched, accurately, by "unthoroughfaresomeness." And theological language would be understood by farm hand as well as by scholar if we said "again-buying" for "redemption."

In the tradition of Trench, but much more violent, William Barnes lamented the linguistic conquest of English and declared the old stock still capable of extension by compounding. Instead of "photograph," we should say "sunprint" or "flameprint." Indeed, all our current Latinisms we should replace out of the "wordstores of the landfolk." Barnes's nominations are all flavorsome; samples are "overyearn" (commiserate), "gleecraft" (music), "outclear" (elucidate), "faithheat" (enthusiasm). He regretted the loss of "inwit" in place of "conscience"; and to serve instead of "subjective" and "objective" (those psychological-philosophical terms which Coleridge introduced from Germany) he suggested "inwoning" and "outwoning."

Barnes had something of a following among literary people; was publicly praised by Patmore, Gosse, Bridges, Hardy. His poetry, early read, Hopkins preferred to that of Burns, liking its "West Country instress." But he learned most from the prose. Barnes's *Speechcraft* [i.e., Grammar], says Hopkins, is "written in an unknown tongue, a soul of modern Anglo-Saxon, beyond all that Furnival in his wildest Forewords

ever dreamed. . . . It makes one weep to think what English might
have been, for in spite of all that Shakespeare and Milton have done
with the compound ["impure" English] I cannot doubt that no beauty
in a language can make up for want of purity. In fact, I am learning
Anglo-Saxon and it is a vastly superior thing to what we have." He cites
Barnes's wondrous "pitches of suchness" (for "degrees of comparison"):
"We *ought* to call them so, but alas!"

Hopkins' characteristic critical and philosophical terminology follows
closely the counsel of Trench and Barnes: that it, it is a compounding of
Old English roots and suffixes to suit new needs and to replace Latinic
terms. "Inwit" (for "conscience") and Barnes's "inwoning" (subjective)
may have suggested "instress" and "inscape." Hopkins explains his special use of "sake" the being a thing has outside itself) by analytic parallel
of the compounds "forsake," "namesake," "keepsake." The terminology
of the *Comments on the Spiritual Exercises* (1880) is particularly Hopkinsian (e.g., "pitch," "stress," "burl"). To Bridges, Hopkins wrote of his
manuscript book on rhythm, "It is full of new words, without which
there can be no new science."

His doctrine of the language for poetry, nowhere exposited, we can
infer to have been quite different. Archaism—the use of obsolete words
for literary effect—he repudiated. His oddities (like "pashed," "fashed,"
"tucked," "degged") are generally dialectal; and it is safe to assume that
his words of Old English lineage were collected and used by him as
dialectal, still-spoken English: not "inkhorn" terms but folk speech. Even
when he thought he was improvising, he was—at least in one instance—
remembering: his alleged coinage, "louched" (slouched, slouching) was,
as Bridges observed, to be found in Wright's Dialect Dictionary.

Whenever Hopkins explained his words (as he always stood ready to
do), their particularity, their compactness and detail, were manifest.
"Stickles—Devonshire for the foamy tongues of water below falls."
"Bole" is not only used by poets but seems technical and proper and in
the mouth of timber merchants and so forth. Of "flit," questioned by a
correspondent, he writes: "I myself always use it and commonly hear
it used among our people. I think it is at least a North Country word,
used in Lancashire, for instance."

His compoundings are another matter. Though analogues can be
offered from Browning, Hopkins came to them, it is probable, by way
of medieval poetry, English and Welsh, and by way of Marsh, Trench,
and Barnes. His defense would doubtless be that to compound freely was
to restore to the English language a power it once had possessed. But
the words thus compounded, or the root and suffix or prefix, were sep-

arately familiar and oral. He writes "spend-savour salt" (the salt which is spending its savor and on its way to being the biblical salt which has lost its savor); "bloomfall"; "trambeam"; "backwheels"; "though worlds of *wanwood leafmeal lie*" ("leafmeal" is on the model of "piecemeal"; suffix means "by bits," "by portions").

Judged by its effect and its internal intent, Hopkins' poetry finds partial parallels in Holst, Delius, and Vaughan Williams. Avoiding the archaism of Warlock and Dolmetsch, they sought to resume the line of English music where its genuine succession was interrupted—at the Restoration, and to go creatively back to the English glory of folksong and madrigal and the modal scales, to Dowland, Bull, and Byrd. Similarly, Hopkins seems to be reaching back, while he is reaching forward, to an "English" poetry. Probably, we may add, to an "English Catholic" poetry; and suppose that his pushing back of the Elizabethans had some incentive in his desire to get back of the Reformation to an England at once Catholic and English.

Like the poetry of the bards and the scops, Hopkins' poetry is oral, yet not conversational but formal and rhetorical. It uses dialectal words without intending, like Barnes's *Poems of Rural Life,* to be local and homely; it uses folk words in "serious" poetry. Hopkins' poems were written for an ideal audience, never existent in his day or ours, composed of literarily perceptive countrymen and of linguistically adept and folk-minded scholars. What his poetry assumed as convention, he had, by artifice, to create. "The Wreck" and "Tom's Garland" suggest or predict a greater poetry than they achieve. Hopkins' experiments are yet more important than his achievement; his comparative failures more interesting than his good "whole poems."

The ideal of poetry must be to instress the inscapes without splintering the architecture of the universe and, expressionally, to make every word rich in a way compatible with a more than additively rich total poetic structure. But in Hopkins' poems, the word, the phrase, the "local excitement," often pulls us away from the poem. And in the more ambitious pieces, the odes as we may call them ("The Wreck," "Spelt from Sibyl's Leaves," "Nature Is a Heraclitean Fire"), there is felt a discrepancy between texture and structure: the copious, violent detail is matched by no corresponding intellectual or mythic vigor. Indeed, "The Wreck of the Deutschland" is an "occasional," commissioned piece at which Hopkins works devotedly and craftfully, like Dryden at his *Annus mirabilis,* but which, like Dryden's poem, falls apart. Hopkins was not a story-teller, and he was not able to turn his wrecks into myths of wreck; they remain historical events accompanied by commentary. "The Bugler-

Boy" and other poems suffer from the gap between the psychological naïveté and the purely literary richness. To try prose paraphrases of the middle poems is invariably to show how thin the "thinking" is. Hopkins' mind was first aesthetic and then technical: he reasoned closely upon metaphysical and prosodic matters. But his reflections upon beauty, man, and nature—his humanistic thoughts—are not distinguished.

The meaning of Hopkins' poems hovers closely over the text, the linguistic surface. The rewarding experience of concern with them is to be let more and more into words and their ways, to contemplate the protopoetry of derivation and metaphorical expansion, to stress the inscapes of the English tongue.

Chronology of Important Dates

1844	July 28: Gerard Manley Hopkins born at Stratford, Essex.
1854	Attends Cholmondesley Grammar School, Highgate.
1859-62	First significant poems: "The Escorial," "A Vision of the Mermaids."
1860	Tours Southern Germany. Had toured the Rhineland in 1857.
1863	Exhibition scholarship to Balliol College, Oxford.
1866	Decision to become a Catholic (July 17); consults Newman at the Oratory in Birmingham (September 20); is received by Newman into the Catholic Church (October 21).
1867	Graduates from Oxford with Double-First in "Greats."
1868	Burns his poems. Enters the Jesuit Order and begins his Novitiate at Roehampton.
1870	Philosophical Studies at St. Mary's Hall, Stonyhurst.
1872	Contact with the works of Duns Scotus.
1874	Correspondence with Robert Bridges begins anew.
1875	December: "The Wreck of the Deutschland." Starts to write poetry once more after a seven year silence.
1877	Ordination to the Priesthood.
1878-81	Preacher in London, then in Oxford and Liverpool. Interest in the working class.
1881	Retreat at Roehampton (Third Year Novitiate).
1882-83	Teaches Classics at Stonyhurst College. Contacts with R. W. Dixon, Robert Bridges, and Coventry Patmore.
1884	Professor of Greek at Royal University College, Dublin.
1885	The "terrible" sonnets.
1889	Dies of typhoid fever, is buried in Dublin.
1918	First edition of his *Poems* edited by Robert Bridges.

Notes on the Editor and Authors

GEOFFREY H. HARTMAN, the editor of this volume, teaches English and Comparative Literature at Cornell. He has published *The Unmediated Vision* (1954), *Malraux* (1960), and *Wordsworth's Poetry* (1964).

F. R. LEAVIS, an honorary fellow of Downing College, Cambridge, was among Hopkins' first and strongest appreciators. His books of criticism and educational philosophy include *Revaluation* (1936), *The Great Tradition* (1948), and *D. H. Lawrence: Novelist* (1955).

YVOR WINTERS, poet and critic, is Professor of English at Stanford.

JOHN WAIN, the English author, critic, and publicist, has written works of fiction and poetry as well as essays in criticism.

ROBERT BRIDGES (1844-1930) is the well-known poet responsible for the first edition of Hopkins' poetry.

ROMANO GUARDINI is Professor of Religion at the University of Munich. He is an eminent interpreter of Dante, Hölderlin and Rilke.

HERBERT MARSHALL McLUHAN, Professor of English at St. Michael's College, The University of Toronto, has published *The Mechanical Bride* (1951), *The Gutenberg Galaxy* (1962), and *Understanding Media* (1964).

J. HILLIS MILLER, Professor of English at Johns Hopkins, has written *Charles Dickens: the World of his Novels* (1955), *The Disappearance of God* (1963), and *Poets of Reality* (1965).

GIORGIO MELCHIORI is Professor of English at the University of Turin, Italy. Besides *The Tightrope Walkers* (1956), which has also appeared in Italian, he has published on Yeats.

F. O. MATTHIESSEN (1902-1950), who taught at Harvard, was a distinguished scholar of American Literature and modern poetry.

WALTER J. ONG, S.J., who teaches at St. Louis University, has published a magisterial work on Ramus. A number of his critical essays have appeared under the title *The Barbarian Within* (1962).

SIGURD BURKHARDT, Professor in the University of California at San Diego, is the author of essays on Shakespeare, German literature, and the philosophy of language.

AUSTIN WARREN, to whom this volume is dedicated, is Professor of English at the University of Michigan and a generous interpreter of the religious sensibility. Among his books are *Alexander Pope* (1929), *Richard Crashaw* (1939), *Rage for Order* (1948), and *New England Saints* (1956).

Selected Bibliography

1. Editions

Poems of Gerard Manley Hopkins, ed. Robert Bridges (London: Oxford University Press, 1918). Second edition, introduction by Charles Williams (1930). Third edition, ed. W. H. Gardner (1948).

The Letters of Gerard Manley Hopkins to Robert Bridges, ed. C. C. Abbott (London: Oxford University Press, 1935 & 1955).

The Correspondence of Gerard Manley Hopkins and R. W. Dixon, ed. C. C. Abbott (London: Oxford University Press, 1935 & 1955).

Further Letters of Gerard Manley Hopkins, ed. C. C. Abbott (London: Oxford University Press, 1938, second edition, 1952).

The Journals and Papers of Gerard Manley Hopkins, eds. Humphry House and Graham Storey (London: Oxford University Press, 1959).

The Sermons and Devotional Writings of Gerard Manly Hopkins, ed. Christopher Devlin, S.J. (London: Oxford University Press, 1959).

2. Book-length studies on Hopkins

Boyle, Robert, S.J., *Metaphor in Hopkins* (Chapel Hill: University of North Carolina Press, 1961).

Gardner, W. H., *Gerard Manley Hopkins (1844-1889), A Study of Poetic Idiosyncrasy in Relation to Poetic Tradition* (London and New York: Oxford University Press, 1958), 2 vols.

Heuser, Alan, *The Shaping Vision of Gerard Manley Hopkins* (London: Oxford University Press, 1958).

Keating, J. E., *The Wreck of the Deutschland: An Essay and Commentary,* Kent State University Bulletin (January 1963).

The Kenyon Critics, *Gerard Manley Hopkins* (Norfolk, Conn.: New Directions, 1945). Essays by Austin Warren, H. M. McLuhan, Harold Whitehall, Josephine Miles, Robert Lowell, Arthur Mizener and F. R. Leavis.

Lahey, G. F., S.J., *Gerard Manley Hopkins* (London, Oxford University Press, 1930).

Peters, W. A. M., S.J., *Gerard Manley Hopkins, A Critical Essay toward the Understanding of his Poetry* (London: Oxford University Press, 1948).

Phare, E. E., *The Poetry of Gerard Manley Hopkins, A Survey and Commentary* (Cambridge, England: Cambridge University Press, 1933).

Pick, John, *Gerard Manley Hopkins, Priest and Poet* (London: Oxford University Press, 1942).

Ritz, Jean-Georges, *Le Poète Gerard Manley Hopkins, S.J.* (Paris: Didier, 1963).

Ruggles, Eleanor, *Gerard Manley Hopkins* (London and New York: W. W. Norton & Company, Inc., 1947).

Weyand, Norman, S.J., ed., *Immortal Diamond: Studies in Gerard Manley Hopkins* (London: Sheed and Ward, 1949). Essays by members of the Society of Jesus with a foreword by John Pick and an "Interpretive Glossary of Difficult Words" in Hopkins' poems by R. V. Schoder.

3. *Shorter Studies* (not collected in the present anthology)

Auden, W. H., "The Knight of the Infinite," *The New Republic,* 111 (August 21, 1944), 223-24.

Blackmur, R. P., "Text and Texture," *Virginia Quarterly Review* 13 (1937), 449-53.

Chevigny, B. G., "Instress and Devotion in the Poetry of Gerard Manley Hopkins," *Victorian Studies,* December, 1965.

Daiches, David, *A Critical History of English Literature* (New York: Ronald Press, 1960), II, 1042-48.

Davie, Donald, *Purity of Diction in English Verse* (New York: Oxford University Press, 1953), pp. 160-82.

Devlin, Christopher, "Time's Eunuch," *The Month,* N. S. 1 (1949), 303-12.

Duncan, J. E., *The Revival of Metaphysical Poetry: The History of a Style 1800 to the Present* (Minneapolis: University of Minnesota Press, 1959), pp. 91-102.

Empson, William, *Seven Types of Ambiguity,* first edition, 1930, chapter 7.

Leavis, F. R., "Metaphysical Isolation," *Gerard Manley Hopkins by the Kenyon Critics,* pp. 115-34.

Lewis, C. D., *A Hope for Poetry* (Oxford: B. Blackwell, 1934), pp. 6-13.

Martz, L. L., *The Poetry of Meditation* (first edition, New Haven: Yale University Press, 1954), pp. 321-26.

Miles, Josephine, "The Sweet and Lovely Language," *Gerard Manley Hopkins by the Kenyon Critics,* pp. 55-71.

Mizener, Arthur, "Victorian Hopkins," *Gerard Manley Hopkins by the Kenyon Critics,* pp. 94-114.

Richards, I. A., "Gerard Hopkins," *The Dial,* 81 (1926), 195-203.

Richards, I. A., *Practical Criticism,* 1st ed., 1929 (New York, Harvest Books), pp. 77-87.

Schoder, R. V., S.J., "What Does *The Windhover* Mean?" *Immortal Diamond,* ed. Norman Weyand, pp. 275-306.

Ward, Dennis, "The Windhover," *Interpretations: Essays on Twelve English Poems,* ed. John Wain (London: Routledge and Kegan Paul, Ltd. 1955).

Warren, Austin, "Gerard Manley Hopkins, 1844-1889," *Gerard Manley Hopkins by the Kenyon Critics,* pp. 1-14.

Yeats, W. B., *The Oxford Book of Modern Verse 1892-1935* (Oxford: Clarendon, 1936), pp. xxxix-lx.

For complete bibliographical information the following sources may be consulted: M. A. Charney, "A Bibliographical Study of Hopkins Criticism. 1918-1949," *Thought*, 25 (1950), 297-326, and J. Pick's essay in *The Victorian Poets: A Guide to Research*, ed. F. E. Faverty (Cambridge, Mass.: Harvard University Press, 1956), pp. 196-227 (these are the best critical surveys of the secondary literature but carry us only through 1950 or so); also Norman Weyand, "A Chronological Hopkins Bibliography" in *Immortal Diamond*, pp. 393-436 (a reliable listing through 1946), Jean-Georges Ritz, "Bibliographie" in his *Le Poète Gerard Manley Hopkins*, pp. 673-709 (quite complete to the early fifties, spotty after that), and W. H. Gardner's listings in the *CBEL*, V (1957), pp. 600-04.

of one of Whitman's merely average productions.[3] Still Hopkins might have justly contended that any group of Whitman's lines would show the same logical consequences of extreme protestantism, of his downright statement that formal verse was as outmoded as sacraments and dogma. Whitman also declared that he had an instinctive "aversion to the church notion of an atonement," because of "its essential vulgarity, its wanton treachery" to what he believed to be the "high and imperative" recognition that man was made to be free. To the Catholic this would furnish the most compelling evidence why Whitman's rhythms had naturally fallen into the final looseness of decomposition. Whitman said that he could not read Tolstoy's *Confession,* since he had never been worried by the question of whether he should be saved or lost. Yet in his desire to keep all doors open, he was willing to grant that the "introspective, sin-seeking" element in the Russian "may better represent the present day than I do." However, his complacence did not leave his view of freedom so undeveloped that he thought any road as good as another or that the individual's impulse constituted the only law. When he surveyed the instances of usurping individualistic lawlessness in the era of the robber barons, he had reached his main position in *Democratic Vistas* (1871): that the crucial task for the American future was some reconciliation of the contradictory needs for full personal development and for "one's obligations to the State and Nation," to "the paramount aggregate." Although this conception of the One and the many would not have satisfied Hopkins, when Whitman went on to say that "most people entirely misunderstand Freedom," which we can attain only "by a knowledge of, and implicit obedience to, Law," he at least approached Engels' disciplined comprehension of freedom as "the recognition of necessity."

It is wholly obvious to us now that Bridges was wrong in his notion that Hopkins' work was a case of "unexampled liberty." His reaction against flabbiness had driven him rather to an excessive control, which finally amounted to constriction. The "terrible pathos" that became his habitual tone sprang never from doubt, but from the bitterest anguish, from the absence of movement in a life driven in on itself, from the unflinching scrutiny of his weakness before the perfection of God. But what is expressed has hardly any of the resolution of tragedy, since all action has been reduced to suffering. In his unsurpassable courage to endure, his world finally became as narrow as the cell in a monastery.

[3] A much more energetically imaginative poem on a similar subject is Whitman's "The Dalliance of the Eagles."

Sprung Rhythm and English Tradition

by Walter J. Ong

. . . Within a rhythmic tradition such as that which was car from Old English into Elizabethan times, it was natural for his [F kins'] contemporaries to single out Spenser as "the new poet." For the tradition Edmund Spenser hardly fits. Something might be don introduce him in part into the tradition on the score of "Februarie" "Maye" in *The Shepheardes Calender,* although this is uncertain, but the important rhythmic achievements of this poet tend to divert Eng verse into pure running-rhythm channels with no sense-stress tributar

We are so close to the Spenserian tradition even yet that it is diffic to realize the extent of the revolution Spenser effected. His full influer in establishing the eighteenth- and nineteenth-century feeling for a "co tinuous literary decorum," which so easily associated itself with the qu throbbing of the smooth alternating-stress verse he perfected, is only I ginning to be recognized as comparable to that of his greater discip Milton, for whom he had everywhere paved the way. Saintsbury was n only making a supposition common in his day, but he was calling atte tion to a fact when he said that Spenser was the Joshua who brougl English prosody into its promised measure and rhyme.[1] Saintsbury's su position would find little support now: that Spenser's achievement w inevitably progress is at best a gratuitous assumption. But the importanc Saintsbury assigns to Spenser is not exaggerated. To appreciate the rev lutionary effect of Spenser's verse, we need only look to the diffidence o Elizabethan prosodists toward the "feet" which become the stock in trad of prosody in the late Spenserian tradition we have known. And to se the extent of his influence long after his death, we can recall that all th

"Sprung Rhythm and English Tradition" (editor's title) by Walter J. Ong. From "Hopkins' Sprung Rhythm and the Life of English Poetry," in *Immortal Diamond,* ed. by Norman Weyand, S.J. (New York: Sheed & Ward, Inc., 1949), copyright 1949 by Sheed & Ward, Inc., pp. 159-68, 170-72. Reprinted by permission of the publishers, New York and London.

[1] George Saintsbury, *A History of English Prosody* (London: Macmillan and Co., 1906-1910), I, 351.

proclaiming in his *History of English Prosody*, "It is the 'Progress of Prosody' which the present writer, not being able to 'sing,' is ambitious to 'say,' " [4] considers it a foregone conclusion that in the march of progress, Spenser is the Joshua. The same tradition accounts for the judgments of a Sir Sidney Lee in the *Dictionary of National Biography*. Without a glance aside at Gavin Douglas or Skelton, Sir Sidney hits with predictable accuracy on Sackville's *Induction* as the greatest poem between Chaucer and Spenser. It "has no rival." [5] The reason is not hard to find: it is almost the only thing like Spenser until Spenser himself.

Other evidence is available in the development of the lyric. In the Spenserian tradition, the lyric of Jonson and Donne, which had built on the strength of declamatory stress a strong idiom of counterpoint now regarded as making the verse too rough, had been discarded in favor of the staid and sober ruminations of Akenside and the Wartons. The tone of direct dialogue is replaced at best by bursts of apostrophe before an audience either unconscious or absent. It is here rather than in the twentieth century that poetry begins talking to itself. And this tradition was in possession when Hopkins put in his appearance. How thoroughly it had proscribed an oratorical delivery by its exclusive exploitation of running rhythm is evident in any representative poem, such as Shenstone's *The School-Mistress*:

> Ah me! full sorely is my heart forlorn,
> To think how modest worth neglected lies;
> While partial fame doth with her blasts adorn
> Such deeds alone, as pride and pomp disguise;
> Deeds of ill sort, and mischievous emprise!
> Lend me thy clarion, goddess! let me try
> To sound the praise of merit, ere it dies;
> Such as I oft have chaunced to espy,
> Lost in the dreary shades of dull obscurity.[6]

Any tendency to develop a pattern built on sense-stress here is entirely masked by the steady drone of the Spenserian meditative machinery. Indeed, the only sense or feeling which can exist here is that capable of moving with the special motion of this verse. Earlier verse had not all known such a restriction: this movement was only a phase in the varied rhythms found in the dramatists, even in their lyrics. But in the eight-

[4] Saintsbury, *op. cit.*, II, 26.

[5] *Dictionary of National Biography*, ed. by Leslie Stephen and Sidney Lee, XVIII (London: Oxford University Press, 1921-22), 586.

[6] *The Works in Verse and Prose of William Shenstone, Esq.* (London: R. and J. Dodsley, 1764), II, 333.

eenth and nineteenth centuries it pretty well held the field all the way
from light lyric pieces to Thomson's staid heroics. It is little wonder that
the mind which restricted poetry to this sort of thing should be disgusted
with Donne and embarrassed to discover in itself a liking for Shakespeare.

In this picture of the poetic heritage of Hopkins' world lies the answer
to the question, What did Hopkins find? Hopkins found a tradition in
English poetry which was older and stronger than the one in possession
in his day. He found a rhythmic tradition which could cut under and
around the "running" or "common" rhythm of the nineteenth century,
not because his new rhythm was the ancient rhythm of English—this
would be a fact of no value in itself—but because it was a rhythm still
inherent in the language and only suppressed by an artificially sustained
tradition. It is indeed strange that between the period when we find
Shakespeare's "cabined, cribb'd, confined" and

> If it were done, when 'tis done, then 'twere well
> It were done quickly, ...

and the later period which finally brought Hopkins' "hearts' charity's
hearth's fire" or "And the sea flint-flake, black-backed in the regular
blow," there is almost nothing to compare with these passages. The place
in poetry where such things fit was kept tightly locked. Certainly such
expressions were not entirely foreign to speech—though they may have
been more foreign to it than we suspect—but the kind of poetic rhythm
in favor left them no room. Hopkins opened a place for them.

In opening this place, Hopkins' achievement was not quite alone.
After the dramatists and the wit poets, there had remained tendencies
to maintain in English poetry the strength of the sense-stress rhythms.
(We must remind ourselves continually that these are not *entirely* unlike
those of the "smooth" or "reformed" numbers of running rhythm, and
hence only rarely will verse be free of at least equivocal instances of
them.) There was the case of Milton, who as a young man had, in *Comus,*
trafficked in the livening rhythms of the stage, but who—as he himself
later acknowledged, telling Dryden that Spenser was his "original"—had
turned away to the rhythms of the non-dramatic tradition. With, however, a scholarly sophistication unknown to Spenser, he had overlaid the
Spenserian numbers with a heavy counterpoint and had finally in his
Samson choruses gone so far as to sacrifice almost completely the rhythm
of the alternating stress. But life was gone: under the spell of the epic
theory, Milton had fallen upon a coagulating poetic idiom which passed
stiff and unyielding to the hands of his successors. Nevertheless, Milton
being an approved author, his work came to Hopkins' attention.

The eighteenth century, after Pope, had been pretty destitute of sense-stress rhythms, but latterly there had come Burns, cultivating the habit of direct address, and the sense-stress counterpoint revives once more with the life of the declamatory verse. Burns' strength, which lies in his satirical pieces, is apparent in *To a Louse*:

> Ha! whare ye gaun, ye crowlin' ferlie!
>
> . . .
>
> My sooth! right bauld ye set your nose out,
> As plump and gray as onie grozet;
> O for some rank, mercurial rozet,
> > Or fell, red, smeddum.[7]

With its three successive stresses tempting the rhythm far from an alternating stress, the last line here is as much a surprise as the first.

Burns is followed by Blake, with his "rhymeless pindarics" and *The Fairy,* which is in genuine skeltonics:

> So a Fairy sung.
>
> From the leaves I sprung;
>
> He leap'd from the spray
>
> To flee away;
>
> But in my hat caught,
>
> He soon shall be taught.[8]

And there was Southey's *Thalaba* and Shelley's *Queen Mab,* done in what was much later to be called free verse, as well as other pieces like those noted by Hopkins, or like Shelley's *A Dirge* ("Rough wind that moanest loud") interesting for a tendency toward juxtaposed stresses. There are stirrings, too, of a new life in Byron, a defender and imitator of Pope. And the Keats of the mature odes picks up a kind of counterpoint verse unknown since the Elizabethans. Lines in the *Ode on Melancholy* can be divided to expose the Old English antiphonal pattern:

> No, no, go not to Lethe,   neither twist
>
> Wolf's-bane, tight-rooted,   for its poisonous wine;

or

---

[7] *The Complete Works of Robert Burns,* ed. by Alexander Smith (New York: Thomas Y. Crowell and Co. [no date]), p. 74.

[8] *The Poetical Works of William Blake,* ed. by John Sampson (London: Oxford University Press, 1914), p. 122.

And feed deep, deep   upon her peerless eyes.[9]

In the *Ode on a Grecian Urn* there is this heavy counterpoint:

> "Beauty is truth, truth beauty," that is all
> Ye know on earth, and all ye need to know.[10]

The whole nineteenth century witnessed a general movement toward this "rougher" verse, a movement which culminated perhaps in Browning, where a revival of counterpoint brings in again sound echoes. Certain lines in *The Ring and the Book,* for example—there are plenty of others—might be halved as four-stress lines:

> Flung with a flourish!   But repentance, too.
> But pure and simple   sorrow for law's breach
> Rather than blunderer's-ineptitude?
> Cardinal, no!   Abate, scarcely thus!

> 'Tis the fault, not   that I dared try a fall
> With Law and straightway am found undermost,
> But that I failed to see, above man's law,
> God's precept you, the Christians, recognize?

> Colly my cow!   Don't fidget, Cardinal! [11]

Apart from the lines divided here, the verse, as is usual with Browning, is not smooth. Had Browning's idiom been more genuine, less pretentiously offhand, its gawkiness less "flung with a flourish," his achievement might have partaken of Hopkins'. As it is, Hopkins says discerningly of Browning's verse, "I greatly admire the touches and the details, but the general effect, the whole, offends me, I think it repulsive," and he has little patience with "the scarecrow misbegotten Browning crew."

While these developments were taking place, sense-stress rhythms had persisted here and there in out-of-the-way places where the tradition of smoothness in verse was not enforced: in songs, including the ballads, where because the verse was subordinated to music great regularity had never been demanded (musical measure has always been able to salve errancy in syllabic count); and in weather saws and nursery rhymes, for

[9] *The Poetical Works and Other Writings of John Keats,* ed. by H. Buxton Forman and Maurice Buxton Forman (New York: Charles Scribner's Sons, 1938), III, 184. Italics mine.

[10] *Ibid.,* p. 157.

[11] XI, "Guido," *The Complete Poetic and Dramatic Works of Robert Browning* (Boston: Houghton Mifflin and Co., 1895), p. 577.